LEST WE LOSE LOVE

LEST WE LOSE LOVE

REDISCOVERING THE CORE OF
WESTERN CULTURE

SCHERTO R. GILL

ANTHEM PRESS

Anthem Press
An imprint of Wimbledon Publishing Company
www.anthempress.com

This edition first published in UK and USA 2023
by ANTHEM PRESS
75–76 Blackfriars Road, London SE1 8HA, UK
or PO Box 9779, London SW19 7ZG, UK
and
244 Madison Ave #116, New York, NY 10016, USA

Copyright © Sohorto Gill 2023
The author asserts the moral right to be identified as the author of this work.

All rights reserved. Without limiting the rights under copyright reserved above, no
part of this publication may be reproduced, stored or introduced into a retrieval
system, or transmitted, in any form or by any means (electronic, mechanical,
photocopying, recording or otherwise), without the prior written permission of both
the copyright owner and the above publisher of this book.

British Library Cataloguing-in-Publication Data
A catalogue record for this book is available from the British Library.

Library of Congress Control Number: 2022950025
A catalog record for this book has been requested.

ISBN-13: 978-1-83998-760-1 (Hbk)
ISBN-10: 1-83998-760-X (Hbk)

ISBN-13: 978-1-83998-761-8 (Pbk)
ISBN-10: 1-83998-761-8

Cover graphic design: Silvina De Vita

This title is also available as an e-book.

CONTENTS

Preface   vi
Acknowledgements   ix

CHAPTER 1	Time for a New Narrative	1
CHAPTER 2	A Threefold Framework for Understanding Love	13
CHAPTER 3	Love as Valuing	33
CHAPTER 4	Love as Relationing	91
CHAPTER 5	Love as Caring	157
CHAPTER 6	Love in Practice	213
CHAPTER 7	Towards a Paradigm of Love	233

Bibliography   247
Index   257

PREFACE

This book is an invitation to all readers to become curious and interested in the notion of love. It is not merely a book that interprets philosophy of love, but instead, it makes it possible for the reader to have an easy access to accounts of love in the Western thoughts. It is not simply a text charting love in our culture, rather it systematically explores these in classical Greek thoughts, Christian theology and modernist and post-modernist ideas. In doing so, it opens the window to a vista of the landscape surrounding ways of loving. It is a call to embark on a voyage, to immerse in the scenery, to encounter, to explore, to see anew and to transform.

There have been many books about love precisely because love is at the core of human existence. In those volumes, what were captured are not only different ways to describe love, there are also innumerable perspectives to articulate what love is and how love can be pursued. Yet, a compelling book is still required to investigate what has been offered by the Western culture to our understanding of love. This investigation is particularly necessary at present time when humanity is once again at a crossroads. The choices we make and actions we take will determine the kinds of legacy to be inherited by our future generations. How we choose and what we do will ultimately make a difference between a path towards collective flourishing and a path of collective peril. In other words, at this point in human history, it is love that matters. How we understand love matters. How we embrace love in our ways of being matters even more.

What makes this book compelling is that it envisions love's wisdom in an innovative way. Rather than locating love in the familiar landscapes of romance and spirituality, it situates love within living the good life in well-being. To do so, it proposes a triadic framework for understanding love: (a) love as valuing, (b) love as relationing and (c) love as caring. Such a framework allows this book to reflect upon and interpret love's contribution to our collective flourishing. Through such a framework, the book can systematically revisit accounts of love already present throughout the history of Western thought and re-consider how love can guide human's continued journeys, lest we lose love.

Avoiding the complexity of defining love as a *noun* and the risk of simplification and reduction when putting love in different categories, this framework enhances our appreciation of the divergent ways that love can inspire our collective pursuit of the common good. For instance, it draws our attention to the important and intrinsically valuable aspects and qualities in people, things and worthwhile causes in the world. It enriches the myriad ways of our relating and emphasises on an overall culture of caring. Through such a framework, readers can be more attuned to how love can be understood, practised and integrated into our everyday life.

There is always a great deal of cynicism around love, especially when we find ourselves in an extremely unloving world. At present, our world is characterised by the continued impact from COVID-19 pandemic, Russia's invasion of Ukraine, the glaring inequality and the intermittent threat of climate change, to just mention a few. These events can make many of us doubt our collective ability to love. Is talking about love helpful when people's lives are ripped apart by diseases, violence, poverty and displacement? What can love do to alleviate suffering and advance social justice? How can love resolve the tensions amongst the global powers? In what way could love be relevant to the present ecological crisis?

Yet, the suspicion of the naïvety of such a love project can be quickly dismissed. In fact, throughout history, humanity has triumphed over atrocities, tragedies and catastrophes and has supported each other in overcoming great difficulties precisely because we live by loving and caring. In loving, we may transcend humans' imperfections and limitations. In caring, we seek to improve our lives and create spaces for other's flourishing.

When I first accepted to do a research into the notion of love in Western culture, I was open to both love's implausibility and love's potentiality. The more I journeyed into the vast landscape of love and encountered the writings of thinkers, theologians and philosophers on the way, the more I became convinced of love's centrality in the good life for one and all. To such an extent, I could not see any other way for humanity to move forward except via the paths of love. The paths here are intentionally plural. As outlined in this book, there are indeed many routes to a better future, each characterised by certain qualities that love can inspire. These are articulated by the accounts of love gathered in this book and they can indeed provide a richer understanding of how love grounds and enthuses caring human actions.

The research on love had not been a mere intellectual task for me. In fact, whilst writing the book, love has already begun to serve as an ethical pillar for a number of projects that I am working on, not least the collective healing initiative we are developing in partnership with UNESCO and the project on positive peace that focuses on holistic human well-being.

Scherto Gill
May 2022

ACKNOWLEDGEMENTS

The research leading to this book was proposed and commissioned by Dartington Solar Quest Charity Trust, in memory of William and Vera Elmhirst, the co-founders of the Trust.

It was carried out with the assistance from Dr Ezra Cohen, Toto Mars Gill, Alice Sommerville and Sebastian Batzer.

This project would not be possible without the support from the Guerrand-Hermès Foundation for Peace, Pureland Foundation and the University of Wales Trinity Saint David.

I am particularly indebted to the encouragement and trust from Chantelle Hibbs, the generous support from Bruno Wang, and the wise guidance from Professor David Cadman.

The book's structure is shaped owing a great deal to the constructive criticism from Professor Kenneth Gergen.

Scherto Gill
May 2022

CHAPTER 1

TIME FOR A NEW NARRATIVE

Since the Symposium [or even before] [...] the general schema of a philosophy of love is at work, [...] and it has not ceased to operate even now, determining philosophy as it understands and construes itself, as well as love as we understand it and as we make it.
—Jean-Luc Nancy, Shattered Love

We are living in an age of bewilderment. This period of lingering perplexity is further exasperated by global crises, in particular, the COVID-19 pandemic, the ongoing humanitarian crisis, the continued refugee crisis, Russia's invasion of Ukraine and the ever-present climate crisis. These problems have disclosed the structural violence and systemic injustice that have prevailed in our socio-economic processes and political institutions.

According to Yuval Noel Harari, the Israeli historian and philosopher, it is bewildering and perplexing because the current narratives that explain who we are and how we shall live have collapsed, and new ones are yet to emerge.[1] Thus whilst this is a turbulent time for humanity, it also provides an important opportunity for us to pause, reflect and respond. Indeed, from around the globe, similar questions are posed, including: 'Why is there so much inequality, injustice and inhumanity in our society?' 'What has led to such exploitation, devastation and destruction to our planet?' 'What kinds of transformation are necessary as we move forward?' 'Which are the most congenial processes and pathways that can take us to a promising future?' For many, these questions are indicating a need for shared inquiry and collective sense-making.

For Hariri, our search for a path to a hopeful future for humanity starts with a new narrative that may transcend the present disorientation and uncertainty. Narrative, in this case, like cultural *mythos*, is fundamental to our

---
1 Harari, *21 Lessons for the 21st Century*.

way of being. Indeed, since antiquity, humanity has always created stories that articulate who we are, what we value and what constitutes the good life. More importantly, narrating or storying is critical to defining who we should become, what we ought to care and how we might live well together.

At this point in human history, with the aforementioned crises looming large globally, the search for a compelling new narrative to take us out of our present impasse seems to be more pressing than ever before.

This book offers such a new narrative.

This new narrative is a *narrative of love*. As I shall demonstrate, although rooted in the evolving accounts of love already present in our culture, the new narrative has meanings beyond these different accounts precisely because it can offer a unifying vision of hopefulness. It is such a narrative that will help re-instil and re-energise the truly transformative potential of love.

Evolving Accounts of the Good Life

Accounts of the good life have evolved over two millennia.[2] To understand this evolution, it is necessary that we delve into the ever-changing articulations of life's meaningfulness, our relationship with what we consider to be valuable in life and how we live out these values in everyday realities.

Since antiquity, Western thinkers and philosophers have always been interested in the question of what constitutes the good life. Luc Ferry, the former French Minister of Education, and philosopher, argues that there is a *progression*, or *evolution*, in the ways that life's meaningfulness has been explored over time. For Ferry, the shift in our understanding of the good life might be construed as a continuum – starting from cosmological or cosmocentric conceptions, progressing to theological or theocentric orientations, then humanist or humancentric arguments and finally, in the last millennium, towards more individual-centric ideas.[3] Curiously, as Ferry points out, this shift in our claims about the good life seems to correspond to the historical development of Western thoughts, although not necessarily in a strictly linear way.

---

2 Singer, *Philosophy of Love: A Partial Summing-Up*, 2. Also see observations from Teilhard de Chardin, Irving Singer, Luc Ferry and Thaddeus Metz, to mention a few.

3 Ferry (2013) suggests this be a deconstructive principle that challenges all grand narratives of cosmos and divine. In this report, we briefly touched upon this term but have used instead the word human-focused to describe the growing concern for human life.

We can see how the 'evolution' plays out in a revision of Ferry's description of these four 'principles' as follows:

The cosmological or cosmocentric principle was developed in antiquity, in classical Greek philosophy. During this time, conceptions of the good life tended to regard the purpose of human life as moving 'from the initial chaos to a reconciliation with the harmony of the cosmos'.[4] Achieving reconciliation and harmony with the cosmos is a matter of finding or identifying a person's 'place in the cosmic order'.[5] This pre-existent cosmic order is believed to be all-encompassing, encapsulating all things and all beings (of which humans are a part and in which humans take part).

Moving away from the cosmic vision, is a theological or theocentric principle as proposed by early Christian theologians. It suggests that the good life must necessarily be rooted in virtues which are the fruit of following holy commandments. Christian accounts postulate that humans are the creations of God and in the image of God. Hence human beings can realise our life's meaningfulness by aspiring to God's qualities. It is only through relating to God in appropriate ways and partaking in God's being as God had intended can humans seek deliverance, redemption and justice. These Christian metaphysical, epistemological and relational claims tend to anchor human life solely within the existence of God,[6] and for the sake of God.[7]

Modernist thinkers advanced the humanist/humancentric principle. This principle determines human's pursuit of emancipation from the constraints of an external authority, for example, the cosmic order or God. It regards the highest human value to be individual freedom, including our ability to move beyond the natural, historical and metaphysical limitations. In this sense, modernist humanist view sees man as defined:

> [not] by a 'nature' proper to him, not even by a history of which he is the prisoner; rather, he endlessly 'creates himself' by making progress in the sciences and the arts, by the conquest of an ever-wider autonomy, by the endlessly increasing mastery of a sometimes revolutionary history.[8]

---

4 Ferry, *On Love*, 12.
5 Ibid., 13.
6 See, for instance, Cottingham, *On the Meaning of Life* and Baggini, *What's It All About? Philosophy & the Meaning of Life*.
7 May, *Love: A History*.
8 Ferry, *On Love*, 15.

For the self-creating and self-made man, the good life would consist in fully actualising freedom through our rational capacities and our pure and almost disembodied self-consciousness.[9]

The last is the post-modernist individual-centric principle characterised by a suspicion of the universal account of what is valuable and good. This suspicion is directed at the *grand* narrative, such as the idea of cosmic harmony, divine quality or an abstract and purely rational human nature. It takes into consideration the unconscious, the anthropological, the economic, the sociocultural, the historical and the multi-faceted relational processes within which humans pursue the good life. In this view, humans are embodied beings, inhabiting the natural world and subject to the myriad forces implied in our inherent constitution and worldly situations. Thus, the post-modernist thought postulates that the meaningfulness of life resides in the individual's localised realities. There is an implicit negotiation between the desire to fully self-actualise in accordance with an idealised image of 'me' and the need to break free from the many sources of influence that underlie such a desire.

Taking the four principles together, and viewing the shift in Western thinkers' articulation of the good life as a continuum, Ferry comments that these evolving accounts of the good life seem to have tended to prescribe life's meaningfulness more and more from outside human life itself,[10] rather than from within it. Hence we may call this a *transcendent* model. What this entails will be explored in this book, so here is only a glimpse of a possible explanation.

Briefly, a transcendent model suggests that humans can only achieve the good life by aspiring to what is beyond ourselves. Accordingly, as already outlined, human life is either believed to be subject to a cosmic order that has inherent harmony and universal goodness; or our salvation is hinged on the power of God for deliverance; or our contentment is defined by an ideal of freedom achieved by a self-conscious rational individual. Given this desire for meaning from beyond human, the post-modernist view of the good life might appear to be an exception. That is to say that it doesn't seem to follow strictly a transcendent model just discussed. From a post-modernist perspective, we are fragmented and embodied subjects whose humanity lies in myriad particularities and multiplicities. There is no one way to perceive the good life. Instead, there is an endless cycle of interpretation, deconstruction and

---

9 Ibid., 16.
10 Ibid.

reconstruction of what it means to live the good life. However, despite this appearance, post-modernist conception does not really escape the transcendent model. This is because it still seeks to derive meanings from outside of persons and lives, such as in those social, cultural, economic and political categories and the cultural-historical, socio-economic and political contexts which tend to define each person and their lived realities.

Now let's review the 'evolving' accounts of the good life as a whole. Here, words such as 'evolution' and 'progression' might give the impression that human understanding of the good life is linear and one-dimensional. As it is already implied, to assume so would be erroneous. Although our understanding and appreciation of the good life have been shifting, nevertheless, the shift does not mean that the earlier principles are no longer relevant to our present challenges. On the contrary, according to Ervin Singer, the American philosopher, there is indeed a deeper ethical thread linking the conceptual horizons across Western accounts concerning the good life. For Singer, this continuous thread is *an ethic of love*.

Connecting Accounts of the Good Life with Love

What does love have anything to do with the good life? According to Singer, Ferry and other writers, love, although complex and touching upon many different lines of investigation, seems to be consistently present in all the major accounts of the good life in Western thought. Hence underlying these accounts are always interpretations and conceptions of love. In fact, alongside the principles inherent in the meanings of life, the articulations of love seem to have also *evolved* whereby novel proposals are introduced over and above the archaic ones. Here is a brief overview of how the conceptions of the good life are animated by an ethic of love. In a cosmic vision, love for the good, the beautiful and the divine invites the human to participate in the sacred harmony. In a theological account, God's love and the love of God inspires us to be virtuous and caring for ourselves and for each other. In the humanist tradition, our love for others and commitment to each other help form and sustain caring bonds between families, communities and societies. To seek emancipation from the power of imposing forces (e.g. represented by the cosmos, God), we have imagined and proposed social structures and institutions to be more loving, fairer and more just. In embracing the post-modernist multiplicity, self-love and self-respect serve to challenge any imposed myths about who we are and what we are. Multiplicity also helps lay emphasis on the divergent ways that we love each other and acknowledge the myriad modes of being human and diverse approaches to acting with love.

This sketch of the connection between an ethic of love and the good life in Western thought is extremely broad stroked. However, despite its brevity, through an awareness of an ethic of love, what we can already see is that the good life not only relies on its being part of the cosmos, God's Kingdom of Heaven, emancipation and personal empowerment, but above all, it also resides in living itself. An ethic of love postulates that the good life precisely lies in our living a richer and fuller life as humans, in communing with other beings in the cosmos.[11] Indeed, it is by living an enlivened, enriched, enriching and even enchanted life that we can achieve life's fullest meanings.

Furthermore, as accounts of the good life *traverse across* times and stages of human development, through the lenses of a love ethic, we can begin to realise that these accounts are increasingly more *humanity-focused*. Here is how. Whilst earlier principles advocate greater transcendence, towards the cosmos, heaven or a distant omnipotent God, by contrast, modernist and contemporary accounts are geared towards greater *immanence*, that is, to locate the meaningfulness of human life in the *here and now* in the living of it. This dynamic between transcendence and immanence will unfold throughout the book. For now, we can simply be curious about the idea of this humanity-focused understanding of the good life as effectively living out our humanness, founded upon, inspired and enlivened by love.

Taking into account the need for a new narrative highlighted at the beginning of this chapter, it might be reasonable to suggest such an emerging narrative represent a further phase of the evolving journey. In other words, after the cosmic, the theological, the humanist and the post-modernist conceptions, our search for the good life has arrived at another turning point. At this (re)defining moment, an ethic of love affirms humanity's renewed awakening. Such an awakening involves becoming aware of the need to move away from a sole concern for any of the following, for example, the universal, the divine, the rational and the individual, towards an increased interest in human's richer and more wholesome experiences in well-being. This is where an ethic of love can make a contribution to an all-encompassing vision, uniting these different orientations. We are therefore on route to explore a new narrative.

---

11 Thomson, *On the Meaning of Life*.

A Narrative of Love

There is ample evidence to support human's awakening through consciously integrating love. Take a closer look at our current epoch. Our time is no doubt marked by crises at multiple levels as already mentioned, but it is also characterised by unprecedented interconnectedness. Human mobility, intercultural encounter, interreligious learning, worldwide commerce, information and communication technology have all contributed to our interconnection. These domains of activities present unique spaces for humanity to re-engage in the good life that has love at its core. In fact, owing to these aforementioned effects of globalisation and as shown during the COVID-19 pandemic, it is not an exaggeration to say that we are currently experiencing an extraordinary sense of humanity on a planetary scale.

There are happenings in the world that can demonstrate how a narrative of love is already in the making. Let me highlight three of its manifestations:

First, no longer isolated in our own cultures or confined by the bounds of our national borders, people in today's world can see the *face* of 'otherness' and encounter 'the other' everywhere we turn.[12] Whilst some people have regarded globalisation as a part of the greater ill, notably in the form of egoism, exploitation and blind pursuit of wealth and profit, others have suggested that it opens the door to empathy, compassion and mutual caring. The latter would cite numerous love-inspired actions at trans-national, national, institutional, communal and personal levels.

Second, there has never been a time in human history when so many people are engaged in concerted voices and actions to condemn and reject dehumanisation and violence, including violence against each other and towards the planet. More people than ever have offered gestures of caring to those in need and shown concern for the plight of strangers, including the ill-being of other beings on the planet. Our collective response to the COVID-19 pandemic is such a powerful testament. The global support for the Black Lives Matter movement marked by solidarity marches, non-violent disobedience and mutual support is another such example. Both demonstrate a willingness amongst many to be united in a common mission to disclose the discriminative institutional practice and challenge the dehumanising economic system.

Presently, there is more awareness than ever that we are part of a greater whole (in a cosmological, ecological and human sense). This is truly extraordinary

---

12 Levinas, *Totality and Infinity*.

for humanity especially considering that it was not so long ago when the West condoned mass enslavement, committed genocides, waged wars, colonised lands and exploited people(s), animals and other beings in nature. Alongside this awareness of the greater whole is a recognition that the wellness and integrity of our planet's ecosystem and human well-being are mutually constituted. This has allowed us to accept a deep history that cannot be explained purely from a human perspective but must be understood from a cosmic perspective. This means that as humans we cannot see ourselves as occupying a special status in the cosmos. Other beings exist alongside human beings, rather than as opposed to humans.

This recognition of deep time and the cosmos might initially suggest the opposite of the humanity-focus identified earlier, but it is not the case. The humanity-focus remains relevant for two reasons. One is that the focus on humanity can help us decentre on human's self interests by ending our self-aggrandising conviction that prioritises our own concerns over and above those of all other beings in the cosmos. The other is that the focus on humanity can help recentre on our responsibility for each other without the desire for reciprocity. Our responsibility also includes our guardianship or custodianship of the planet's ecological integrity. Both decentring and recentring are humanity-focused and together they point to a paradigm of love.

We still have a long way to go in our collective journey towards the good life and flourishing of all. Thus a narrative of love pointing to a new paradigm of living becomes imperative. It provides a fresher appreciation of love as the energising force present in the different ethical frameworks and meaning schemes investigated throughout the Western thought. Taking a long-view and drawing on our preceding discussions can allow us to see that conceptions of love as the basis of our understanding and living the good life oscillate between two poles, mirroring what I already touched upon in the afore-mentioned overview:

On one side, there are accounts that emphasise love's rootedness in the cosmos and the divine, which can seek to enliven the human spirit and offer deliverance and salvation. In short, these accounts stress a vision of love aimed at greater transcendence. On the other side, there are accounts that focus on love's embeddedness in the particularities of being human and in our complex day-to-day lived realities. These latter accounts accentuate greater immanence, to be located in the here and now. As conceptions and practices of love swing between these two poles, transcendence is integrated with immanence, in the mundane; whereby the spiritual is grounded in the material and the embodied.

In between transcendence and immanence, there are many variations in the way love animates the good life. This suggests that a paradigm of love must not privilege merely the divine vision, nor solely the humanistic ideal, but instead, it must seek an equilibrium between these two.[13] Only love can integrate transcendence and immanence; only love can connect the cosmos, divine, human and nature.[14]

This integration marks the new narrative that humanity seeks, an epitome that carries with it a vision of an *attainable utopia* – a truly promising future for humanity. In many ways, this new narrative draws on as well as proceeds from major principles of the good life identified in the history of Western thought and in the conceptual underpinnings of many social and political movements. Through a narrative of love, we can re-engage and re-imagine key ideas underlying our economic, political and communal lives. For instance, a narrative of love can enable us to challenge the 'Just War' theory and prevent violence in the name of 'justice'. Similarly, a narrative of love may inspire values-based economic systems and equitable practices in social institutions. Love rejects any form of structural dehumanisation.

A narrative of love invites us to bear in mind the historical contexts within which to explore conceptions of the good life and well-being. Otherwise, each account would be detached from the rich human circumstances and situations in which understandings are rooted and from which they are further developed and enriched. More importantly, a narrative of love, as already indicated, can stress the imperative for humans to take the responsibility for caring for each other and other beings on the planet and ensuring humanising global systems within which all can flourish.

The Inquiry and Key Learnings

The inquiry captured in this book was aimed at mapping major conceptions of the good life through the lens of love. It surveyed significant arguments concerning love in Western thought.[15] It aimed to identify convergence and

---

13 In fact, this integral view of love has already been proposed by the Stoics in antiquity (see Chapters 2 and 6), arguing that love enables transcendence through immanence. A similar view was developed by De Beauvoir in the twentieth century (see Chapter 5), for instance.
14 More on this is found in Simone De Beauvoir's philosophy in Chapter 5.
15 This book is an important part of a larger project which seeks to explore conceptions of love in interdisciplinary literature, including classic Eastern philosophy, such as Daoism, Mohism, Confucianism and Buddhism; the Western history of ideas; religious teachings in the Abrahamic tradition; and so forth.

divergence in the relevant conceptions, as well as highlight gaps in the existing accounts, whether these are in relation to humans, the idealised notion of goodness, God, nature or the wider cosmos.

The following core question guided the research: 'How is love conceptualised in Western thought?' This has lent itself to three sub-questions: (1) How has love been conceived of in connection with accounts of the good life in Western thought? (2) How do these conceptions of love converge and diverge over time? (3) Given these significant insights, what implications might we draw from a paradigm of love that are significant to our collective lives?

The research started with a broad survey and critical reflection on accounts of love within Western thought, which pointed to a deep connection between an ethic of love and living the good life. The focus on how an ethic of love can inspire the good life in turn determined that the criteria of selection would be the exemplary work on the nature of love within the extant of moral philosophies or ethics.

What did I learn through this research?

I have learned that first of all, since the time of Plato/Socrates, Western thinkers have never ceased to be interested in the notion of love and the significance of love in attempts to seek to live a good life. In other words, love has been a consistent focus of ethical investigations and has always been regarded as, in part, the quality that truly makes life worth living.[16] In foregrounding love, it also became clear that the ethics of love ought to concern the *verb* form of the notion, rather than its *noun* form. This is because in loving actions, we will experience the proactive ways that love is significant to our lives. Love as a verb de-emphasises the need to define and categorise love and stresses what it involves to practise an ethic of love. The interest in living a good life is thus sustained.

What I also learned, as illustrated in Chapter 2, is that an ethic of love ought to be located within a threefold conceptual framework – love as valuing, love as relating or relationing and love as caring. This conceptual framework can effectively enable us to see persons as bearers of non-instrumental values. In addition, as demonstrated in Chapters 3, 4 and 5, this threefold conception of love can allow me to provide dedicated discussions on specific accounts of love and the good life without cramming them all together. Moreover, locating an ethic of love within the triad, that is, valuing, relationing and caring, calls for our creative response to the current multifarious crises already described at the beginning of this chapter.

---

16 Singer, *Meaning in Life: The Pursuit of Love*, 1.

Organisation of the Book

Chapter 1 presents the urgency of the need for a new narrative to guide our collective journeys. It points out that within the Western culture, there already lies the seed for transformation in its continuous interest and articulation of the connection between an ethic of love and the good life.

Chapter 2 outlines a historical trend where love has been explored as a rich and evaluative concept, including how we might appreciate values in life, the way we connect to the intrinsically valuable aspects of things, people and acts, and how we might live out these worthwhile aspects in our personal and political lives. With this understanding as a basis, I further develop a threefold framework, consisting in (1) love as valuing, (2) love as relationing and (3) love as caring, which in turn will serve as the 'programme' for this book.

The next three chapters investigate an ethic of love from each of these lenses. Examining these interlocking accounts within the threefold framework, these sections of the book depict an ethic of love that has human values, the right relationships and genuine care at its core. As mentioned earlier in this chapter, the narrative of love emergent in this process of analysis is particularly helpful in resolving some of the existing (false) dichotomies when discussing and understanding love. These dichotomies include the personal versus the political, the inner versus the outer, the spiritual versus the material and transcendence versus immanence. Indeed, this threefold framework provides an opportunity for us to realise that love can support the restoration of and returning to a state of harmonising through a co-creative and generative process that transforms contradictions, tensions and separations.

Chapter 6 explores how love has already been and can become a core ethical pillar of our systems, including our economic, political, communal, educational and ecological, as well as the principal underpinning our collective action. As Luce Irigaray, the French philosopher, points out, in our time, we need the wisdom of love:

> that joins together, more than it has been done in the West, the body, the heart and the mind; that it is not founded on contempt for nature. That it does not resort to a logic that formalizes the real by removing it from concrete experience; that it be less a normative science of the truth than the search for measures that help in living better: with oneself, with others, with the world.[17]

---

17 Irigaray, *The Way of Love*, 2.

Therefore, the book captures significant implications of love in various aspects of human life, actions, relational processes and lived experiences. These practical examples serve to illustrate how love-inspired actions can enhance the good life for one and all, advance human well-being and support cultural development in harmony with all that is.

Chapter 7 concludes that as humanity journeys through an evolution of consciousness, love must continue to inspire compelling visions of how we should live. It also recognises that parallel to this promising evolution is the structural traumatisation born out of a lack of love, such as in the neoliberal capitalistic brutality, nationalism and identity politics. Capitalism reduces the values in humanity, beauty and goodness to materialistic wealth; nationalist approach ends congenial relationing, divides people(s) and communities and dehumanises persons of difference; and egoistic identity limits our caring and rejects any commonality and fashions a narcissistic singularity of otherness. To heal these wounds, only an ethic of love can ground the pillars of our global processes, economic structures, community relations, educational approaches and ecological systems. An ethic of love supports our collective healing and co-flourishing with other beings on the planet because only through loving, caring and mutual concern and commitment can we overcome feelings of brokenness and woundedness and return to a sense of wholeness. This is where life's spiritual significance lies – the profound appreciation of the transcendent and the immanent as values in life – an unfolding process of human growth. It is here that a paradigm of love can make a genuine difference.

CHAPTER 2

A THREEFOLD FRAMEWORK FOR UNDERSTANDING LOVE

For love is not merely a contributor – one among others – to meaningful life. In its own way it may underlie all other forms of meaning [...] by its very nature love is the principal means by which creatures like us seek affective relations to persons, things, or ideals that have value and importance for us. Seen from this perspective, meaning in life is the pursuit of love, circuitous and even thwarted as that can often be.

—Irving Singer, *Meaning in Life: The Pursuit of Love*

Love has always been present in Western thought, from classical Greek philosophies to Judaeo-Christian teachings, from modernist conceptions to post-modernist/contemporary ideas. However, although a few major propositions have been continuously explored, interpreted and interrogated, such as Plato's philosophy of love outlined in *Symposium* and the three kinds of love (erôs, philia and agapē) advanced by Aristotle, Western thinkers' reflections on love presented in this book have mostly been sidelined. For instance, most people are familiar with Adam Smith's thesis about the 'invisible hand' as put forward in his book *An Inquiry into the Nature and Causes of the Wealth of Nations*, yet few recognise that in Smith's first book (and to a certain extent, also his last book because he returned to revise it towards the end of his life), *The Theory of Moral Sentiments*, he developed an ethic of love (see Chapter 4 for details). Likewise, many would recognise Simone de Beauvoir as an author with a significant feminist voice that challenges the patriarchal status quo, but few would connect her work, such as her book *Second Sex*, with a theorisation of love (see Chapter 3 for further discussion). Clearly, love has been a consistent theme throughout the ages developed in many thinkers' texts and reflections. Notwithstanding love's continuous presence in our ethical thinking, why is love being sidelined in the mainstream discourse, such as in public policies, and political discussions? Here we might make a few educated guesses:

First, it could be owing to the fact that love has long been associated with romance, a passionate physical attraction and an emotional attachment. In Western history, romantic love, when first introduced in eighteenth-century Europe, was regarded as a liberation of men and women from the strictly instrumental view of marriage. Marriage, at the time, was conceived as an institution established to seek political or economic advantage, or to consolidate power and wealth. Romantic love was important in that epoch because it had empowered young women and young men (through courtship) to enjoy (some) freedom to follow their heart and decide to whom to marry.

A letter quoted here during this period can offer a glimpse of romantic love's intensity:

> Antonia, I love you. Three simple little words and yet never uttered or inscribed in ink by me to another living soul, only to you. I will never love another as I love you. I will never cherish another as I cherish you. I will always love only you.[1]

Later, the discovery of lovers as emotional beings characterised by spontaneity and closeness to nature marked philosophical Romanticism at the turn of nineteenth century. Romantic love privileges feeling and emotion over pure reason, intuitive yearnings and impulsive urges over norms and traditions. This further shifted to a gendered performance of love – men in power and wealth-seeking women who embodied beauty, social dexterity and motherhood. Despite in Jane Austen's novel, Elizabeth Bennett's courage to seek romance, the connection between social economic conditions of marriage and the possibility of enduring love was implied. Therefore true emancipation remained wanting, at least in Regency England.

Liberation from social, economic and power considerations in the twentieth century was marked by an absolute desire for sexual freedom and physical intimacy without the burden of responsibility. Love is individualised. This means that love is subjective, unique to the individual who is experiencing love and engaging in the activities of lovemaking. When '[l]ove is a many splendored thing' was sung ever so splendidly by Nat King Cole, it could be any romantic

---

[1] The first verse of a love letter from Renard, Duke of Roxton, to Antonia, Duchess of Roxton, which was left on Antonia's dressing table the morning after their wedding night. Quote from Lucinda Brant, *Eternally Yours: Roxton Letters Volume One: A Companion to the Roxton Family Saga Books 1* (Queensland, Australia: Prigleaf Pty Ltd, 2019).

vision one imagines and desires it to be, a personalised or individualised love. Amidst such a shift, the potency of romantic love perceived in the previous centuries became diminished.

The second reason that love is sidelined might have something to do with the commodification of love and commercialisation of love. With romantic love arrives the commodification of love through 'products' as symbols of love, such as a diamond ring, luxurious gifts, and even cosmetic procedures as enhancement of love, or augmented physical attractiveness. The example of New England Valentine Company reaching an annual gross sale of Valentine cards for up to $100,000 in the 1880s was a clear illustration that 'love sells'. There is also the commercialisation of love aimed to make romance work through payable services, such as matchmaking, couples counselling and love coaching. Books on romantic relations, romance themed tours, dating agencies, love shows, are amongst the packages to commercialise love. When 'love' becomes a tradable good, or purchasable items, it is no longer the liberation from the institution of marriage that is being sought. Instead, lovers return to the same entrapment, although by a different kind of instrumental end – wealth, status and other privileges. It almost feels as if romantic love has lost what makes it romantic.

A third reason why love is sidelined might have something to do with the fact that love has often been mentioned in religious/spiritual discourses. Therefore, in an increasingly secular world, it can be somewhat off-putting when love is portrayed as belonging to the practices of religion. For example, many of the world's religions, not least the three Abrahamic religions, tend to regard love as foundational to their faith, albeit in different ways. Adding to this list is love's connection with new-age spirituality. Many spiritual practitioners tend to base their teachings on love, empathy and compassion, describing love as its essence, the sole pathway to personal development and salvation. In both these situations, love has become too generalised, too broad, especially in phrases such as 'All you need is love!', risking of losing its meaningfulness altogether.

Still, it is not clear whether these shifting phenomena are the reasons why cynical attitudes are found in people who might otherwise have more respect for love. Is commercialisation or commodification reducing love's potency? Does spiritualising love, and portraying love as a force both omnipotent and vague, render it almost empty?

Whilst love is being side-lined in public agenda, at the same time, we find ourselves yet to consider how to relate to the fact that at a grassroots level, love has gradually become a language, a culture and a way of being in its own right. For instance, we are seeing burgeoning proposals for acts of love to be the answer to our contemporary problems. The global challenges to be responded to by love are far-ranging, and let's just review a few. From addressing racism to narrowing the widening socio-economic gaps, from healing mental ill-health to resolving workplace burnout and from transforming intercommunal conflict to dealing with ecological degradation. As examples of love-based responses, there are mindfulness, heartfulness, soulfulness and other such journeys towards the transcendent, all intending to lead to an idealised society characterised by love and care. The *stairways to heaven* are varied, including courses, practices, emergence of intentional communities, Gaia-centric approaches to regenerative agriculture and more. The magic potency of love chanted in popular songs seems no longer a mere unattainable ideal, but rather it is being proactively pursued by communities worldwide as an antidote to systematic political failings. These activities, approaches and practices categorised within the bracket of 'love' are not romance, nor are they limited to religious/spiritual teachings. What they exemplify tend to be more about social justice, ecological integrity, peaceful and harmonious communities and non-antagonistic congenial political processes.

So the question we are left with becomes: 'What is love anyway?'

Understanding Love

The Latin root of love is 'amor' and the verb form is *amarer*, referring similarly to 'affection' and 'friendship'. It suggests that the notion involves two broad kinds of meaning. The first kind is what we commonly describe as general feelings of love, including 'romantic sexual attraction', 'affection', 'friendliness' and 'the love of God'. It locates the meanings of love within a relational realm, concerning passionate and affectionate feelings in relation to someone or something. The other kind refers a certain action such as 'to praise' or 'to appraise' or 'to care' or 'to desire'. This latter interpretation situates the meanings of love in acts that express intimate connection, affection, and friendliness.

In a recent Netflix documentary series (2021), *Stories of a Generation*, Pope Francis is being asked by young people: 'What is love?', and responds that it is akin to asking the question, 'What is air?' This response implies that love is absolutely essential for our existence, our life. Other elders in the documentary also affirm that to love is to come to life more fully, to live our life more vivaciously.

In a Colombian school named 'Colegio Amor' where I did research some years ago, a question was posed to the school's founders, 'Why is the school called Amor?'. Their answer was surprising. Instead of connecting the school's ethos to love, the school's founders articulated that amor, for them, derives from the word *morir* (meaning to die). With the prefix of 'a', a-morir, to-not-die, a-mor becomes a celebration of life. It is about living well, with liveliness or aliveness.

So is love the animating and energising force of life?

According to Henri Bergson, the twentieth-century French philosopher, there is a revitalising force that propels us towards human becoming and self-transcendence. He terms this force, *élan vital*, which lies at the core of life. For Bergson, *élan vital* is denoted by all the forces that contribute to our aliveness, as well as those that distinguish the vivacity of life from non-life, such as materials. This life force or *élan vital* enables life's evolution, progression and transformation. It also determines that life is in a perpetual flux of shifting, growing and becoming. In this sense, life is that which embodies this dynamism within itself, and that which enables life to advance beyond itself. Life is thus an endless process of becoming, through an accumulation of the past (memories) infused with the present momentum and action, towards the emergent innovation into the newness of future.

From a Bergsonian perspective, life consists in a dual orientation: (a) outwardly directed at a world of matter, such as objects, things, states, quantities and so on. (These are generally discernible through mathematical analysis, and in terms of laws or universal principles, or the elements in units such as systems). The world of matter is that to which living beings respond, through movement, action and evolution; (b) inwardly through engaging with consciousness, including our memory of past experiences, our awareness of lived experience and continuity. Life and its trajectories cannot be perceived purely from a mechanistic view and must be realised by integrating our consciousness. For living beings such as plants and animals, life's vivacity is instinctive; by contrast, for humans, life's vivacity is conscious. Our self-conscious awareness of life as a whole can inspire us to seek out things of values, qualities, activities, practices and processes that enable us to engage in creativity, self-transcendence and social transformation. Under this particular tenet, *élan vital* contains in itself a profound act of love.[2]

This fresh perspective is particularly interesting as it adds a new dimension to our understanding of love. It allows us to explore love from the perspectives of life, the good life, good living or living with dynamism. In other words, understanding love requires a conception of the good life. This is the kind of

---

2 Schott, "Bergson's Philosophy of Religion"

exploration that is typically treated as an inquiry about the 'meaningfulness' of life, under the overall theme of ethics. This has been a perennial philosophical endeavour that has become intensified and has been divergently engaged, particularly in recent decades.[3] Questions explored included, for instance, 'What constitutes a good life?', 'What makes life meaningful or worthwhile?' and 'How should one live?'

Understanding the Good Life

When we inquire into the good life, the first thing to clarify is that we are interested in human beings who are living a good *human* life. In other words, our concern here suggests persons must be regarded as bearers of values in life and holders of life's meaningfulness. It has long been argued that being human should have primary (non-instrumental) value, regardless of who we are, where we are from, what we are and what we do.[4] As primary bearers of non-derivative prudential value, our life must have meaning in itself.[5] This valuable nature of human life implies that the experiences, activities, processes, relationships and our self-conscious awareness that constitute our life also have such (non-instrumental) value. Put simply, human life must be non-instrumentally valuable. That is to say, the nature of our life is essentially living for living's sake. The meaningfulness of life lies precisely in living the life itself, which is valuable in its own right.[6] Life cannot merely have instrumental value, nor should it be treated purely instrumentally. What is of instrumental value will be meaningless outside of the goals it is intended to serve, such as a wheelbarrow or a delivery truck. When our life only has instrumental value, for example, life in enslavement, we experience profound ill-being.

We also live our lives with others in communities, with other people, other sentient beings in the cosmos, such as animals and trees and spirits. This *being-with/living-with* in part consists in our living for living's sake. Other people, other beings and things are already constituted in our flourishing, and they should equally have intrinsic non-instrumental value in our life. Purely treating other people and other beings as means to our own happiness will defy the

---

3 Thaddeus Metz, "The Meaning of Life,"
4 To see a fuller account of such claims throughout the ages, please refer to Thomson & Gill, *Happiness, Flourishing and the Good Life*
5 Ibid.
6 Thomson, On the Meaning of Life

imperative of our living for living's sake. This *with*-ness can also be extended to our activities and experiences in the sense that in life, we engage with activities and experiences with other people, such as building a house, and with other beings, such as cultivating a garden. Doing-*with* and acting-*with* others are therefore included in the meaningfulness of our life, which cannot be reduced to a purely instrumental relation.

This way of perceiving humans (and other sentient beings) as bearers of primary values does not rely on the exclusive characterisations of persons as rational beings who can carry out autonomous actions based on reasoning. Indeed, humans are not just rational beings; we are also embodied beings who live our lives in an embodied way. This perspective recognises the important aspects of human conditions and key contents of meaningful life, such as multifarious activities and experiences, relational processes and actions including working, caring and serving, taking delight in things, being playful and having fun.

Furthermore, how we perceive ourselves as bearers of values can determine how we live our lives. This awareness matters to our dignity. In other words, our self-conscious awareness of ourselves as beings of intrinsic non-instrumental value is essential to our self-respect, self-dignity and self-love.[7] This also means that any attempt to treat oneself, others and life itself purely instrumentally is a violation of human dignity. Acts that treat people solely as means to an end, such as human trafficking and child labour, are dehumanising.

Life of dignity is a life of well-being. In this book, I draw on a conception of well-being developed through an earlier research project that I led. Well-being is understood as *being well* and *living well* in a holistic sense.[8] Through Bergsonian perspective on life's propensity towards human becoming, Michel Foucault's point on life's orientation towards change[9] and Gilles Deleuze's idea on the becoming subject,[10] we can see that becoming is always already regarded as an integral dimension of life. So to *being well, living well*, in this book, I add another dimension, *becoming well*.

---

7 Ibid.
8 Ibid.
9 In one of his lectures, Foucault points to life's orientation towards becoming in 'an effort to restore to things their mobility, the possibility of being modified or of changing' (Michel Foucault, *About the Beginning of the Hermeneutics of the Self. Lectures at Dartmouth College* p. 127).,
10 Gilles Deleuze and Félix Guattari, *A Thousand Plateaus: Capitalism and Schizophrenia*

In this definition, well-being is not an emotional or mental state of contentment and happiness, whereby a person feels that they have all their needs and desires fulfilled. Instead, well-being is a verb form, an active and proactive process of living for living's sake. Another word that expresses this process is flourishing. A flourishing life has value beyond individual self-interest. It recognises that our life's activities and experiences can have meaning beyond ourselves. At least, the intrinsic non-instrumental value of life's content can be appreciated not just by one person individually but also by other people and other communities. It is possible that our personalised activities and experiences are not always shared by others, but certainly the values in these activities and experiences can be similarly appreciated and cherished. At best, we share a flourishing life with others through engaging in actions and projects such as learning, creating arts, playing music, building communities, serving the common good, or challenging social injustice. These are the embodied, relational and even spiritual processes of living a good life.

Hence this non-instrumental understanding of life and well-being does not reject the fact that the ways we live our life can have a meaningful impact on others. In living a good life, we can make a helpful contribution to the experiences of other people, the vibrancy of our community and the betterment of our society. Our doing-*with* and acting-*with* is aligned with doing-*for* and acting-*for* where we express our caring for each other and for the world we live in. Although doing-*for* or acting-*for* seems to be instrumental as it is goal-oriented, however, it doesn't necessarily have merely instrumental value. Instead, as argued by Shelley Kagan, the instrumental value, in this case, is also intrinsically and non-instrumentally valuable. Doing things for other people and engaging in good causes in the world can enlarge our life and expand our life's meaningfulness beyond our self-interest. This is where non-instrumental and instrumental values come together in mutually supportive ways.

Perhaps we may use doing work as an example to illustrate this mutually constitutive aspect of living the good life and how it in turn contributes to the enrichment of the good life. All human life has an element of doing work. There are at least four interrelated facets to this idea of doing work.

First, as previously mentioned, doing work as an important activity and constituted part of life's process (through our profession, vocation or job) should be integral to our well-being. Rather than treating it purely as a means to an end, or making a living (e.g. paying bills, mortgage, or buying food, etc.) and commodifying our talents (e.g. offering our qualities and skills for employment tied up to payment), work should be regarded primarily as part of the desirable activities of our life, intrinsically and non-instrumentally valuable in the first instance, fulfilling, meaningful and genuinely enjoyable. In this sense, work can be central to one's being well and living well, or the good life.

Second, doing work should be encapsulated in the processes of human becoming. Whilst we engage in initiatives, creativity and innovation, work continues to shape and nourish our talents, interests and aptitudes. Instead of repetition, boredom or alienation, doing work can help expand on what we are already interested in, enhance our personal qualities and competences, and enable us to take delight in a renewed passion for what we do. Using a common phrase, work is part of our lifelong learning and continuous personal development.

Third, doing work should provide spaces through which we can partake in relational processes and live out (caring) relationships with others. (As already discussed, these congenial relationships and relational processes are already encompassed in the good life and well-being.) For instance, doing work can facilitate our being-*with*, doing-*with* and acting-*with* others. By engaging in socially affable processes such as collaboration, co-creation and dialogue, doing work can enrich our shared life with others in a given context, for instance, in a company, an organisation and a society. That is to say, work can also be part of community building.

Lastly, doing work should consist in the ways by which we care (for ourselves and for each other), serve others and contribute to the betterment of the world. Doing work not only provides livelihood, sustains well-being for oneself and others, enhances dignity, supports social transformation, and helps direct our actions towards what we value and care about. It is thus values-generating and values-inspiring.

These four facets of doing work are characterised as being and becoming, relating, serving and contributing. They also articulate the ways by which human beings, in living a good life of well-being, can simultaneously transcend our limits, improve our personal and collective lives and transform our communities, societies and even systems. Clearly, this innovative conception of doing work balances and harmonises instrumental and non-instrumental values.

Others have offered similar arguments concerning an integration of instrumental and non-instrumental values in the good life. For example, Susan Wolf maintains that a meaningful life is one that a person finds both fulfilling their own passion and interest and contributing to or connecting positively to things of value beyond themselves.[11] In her argument, Wolf separates two

---

11 Susan Wolf, *Meaning in Life and Why It Matters*

kinds of value – subjective vs. objective – and suggests that '[m]eaning arises when subjective attraction meets objective attractiveness'.[12] This is how the justification of motivation for life is aligned with the appreciation of life's values. For Harry Frankfurt, these are *reasons for love*.[13] In Wolf's conception, love is an act of value-recognition and value-appreciation, which is 'neither subsumable under nor reducible to either happiness or morality'.[14] What lies in between happiness (which tends to be subjective and concerned with our personal life satisfaction, good feelings and self-actualisation) and morality (which refers to what is impersonal and an objective judgement of righteousness) is the satisficing and fulfilling experience. In this book, I argue that what makes life satisficing and fulfilling is when life is lived for living's sake. The next question to arise is 'What has love got to do with the good life?'

The Place of Love in the Good Life

Love brings our attention to those features of life that are in total contrast to an unanimated existence or non-existence. Vivacious life or flourishing is embodying, experiencing, expressing and expanding the dynamism in our life forces through engaging in activities and processes that comprise our life. The reasons for love are what motivate a life of well-being. This means our love (and passion) for learning, doing work, such as teaching or gardening, listening to music, playing football, taking a walk in nature with our friends or volunteering can accentuate our appreciation of life's valuable contents and the meaningful processes of living such a life. Similarly, the more we are tuned to the valuable aspects of our life, the more we relate to these values with greater awareness and the more fully we engage with life and live our life. As already discussed, included in the good life and well-being is our consciousness of the non-instrumentally valuable aspects of the activities and processes as meaningful in themselves. Our self-conscious awareness of our own interests, needs, wants and yearnings can determine our evaluative appreciation of the non-instrumental values in persons, doings and causes. Our self-conscious awareness is rooted in love that can truly highlight the intrinsic non-instrumental value of those activities, processes and relationships constituted in our well-being. Love is a driving force for our

---

12 Susan Wolf, *The Variety of Values: Essays on Morality, Meaning, and Love* , 112.

13 Harry Frankfurt, *The Reasons of Love*

14 Wolf, *Meaning in Life and Why It Matters*, 9.

appreciative attention and our active involvement in life. We are drawn to deeds, endeavours, people, communities, projects and initiatives that are valuable and worthy of our love. It is towards these valuable aspects that we direct our loving attention.

Like well-being, which is defined as being well, living well and becoming well, love must also be understood in its verb form, rather than a noun form. It is precisely by using love's verb form that this book attempts to avoid the typical difficulty that philosophy tends to encounter – the need to define what is and what is not, what to include and what to exclude in such definitions. Instead, when we understand love as a verb, it emphasises the kind of activities that humans should engage in and how we should engage in them.

In this book, I apply a three-fold framework to capture love's meaning and potency in its verb-form:

First, from the perspective of living for living's sake, love is primarily an act of valuing. By valuing, love enables us to appreciate the valuable nature of that towards which love is directed. Irving Singer suggests that love be an appreciative stance one can take towards another person, an object or a cause in the world. Thus, in loving someone or something, we recognise and affirm the goodness or the valuable aspects of the beloved. This means that the goodness to be identified and acknowledged is already there in the first place and the act of love as valuing allows us to direct our attention and appreciation at the goodness.

Singer uses two notions, 'appraisal' and 'bestowal', to describe love as 'a way of valuing something'.[15]

On love as appraisal, the appraising or loving must go beyond the mere empirical or objective fact-finding for the sake of ascertaining the (monetary or quantifiable) 'value'. Let's take a person's appraising the value of their garden and doing the gardening as an example. If, for instance, the person's love for a beautiful garden is such that they and their family may be seen to be more respectable in the eyes of neighbours, friends and visitors, then their 'love' or 'appraisal' of the garden and their own gardening activities is based on an instrumental mentality – treating the garden and gardening purely as a means, as having merely instrumental value. In this case, it may even be preferable to hire someone to do the gardening and to make the garden look good. The garden and gardening are therefore not part of this person's well-being. To love the garden and gardening, love's appraisal must engage one's interests, needs

---

15 Singer, *Philosophy of Love: A Partial Summing-Up*, 3.

and desires in seeking what makes the garden a true object of one's heart's yearning. When, for example, a person loves their garden because the spaces are where some activities and experiences central to their well-being take place: they love spending quality time in the garden with neighbours and friends; they cherish the memories of children growing up playing in these spaces; they treasure the beauty of the flowers and plants whilst sitting in the garden; they enjoy caring and nurturing the beings in the garden, and take delight in anticipating the garden's bloom. When applying these non-instrumental lenses, we see that love can fully appraise and appreciate values.

On love as bestowing, Singer argues that to love is to offer to others what is of value, which is beyond something of purely materialistic worth. The word C.S. Lewis chooses to describe bestowing is 'gift-love', or gifting.[16] Both Singer and Lewis suggest that by bestowing, giving or gifting, love *creates* or *engenders* value and enables us to recognise the valuable aspects or goodness in the thing/person/project from a new perspective. According to Singer, what is being loved is 'created by the affirmative relationship *itself*'.[17] In other words, in valuing, love begets added value(s) or more goodness.

Appraising and bestowing are interrelated because in appraising, the valuable aspects of things, persons or activities become more present and more accessible to us; and in bestowing, love creates 'affective value'. This is where applying non-instrumental self-conscious awareness is imperative. Otherwise, with appraisal merely at a material level and from an instrumental perspective, all can just be like commodities, being assessed and measured for their material deservedness or worthiness to be loved. Through appreciating the valuable aspects consciously, love brings to the fore life's meaningful contents more vividly.

In Chapter 3 of this book, we will demonstrate the ways that many thinkers have supported this notion of love as valuing. However, there are also objections to this idea, such as that of Harry Frankfurt. In the quote below, he explains his objection:

> It is entirely possible for a person to be caused to love something without noticing its value, or without being at all impressed by its value, or despite recognizing that there really is nothing especially valuable about it. It is even possible for a person to come to love something despite recognizing

---

16 Lewis, C. S. *The Four Loves*
17 Singer, *Philosophy of Love: A Partial Summing-Up*.

that its inherent nature is actually and utterly bad. That sort of love is doubtless a misfortune. Still, such things happen.[18]

How does one respond to such a critique of all that just discussed on love as valuing? Frankfurt's statement suggests that love is caused by something, a reactive response to something desirable but without one's necessarily identifying it as valuable. Well, we can respond by saying the following. It might be true that sometimes we can be captivated by a certain quality in the *beloved*, and we find ourselves moved to love them, say blindly. However, such experience might be categorised as an infatuation, attraction or even an enchantment. It *cannot* be an act of love. When we understand love as valuing, it necessarily involves an evaluative self-consciousness that enables us to appreciate the valuable aspects of life, human beings and other beings in the world. The value we take delight in, however, does not concern the moral inclinations of people or their nature being good or bad. Rather, it is because we recognise that persons are bearers of value and hence we love and appreciate beings of intrinsic non-instrumental value as such.

Second, from the perspective of well-being, love can be perceived as an act of relating/relationing. Love can enable, enhance, enrich and engender relationships. In the minimal sense, love, being almost always construed as loving something or someone, by virtue, already involves the act of relating and relationship between more than one entity. Even self-love entails a relationship to one's self possibly as an 'other'.[19] Therefore, it would seem obvious that any understanding of love must be a relational conception. Still, what makes this framing beyond a statement of platitude is that love gives prominence to the act of *relationing*. Relationing refers to those aforementioned activities of enabling, enhancing, enriching and engendering relatedness. Indeed, the activities and processes that comprise meaningful life have a relational dimension in that we are always interacting with what is in the world, our body, other people, groups, places and spaces, society and other beings in nature. Some of these relations are comprised in our well-being precisely because they are so due to the act of loving. Love connects things, persons, groups, communities and other beings in the world.

---

18 38, Frankfurt, Harry G. *The Reasons of Love* (Princeton, NJ: Princeton University Press, 2006).
19 See Ricoeur, *Oneself as Another*.

To clarify this point requires that we rehearse an earlier idea on persons and other conscious beings as the primary bearers of non-instrumental value. In this case, our activities, experiences and processes matter because as value-bearers, *we,* or *persons* matter. Love enables us to be open to relationships and engage in relational processes with other people and other sentient beings because they have primary non-instrumental value in themselves to which we can connect and relate. Insofar as we can connect and relate appropriately to the value of other people and other beings, the values they encompass and exemplify can become part of our own life. It is almost like by loving and through relationing, our respective lives have been enlarged and our well-being expanded and enriched. Enlarged life contains other people and other beings who are now comprised in our well-being. Whilst acknowledging their place in our well-being, however, family, friends, colleagues, people in our community and beings in nature are not to be instrumentalised for the sake of our well-being. Love as relationing can ensure just that.

To recognise and appreciate the intrinsic non-instrumental value of our own activities and processes is primarily self-regarding. When we engage with others and connect with the value in their activities and processes, it makes our life other-regarding. Referring to the earlier example of doing work, when we engage in doing-*with*, love as relationing is already comprised in it, in virtue, of this mutually regarding connection. Love invites people to become mutual-regarding – as if love can hold and maintain the space(s) and sustain relatedness between people. This in-betweenness includes that which is between two persons, amongst a large number of people, such as groups, as well as the space(s) and relatedness between humans and other beings. Other beings, in this case, can include the Spirit (as in cosmology, the Spirit of the universe), God (as in theology), beings in nature and beings in the cosmos.

Although there can be a tendency to see other-regarding and self-regarding as opposite or binary, many have rejected this view. Take the French philosopher, Jean-Luc Nancy's argument as an example. He maintains that although other-regarding (in which one loses oneself without reserve) and self-regarding (in which one recuperates oneself) seem to suggest antagonism and binary, introducing self-regarding and other-regarding as mutual-regarding as the fruit of loving can overcome the antagonism and transcend the binary. Nancy writes that when we love, our heart 'exposes the subject'.[20] However, the self, or the subject, 'is never an autonomous existent but is always in relation

---

20 Nancy, "Shattered Love," 254.

with others. Love shatters the atomistic being [...] introducing alterity into the heart of being'.[21] The shattered subject reaches out to different people and things, which in turn become part of a loving subject. It is precisely in the act of loving, the self- and other-regarding binary is overcome:

> This overcoming is achieved not by subsuming one within the other, through a dialectical sublation but through the actions and effects of love, actions which transform the subject, who, in love, or through love, is broken into, touched and fractured by love.[22]

In this sense, 'love is the act of transcendence',[23] an opening, a 'crossing'.[24] Moving beyond the limitations of dialectical oscillations which result in sublimation or fusion of the self and other into a transcendent singularity, Nancy proposes that love provides the model for the endless dialectics of being-becoming, whereby love *shatters* the dialectic and *lives* through exposition. Similar to Levinas's idea, love does not *appropriate the other*, instead, an act of loving can give to the other, which in turn exposes the self or the subject to itself.

Love as relationing creates a space for all to partake in relationships with each other and with things and beings in the world. Relationships unfold in the spaces of in-between. By stressing this in-between-ness,[25] this framing of love as relationing brings to the fore love as a meeting of co-subjects, as a way of being well, living well and becoming well *in* and *with* the world.[26] The relational bonding defines the nature of our communal and social spaces where we can take delight in the presence of one another and seek joy in this meeting. Through mutual-regarding, we experience, enrich and enhance mutual well-being.

Lastly, love involves our self-conscious awareness of the valuable aspects of what we love, also referred to as love's directedness, a form of caring. When love as caring underpins our actions, it is directed, as we have seen, at the intrinsic non-instrumental value in persons or things in themselves. To love is to care about such values and act in ways that express concerns for those in whom and

---

21 Linnell Secomb, 'Amorous Politics: Between Derrida and Nancy' 451.
22 Nancy, "Shattered Love," 145.
23 Ibid., 261.
24 Ibid., 262.
25 See Luce Irigaray's discussion on this in-between-ness in Chapter 4 of this book.
26 Freire, *Pedagogy of the Oppressed*.

in which such values are incarnated and embedded. Value-directedness is the most desirable attitude and action that love urges us to adopt and enact.

Love as caring invites us to act in such ways that enable the value of living for living's sake to radiate and expand. In caring, we engender value in people, activities, things, causes and other beings that we care. In caring, they will bear upon us even more.[27] Insofar as we care, love can make these important constituents of our well-being more vivid and more enriching. Thus love as caring attributes greater meaningfulness to our life. Caring enacts our love of living for its own sake. Through love as caring, we contribute to the enrichment of our well-being.

Love as caring further allows us to balance the seemingly conflicting intuitions where we might otherwise be torn by persons, things and causes of value that demand our caring at once. For instance, we often feel that when deciding on how to spend time, a choice must be made between loving and caring for our child (e.g. spending the afternoon with our children cycling) and loving and caring for our project (e.g. connecting with our team and discussing latest feedback). Love as caring can balance these two by suggesting that giving time to either will be part of the good life, and we are not compromising on one over the other, but instead, we can be caring for both. This means that when we find sensible ways to divide our time, we are caring for things of value in their own right.

The conception of love as caring is as ancient as it is modern. Love as caring is a source of volitional necessities whereby love gives rise to our simply *having* to do certain things that are valuable and about which we care.[28] It is as if love demands that we be and become certain sorts of people, and these reasons provide impetus and motivation for our (voluntary) caring action.

Love as caring is in the ethical realm of life where caring inspires and energises our attention and our acts, directed at the goodness in the world. In this ethical realm, we reject acts and relationships that are unloving and uncaring. In caring, as in valuing, we seek out the goodness in people, things, activities, causes and other beings in the cosmos and become curious about them. Through caring action, we participate with them in processes that are yet to be imagined and created, including how to act differently.[29] Hence love

---

27 Chapter 2 of Frankfurt, "Autonomy, Necessity, and Love".
28 Frankfurt, "Autonomy, Necessity, and Love".
29 Foucault offers three similar moral principles, including 'refusal', 'curiosity' and 'innovation'. See Foucault's Dartmonth College lectures, 2016, 128.

as caring is not solely about our concern for what is already there, but more importantly, caring is about what might come forth. It stresses the importance of creatively living out those valuable aspects, embracing new forms of relating and engaging in novel ways of being. By caring about what matters to us and to the world, innovative acts create new forms of living, in and through which we become and we self-transcend. Love as caring also inspires us to take active responsibility for persons, causes and goodness in the world – self-transcendence and worldly transformation are integrated.

A Triadic Framework for Understanding Love

I started by suggesting that love is always connected to the meaningfulness of life. This is the essence of an ethical life. Such an inquiry has led us to highlight the importance of recognising that persons are bearers of values and therefore our life has primary intrinsic non-instrumental value and is constituted by non-instrumental goodness along the necessary dimensions. These dimensions include our activities, experiences, processes and relationships, all of which require self-conscious awareness of the non-instrumental value of these. In doing so, this book offers a view of life's meaningfulness which lies in life itself or living for living's sake. This characterises the nature of our well-being, conceived as being well, living well and becoming well.

The interlocking dimensions of the good life then give rise to understanding love in its verb form through a threefold framework: (1) love as valuing, (2) love as relationing and (3) love as caring. None of these conceptions of love is unfamiliar, still, when these are discussed together, we can re-familiarise ourselves with love anew. This threefold framework effectively demonstrates the interconnection between values, relational processes and actions. In its verb form, love is enacted by bearers of values and in turn, it enriches and enhances the meaningfulness of our life and our well-being. Throughout this book, I will use this framework of an ethic of love as the basis to present the evolving Western conceptions of love.

Love as valuing accentuates that our well-being has primary value. Moreover, our well-being is always shared with all the forces underlying our living systems as a whole, including, for example, not only other people, communities, societies, but also the climate, the oceans, the lands and the interactive dynamics out of which life is formed and transformed.[30] This

---

30 Deleuze and Guattari, *A Thousand Plateaus: Capitalism and Schizophrenia*.

naturally connects to love as relationing that ensures congenial and hospitable relational spaces and processes between and amongst beings , inviting co-flourishing, rather than mutual, exploitation. Love as caring points to that human well-being consists in our engaging in social, cultural and political processes with each other in the material world. Our life is aligned with both living and non-living forces that provide the conditions for life to be created, enriched and innovated.

By underscoring the three interconnected dimensions that give rise to an ethic of love, we bring our attention to the importance of non-instrumental value, such as love-friendship in flourishing life, including civic friendship. Likewise, an ethic of love underlines those ideas that point to the interdependence between humans and other beings in nature and the imperative to condemn the devastating effects on nature by human's economic pursuit and other ego driven activities, such as geographical expansion that intrudes on the habitats of other beings in nature. Therefore, an ethic of love can help humans to engage in being, living and becoming well in harmony with the flourishing of all others.

The next three chapters outline a historical trend where love has been understood as a rich and evaluative concept, including how we appreciate values in life, the way we relate to what we consider as valuable and how we live out these worthwhile aspects of our being in personal and political lives. The threefold framework, that is, valuing, relationing and caring, will serve as the 'programme' of the book.

Selection of the Works on Love

Love has no doubt a history. Throughout the ages, philosophers have continued to interpret their predecessors' theories of love and further develop their own ideas by critiquing, building and expanding on others' thoughts. Therefore, in this book, under the threefold themes of *Love as Valuing*, *Love as Relationing* and *Love as Caring*, I have managed to focus on identifying a major thread of love's evolution, that is, from the cosmocentric to the theocentric views, from the humanistic towards the more human-centred standpoints. Unfortunately, due to the word space limit, I could only select the most relevant ideas rather than presenting the entire vista.

The broad periods of Western thought include: (a) the Greek tradition (from c470 BC to 86 BC, including the classical period, e.g. Socrates, Plato and Aristotle's philosophies and Hellenistic period, especially Stoicism); (b) classical antiquity (e.g. Judaeo-Christian theological thought or from 300s till sixteenth century); (c) modernist period (starting from eighteenth century to late nineteenth century); and (d) post-modernist/contemporary time (from twentieth century until now). I have left out the Renaissance period altogether because philosophical inquiries at this time were mostly about reengaging with classical Greek thought, including reinterpreting theories of love in, for instance, the texts of Neo-Platonists, such as Marsilio Ficino or Baldassare Castiglione, Leone Ebreo and Giordano Bruno who embarked on novel interpretations of Symposium and re-developed their own theories of love. There is an exception though: I have included Michel de Montaigne in this book, listed under those ideas within the theological principles.

In some periods, such as the ancient Greek, it was relatively easier to identify the key voices, the omission of which would not allow a foundational understanding of the concept. However, since the Middle Ages, it is not at all straightforward in identifying the foundational ideas. Selection becomes strenuous, and I took an approach as if following the breadcrumbs, for example, St Augustine and St Thomas developing their ideas by following Plato and Aristotle, Martin Luther's continuing the Greek tradition and their predecessors, and so forth.

The selection to follow was based on those arguments that can support the overall direction of this project. For example, although Spinoza and Kant's theories on love are not necessarily the core of their oeuvres, Spinoza's argument on the wholeness of our being and Kant's categorical imperative have truly established the paramount importance of respecting human dignity, which does not solely rely on divine bestowal. These views have heralded a milestone in love's evolution. Hence their inclusion.

Similarly, Schopenhauer and Nietzsche's philosophies establish the values of human life and equally the worthwhileness of pursuing a good life in its own right as part of human striving. These open doors to discussions that do not rehearse the already visited arguments even through their critique.

When selecting modern perspectives, I tended to stress voices of women philosophers, which are found wanting in the earlier discussions. For instance, Tullia d'Aragona and Emma Goldman, whose perspectives on love as emancipation for women are significant additions and the same applies to Simone de Beauvoir, whose unique conception of love takes the notion into the realm of culture. Including Hannah Arendt's interpretation of St Augustine's ideas on love and providing a space for Arendt's political philosophy through the perspective of love is very important because it encourages a reflection on the role of the state in ethical governance. Other significant women philosophers' voices, such as Nussbaum's re-reading of Plato and Aristotle, Amelie Roty's interpretation of Spinoza and Kathryn Morgan's analysis of de Beauvoir, have been included as constructive commentaries and critical analyses.

I confronted a few challenges when deciding whose accounts to include and not include in this book. To begin, it was the challenge of deciding how to include accounts of love from thinkers and writers who might *not* want their works to be labelled as *Western*, such as those by African American writers, bell hooks, Cornel West and authors from the Latin America, especially in the case of Paulo Freire and other contemporary scholars of decolonial studies. After consulting some of my colleagues, I have decided to include these voices for constructive critique when engaging with perspectives captured in this book.

The other challenge concerned dividing the key accounts of love into three chapters in order to present conceptions of love through the triadic framework for understanding love. This has proven to be extremely difficult because to do so meant that the book would have three particularly long chapters. Therefore, I have intentionally captured the main ideas in each of the thinker's relevant arguments without over-elaborating them. The end result is that although there are three long chapters, each is punctuated with shorter and extremely digestible and accessible entries.

Lastly, there has been burgeoning contemporary literature exploring love's place in the good life, including books, scholarly articles and other entries on blogs and social media. The plurality of voice is pleasing, demonstrating a growing interest in the power of love and the practice of love in all domains of human endeavour. However, it is impossible to provide a space for these voices in this book. So what I did was to include the fruits of these interests in a chapter that illustrates love in action. These are by no means sufficient, but at least, we can have a glimpse of a new movement inspired by love.

CHAPTER 3

LOVE AS VALUING

Wicked men obey from fear; good men, from love.

—Aristotle

In Western history, love has been conceptualised by many as a supreme value. On love as valuing, earlier thinkers tend to stress two contrasting ideas: one is the imperative of self-knowledge that enables us to seek out the valuable aspects in things, persons and activities; and the other is the requirement of disinterested interest, independent of our self-knowledge, personal desire or preference. On the latter, for instance, the classical Greek thinkers might propose that we affirm and appreciate the goodness and beauty in things and persons because they mirror the ideal forms already present in the cosmos. In this sense, to love is to value and cherish anything that is reflected in the cosmic order of harmony. In a similar vein, a theological argument might suggest that because we are creations of God, to revere the beauty and goodness in the world is to revere God's divine qualities reflected in humans. Moreover, valuing cosmic and divine qualities in humans and in other beings in the world may necessarily involve self-love which in turn requires self-knowledge. Here self-love and love of what is beyond the self are regarded as mutually constituted because without love of the self, a person cannot extend affection and compassion to others.

Modernist perspectives on love as valuing are directed at the valuable nature of persons, the good life and our well-being in their own right, rather than merely for the sake of the cosmos, the divine or God. Following this turn also arrives the post-modernist passionate appraisal of the rich particularities of the atomic singularity. These particularities reflect the diverse aspects of an individual person, including their gender, sexual orientation, ethnicity, class, capability and belief. In this light, for some (especially the libertarians) what is being valued involves the individual's rights, freedom and each person's deservedness of their due, all of which have socio-economic and political implications. For others (especially the communitarians), love as valuing inspires solidarity, harmony and collaboration across the particularities and differences.

However, the contemporary passion for individualistic success has subtly marked an underlying shift from love's championing intrinsic non-instrumental value to love becoming a means to the ends of self-directed gains. We have observed love as valuing being replaced by serving self-interests, such as meeting personal needs and desires, seeking hedonic sexual pleasures and procreation. Self-interests are now effectively the main impetus for the design of socio-economic and political systems. These systems are therefore structured to maximise wealth accumulation and growth-oriented market development. Instrumentalisation has resulted in a contemporary malaise – perceiving human being as means to keeping alive the economic engine for materialistic gains. Instrumentalisation thus causes a sense of alienation and isolation that characterises some contemporary Western societies. It also allows the annihilation of other beings on earth and even violation of the integrity of the entire ecosystem itself.

Dehumanisation is the opposite of love and cannot be a source of ethical living for humanity. It is therefore unsurprising that some contemporary philosophers have reconsidered the value that love inspires and come up with proposals to re-envision the cosmos, God and supreme values of goodness, beauty and wholeness to be reintegrated in the meaningfulness of life.

Classical Greek Thought on Love as Valuing

The legacy of Greece to Western Philosophy is Western Philosophy.
—Bernard William, *The Legacy of Greece: A New Appraisal*

It is love that makes the world go round
—Ervin Singer, *The Nature of Love: Plato to Luther*

Donald Levy once suggested that, for anyone who wants to understand love, the only way to begin is to reflect on the problems first raised by Plato.[1] Plato tends to use the voice of Socrates in developing his philosophical ideas. From this beginning, Western philosophical tradition has continued to explore a connection between love and value and regarded it as central to a proper understanding of how to love and how to be loving.

Western philosophy started in ancient Greek times,[2] and part of 400 BC enjoyed a brief period of the 'golden age' where Athens became a cultural centre. During this time, arts and philosophy flourished, as well as democratic practices where power was distributed amongst citizens, rather than residing in the hands of the aristocrats. Around this time, the ancient Greeks discovered a systematic approach to inquiry through both reasoning and empirical observation, allowing them to understand natural processes and the principles and laws underlying them. Such systems of thought were the foundation to the ethical (and political) theories of Socrates, Plato, Aristotle and the Stoics, and they remain relevant to today's philosophical approaches.[3] The continued wars and the Spartan rule through oligarchy (which resulted in the death sentence of Socrates around 399 BC) ended this golden age.

In classical Greek thought, the idea of the *whole* is important, and seeking the good life through identifying our appropriate or rightful place in the *whole* has become a perennial human quest.[4] To do so, it requires the idea of the cosmos – an all-encompassing universe within which people, things and other beings interact in the grand order of things.[5] On this, Plato has argued for

---

1 Levy, "The Definition of Love in Plato's Symposium".
2 Russell, *A History of Western Philosophy and Its Connection with Political and Social Circumstances from the Earliest Times to the Present Day.*
3 Thomson, *Ancient Philosophy.*
4 Ferry, *A Brief History of Thought.*
5 For Socrates, Cosmos is an Order over Chaos. This order of nature is the outward reflection of the inner order of reason.

the existence of universal forms.[6] These forms define what counts as just and good and depend on knowledge and language, or *logos*, to describe and explain (the forms). For Plato, through such forms arise epistemology, education, metaphysic, ethics, art and politics. Justice and goodness in the forms are ideals drawn from the *cosmos*. However, for Aristotle, although recognising that universals – such as Plato's ideal forms – do exist, he maintains that their existence is derivative of what is found in nature (which is the *whole*). In other words, the forms embodying goodness and beauty are immanent in our world rather than from beyond our world. The Stoics go even further and believe that the cosmos or the *whole* is a living organism, within which each element is ordered, coordinated and harmonised with other elements in support of the *whole*. This is a vision of cosmology. Within such a cosmos, there exists an order and a form of harmony that affects what is right, just and good. As long as we can discern the principles of harmony and values of aesthetics and ethics, we can pursue the goodness through such models.

According to the ancient Greeks, there are two challenges confronting humanity when aspiring for the good life. One is that we are always already situated within our own reality. As our reality is merely a minute corner of the cosmos, it is therefore impossible for humans to observe and appreciate the order, the harmony, the beauty and the rightfulness from the perspective of the whole. To go beyond our limitation, there is the need for learning, for surpassing our current situations. This surpassing requires transcendence. The other challenge is that human's life is finite, and we will eventually face mortality. Although from an early time, humans already recognised that some activities could help extend life, including through procreation, perpetuating stories of heroic deeds, building statues and monuments, the fear of finitude has continued to haunt us. This fear urges us to seek salvation, and salvation requires transcendence.

An important pathway towards transcendence is love.

From the beginning, there is an idealisation of love in classical Greek thought. This idealisation places love within the realm of the perfect good, the object of ultimate human desire. Love is translated into supreme virtues, the qualities to be pursued and experienced as part of a good life. At the time, the good life is only defined as the kind of life enjoyed by the gods. Accordingly, love determines, in part, human's ceaseless striving and becoming (more like

---

6 Thomson, *Ancient Philosophy*.

the gods). Equally, love postulates the important god-like virtues that are worthy of our cultivation.

There are various principles that prescribe love as valuing. For example, by applying the principle of rationality, love invites the perfection from the beloved.

Indeed, the Platonic 'erôs' identifies the absolute perfection as the object of love. In seeking such perfection, the lover is en-route to a gradual ascension, as if climbing a ladder, towards the good life (enjoyed by the gods). By contrast, Aristotle presents a vision of love, 'philia', experienced as friendship. For Aristotle, love is bound up in reason (versus emotion) and inspires (intellectual) companionship in mutual yearning for the good. Perfect friendship is delightful and joyous, not in the sense of pleasure-seeking, but in the common recognition of the goodness and virtuous qualities amongst the friend-lovers. It is these qualities that have intrinsic values and thereby constitute in part the good life.

Stoicism seeks to articulate a coherent account of reality, including the systemic nature of the world, as well as the holistic nature of human life. For the Stoics, 'logos' (reason and rationality) provides an overarching structure for understanding the world, and logos have been identified with the creative force, such as God. Through the universal logos, order is created, where everything shall find its rightful place in the cosmos. Hence a flourishing life is a well-reasoned life, in harmony with the values put forward by logos. Highly influenced by Aristotelean philosophy, Stoicism advocates the cultivation of virtues as the core of a good life and stresses that wise persons are those who practise virtues and live a virtuous life.

***

Plato (428–348 BC): Love as valuing the good

Symposium is one of Plato's two dialogues on love.[7] In this dialogue, Plato re-accounts a drinking party when the host, Phaedrus, claims that the God of love, Erôs, has been neglected by the Greek poets. For this reason, he invites his guests to give speeches to praise love. Amongst these praises of love, two are particularly relevant to the theme of love as valuing.

---

7 The other dialogue is *Phaedrus*.

Agathon is the fifth contributor who speaks about love.[8] In his speech, Agathon introduces the idea that love is always directed at a certain kind of value, such as beauty and is a response to this particular value: 'all goods came to gods and men alike through love of beauty'.[9] Interestingly, the original Greek word καλόν meaning beauty, or 'the beautiful', can also be translated in English as 'the fine' or 'the noble'.[10] Love, according to Agathon, is what is taken to be the beautiful. The beautiful, however, is not merely an aesthetic quality, though the aesthetic sense is prominent. Instead, beauty or the beautiful is an ethical value that might also be exhibited in qualities of the mind, action and character. Agathon concludes that love seeking the beautiful, the refined and the noble is said to be responsible for all goodness.

The next to speak is Socrates who picks up the themes advanced by the previous speakers and develops them further. To begin, he says that we must realise that to love is to desire beautiful things. While it may seem to make sense for someone to want what is beautiful when they already possess it, love, Socrates proposes, is the desire to pursue the beautiful and continue to do so in the future. He refers to a dialogue between himself and Diotima, a prophetess and philosopher, from whom he has acquired understanding of love.[11]

According to Diotima, we desire or take delight in what is *good*.[12] Since, as Socrates already established, whatever is good is also beautiful, love is the desire

---

8 The other speeches before Agathon are given by Phaedrus (speech begins 178a); Pausanias (speech begins 180c); Eryximachus (speech begins 186a); Aristophanes (speech begins 189c).
9 Plato, *Symposium*, 197b-c.
10 Cooper, *Reason and Emotion*.
11 It is striking that Socrates portrays a woman as an expert, superior to himself, on the nature of love, especially given the context of the *Symposium* as a whole, in which male and homosexual love tend to be emphasised and elevated. For discussion, see Halperin, "Why is Diotima a Woman?" . By putting this account of love in the reported words of Diotima – who is not present at the party – Plato also places it at one further step of removal from both Socrates and himself.
12 "'Now there is a certain story', she said, according to which lovers are those people who seek their other halves. But according to my story, a lover does not seek the half or the whole, unless, my friend, it turns out to be good as well. I say this because people are even willing to cut off their own arms and legs if they think they are diseased. I don't think an individual takes joy in what belongs to him personally unless by 'belonging to me' he means 'good' and by 'belonging to another' he means 'bad'". Plato, *Symposium*, 205e.
Diotima here offers a crucial revision of the myth recounted earlier in the dialogue (189d-193d) by Aristophanes. According to that myth, in a Golden Age, people were

for what is beautiful as whatever is desired is in effect desired as something good. Diotima concludes that 'what everyone loves is really nothing other than the good'.[13] With this revision, Diotima reformulates Socrates's earlier proposition: 'In a word, then, love is wanting to possess the good forever.'[14]

Every person, in Diotima's view, wants and acts for the sake of something they take to be good. This longing for the good, which she equates with happiness or flourishing (*eudaimonia*), is love.[15] The main point, she tells Socrates, is that 'every desire for good things or for happiness [eudaimonia] is the supreme and treacherous love' in everyone'.[16] The good, or the beautiful, that Diotima instantiates is the absolute beauty, which

> neither comes into being nor passes away, neither waxes nor wanes, [...] is not beautiful in part, [...] nor beautiful at one time [...] is not beautiful in this relation [...] nor beautiful here [...] as varying according to its beholders [...].[17] Instead, such beauty is absolute because it is 'existing along with itself, unique, eternal and all other beautiful things as partaking of it [...] [and] neither undergoes increase or diminution nor suffers any change.[18]

Love is hence valuing the absolute beauty, eternal, independent of persons, time and space. Absolute beauty is the very essence of all things beautiful, such as the many instances in the beauty of trees, the beauty of blue colours, the beauty of persons and so forth. What is being valued is the ultimate structure of the universe, captured in the *tree*-ness, *blue*-ness and *human*-ness. It is precisely this *what*-ness (the qualities that define what things are) that love yearns for and lovers ought to pursue. When we value goodness or beauty in this way

---

eight-limbed powerful creatures, so filled with hubris that they threatened the gods. Zeus order them sliced in half, and thereafter these (we) 'half people' search for their (our) other halves. Sexual desire and intercourse are derivative from a prior urge for reunification in the myth, introduced only after Zeus orders the sexual organs to be relocated to people's soft, forward-facing side. The revision that reunification is desired only on the condition that it is something good fundamentally changes the myth's significance: love becomes a longing for the good, rather than bodily longing for conjugation. Cf. Singer, *The Nature of Love: Plato to Luther*, 52–3.

13 Plato, *Symposium*, 206a.
14 Ibid., 206a11-12.
15 cf. Kraut, "Plato on Love", 290.
16 Plato, *Symposium*, 205d.
17 Singer, *Philosophy of Love: A Partial Summing-Up*, 56.
18 Ibid., 56.

and when we are consciously aware of our appreciating these valuable aspects of things, persons and nature, love fills us with absolute joy – an experience of true happiness or eudaimonia.

Singer interprets this as implying that, in Plato's view:

> all human activity is motivated by love [...] since everything – not just man – strives for the attainment of some good, the entire universe would seem to be continuously in love [...] It is love that makes the world go round.[19]

Love not only values the perpetual goodness and beauty in all things, at the same time, love invites and energises the goodness and beauty in all that is. In her striking phrase, Diotima teaches that in pursuing the good, lovers seek to 'give birth in beauty',[20] which alludes to all manner of creative pursuits in which lovers engage. Here, Diotima highlights three kinds of creativity suited to different sorts of people. Some, she tells us, are 'pregnant in body and for this reason turn more to women and pursue love in that way, providing themselves through childbirth with immortality and remembrance and happiness [eudaimonia]'.[21] Some, she suggests, seek to possess the good forever in heroism and honour through acts of courage of which they are the author. They do so in the hope that their memory will be immortalised through dramatic or poetical recounting of their deeds.[22] Others (and apparently the best), according to Diotima, 'are pregnant in soul' who pursue love through the cultivation of virtues. Amongst the virtues, Diotima highlights the kind of 'wisdom' that 'deals with the proper ordering of cities and households [...] called moderation and justice'.[23] When two people come together in love to

---

19 Singer, *The Nature of Love: Plato to Luther*, 54.
20 Plato, *Symposium*, 206b7.
21 Ibid., 208e3-5.
22 Ibid., 208c4-e2.
23 Ibid., 209a. The notion of virtue invoked here, nowadays much less of a live concept than in the ancient world (except as it figures theological ethics and some recent moral philosophy), is the notion of that psychological condition which forms the basis of one's ability to lead the best kind of human life, and therefore the goal of ethical training and (in the Socratic tradition) philosophical enquiry (Cooper 1999: 77). In the *Republic*, Plato offers a tripartite theory of the soul as consisting in Appetite, Spirit and Reason, arguing that a person's being just and virtuous is a matter of these being in proper harmony, with their Reason governing, and, with the aid of Spirit, controlling their Appetite. The three sorts of people, and their associated forms of 'giving birth in beauty', seem to correspond

bring forth their (natural, practical or intellectual) offspring, Diotima teaches, 'this is a godly affair [which] cannot occur in anything that is out of harmony [...] Beauty, [...] is in harmony with the divine'.[24]

In this part of the *Symposium*, Plato stresses love as a perpetual pursuit of the value (as in goodness and beauty) in immortality where divine goodness or divine beauty resides. This is often regarded as a spiritual pursuit, or a striving for transcendence, the end of which can only be reached by aspiring for and procreating what is closest to the perfect good and the absolute beauty. One such greatest lover is, accordingly to Plato, the philosopher who can become god-like by contemplating 'a world of unchanging and harmonious order'.[25] Possessing goodness and beauty is to be possessed by goodness and beauty. However, the notion of 'possessing' is not the same as owning a house. Instead, to possess something is to behold and bring forth those valuable qualities that reside in the what-ness of things. Procreation is the closest to immortality and perpetuity.[26] This generative dimension of love has been connected to education and learning.[27]

To conclude, Diotima illustrates a ladder of love, through which lovers can ascend, step by step, in valuing, appreciating and following love's true nature, from beauty in the body of a particular person to beauty in the soul, so as to 'go aright, or be led by another, into the mystery of love'.[28] The ascent involves adopting an increasingly more encompassing view of the multitude of beauty. At the pinnacle of the ladder, the lover will gain a full understanding of beauty or goodness itself, which, Diotima suggests, is the perfection of love and that 'there if anywhere should a person live his life, beholding that beauty',[29] is the supreme value.

Love as valuing deepens the lover's understanding of goodness and beauty. Thus the lover will know what to value and how to value. They will know 'what makes laws well designed, which practices should be adopted and which

---

to people in whom one or another of these three parts of the soul is dominant (cf. Kraut "Plato on Love," 292). For discussion of Plato's moral psychology in the Republic, see Cooper (*Reason and Emotion*), and also Morris (2006).
24 Plato, *Symposium*, 206c-d.
25 Plato, *Republic*, 208.
26 Singer, *Philosophy of Love: A Partial Summing-Up*, 63.
27 Kraut, "Plato on Love," 291; Nussbaum, *Upheavals of Thought*, 491–3.
28 Plato, *Symposium*, 211c.
29 Ibid., 211d.

branches of knowledge should be studied'.[30] In this way, love as valuing also provides indications for the economic and political structure of a society, which we will draw upon in the later chapters.

***

Aristotle (384–322 BC): Love as valuing human qualities and virtues

Aristotle develops a conception of love through the idea 'philia' or the ideal friendship, which is also supposed to refer to as being responsive to the good qualities of a friend. Philia is 'the friendship of men who are good and alike in virtue'; and for those friends who 'wish well alike to each other qua good, [...] they are good in themselves'.[31] Love as the ideal or perfect friendship is thus valuing the good characters and qualities in the friend and cherishing the perfect friendship. Love in this sense involves taking mutual delight in the friend's company, qualities, but also their rationality. This is because to be able to recognise and appreciate the perfect qualities in each other, philia must involve reasoning, for instance, to distinguish what we love (e.g. the good) from what is good for me. This is an evaluative exercise through rationality. In evaluating the good qualities, love bestows value upon those whom the friend loves. By loving, or in this case, by entering into a friendship with another person, one gives significance to the good qualities in them. Philia's rationality points to a non-emotional response to the goodness in the friend. In contrast to erôs' passion and intensity, philia is objective and prudent.

According to Aristotle, there are three forms of friendship, each of which is grounded on the concern for and the well-wishing towards one's friend. Some forms of friendship are founded on the basis of three categories of recognition: (1) the friend's moral goodness, (2) the pleasure the friend brings and (3) the opportunity to attain advantage in the association with the friend. Comparing these three, Aristotle highlights the first, that is, the one that values the friend's moral goodness or virtues, to be true or perfect 'philia'. Here, Aristotle emphasises the non-instrumental nature of love – love for the good qualities and virtues in the friend and valuing these for their own sake. The latter two suggest instrumental motivation as they seek friendship on the grounds of

---

30 Kraut, "Plato on Love," 298.
31 Ross, *The Student's Oxford Aristotle*, L1; 1156b.

other ends. We shall return to this point later in the book when discussing love as relationing.

Perfect friendship is when there is mutual recognition of the moral goods in each other and mutual valuing of these goods for their own sake. For Aristotle, the good qualities 'are essential properties of humankind',[32] suggesting that these are in part constituted in the fundamental nature of being human and what it means to live a good life.

Perfect philia contrasts with instrumentality and is intrinsically meaningful in itself. When people enter into friendship on such a ground, although they may also receive pleasure and gain advantage, these benefits are merely incidental rather than intended.[33] Ideal friendship, in the words of Aristotle, involves 'friends without qualification'.[34] Love as valuing is an ethical act that seeks goodness in others and wishes them well for their own sake. Valuing others' excellences and moral goodness non-instrumentally can guide our living in pursuit of truly right ends – of perfect goodness in each of us.

However, if love is a mutual exchange of recognisable excellence and goodness amongst friends, what would happen when one party becomes less excellent and less good? On this, Aristotle suggests that perfect friendship 'will tend to be continuous and permanent, since it is grounded in knowledge of and love for one another's good qualities of character and such traits, once formed, tend to be permanent'.[35] Despite some interpretations to suggest otherwise,[36] moral virtues can be cultivated, according to Aristotle. They can continue to constitute a person's life. This does not undermine love nor make it a condition of love. For instance, two people with perfectly excellent qualities can encounter and further develop and deepen their friendship in and through mutual striving.

Additionally, the mutuality of perfect friendship suggests that if one loves and values the good qualities in the friend in their own right, one must likewise love and value these in oneself.[37] Self-love for Aristotle sets the foundation for one's love for others – one must first be one's 'own best friend' to be able

---

32 Cooper, *Reason and Emotion*, 324.
33 Ibid.
34 Aristotle, *Nicomachean Ethics*, 1157b4.
35 Ibid., 1156b11-12.
36 Such as May's (2011) interpretation that Aristotelean love is conditional.
37 Cooper, *Reason and Emotion*, 333.

to be a friend to others.[38] Conversely, a friend is effectively 'another self'.[39] Indeed, the highest friendship and loving others (through self-love) comprise our eudemonia or flourishing.[40] In other words, we flourish by loving others, whose flourishing expands our own. Love as valuing and appreciating others is equivalent to valuing and appreciating one's self. Human flourishing involves the processes and activities we engage with our friends and the experiences of loving friendships found in 'philia'.[41]

Moreover, Aristotle regards philia as justice – each person valuing the goodness in the friend who warrants such goodness and deserves being treated fairly.[42] However, for Aristotle, justice is not a qualification, but a mutual appreciation of and mutual participation in the good. Following Plato, Aristotle accepts a pre-existent essential order of the cosmos – a just order – to which all beings must be attuned as part of their flourishing. Love, in this sense of justice, is the universal principle of harmony. By being part of and contributing to this cosmic harmony, humans have the potential to transcend ourselves towards coming ever closer to the perfect goodness.

The appreciation of valuable aspects in these activities requires an awareness that one is conscious of what one values and what underpins one's actions. Self-awareness/self-knowledge is the basis of self-perfection which requires friendship. This is the principle of 'phrónēsis' or practical wisdom that determines how we should act, which makes Aristotelean philia a praxis of the good life. Accordingly, the most desirable form of life is the contemplative life in which, through reasoning, we can appreciate and aspire to the highest qualities/virtues. As an ethical speculation, love as valuing articulates how humans must live our lives, pursue just causes and act in accordance with the accounts of the good.

***

---

38 Aristotle, *Nicomachean Ethics*, IX. 8. 1168b2-4, in Barnes, *Complete Works of Aristotle*, 1846–7.
39 Ibid. IX. 2.1156a11, b10.
40 Ibid. 1159a11–12.
41 In Thomson & Gill, *Happiness, Flourishing and the Good Life*, one's life processes, such as spending time with friends, thinking, taking a walk or having a conversation together, as well as one's intimate relationships, such as friendships, are in part constituted in human well-being.
42 Thus giving the other his due – a truest form of justice. CF Singer, *Philosophy of Love: A Partial Summing-Up*, 95.

Epictetus (c. 50–130): Love as valuing the nature of things

Epictetus's philosophy has been regarded as key to the earlier development of Stoicism.[43] Most importantly, Epictetus's contribution to Stoicism lies in his view that a flourishing life is living in accordance with nature or logos. For Epictetus, some virtues are more fundamental than other and the fundamental ones can provide humans with true freedom:

> Pay attention, therefore, to your sense-impressions and watch over them sleeplessly. For it is no small matter that you are guarding, but self-respect, and fidelity and constancy, a state of mind undisturbed by passion, pain, fear, or confusion – in a word, freedom.[44]

What is also implied here is that an undisturbed mind or a state of reason is a superior state than some of the emotional states and therefore when one is not subject to these emotions, one can experience freedom.[45]

In *Discourse*, Epictetus outlines two aspects of his thought that are relevant to love as valuing.

The first concerns the notion of control, or what is *up to us*. Although this aspect was already part of the Stoic tradition, Epictetus furthers the idea as follows: What is up to us is what can be placed under our ethical consideration or through reasoned evaluation. This is what we can have *control* over. For situations that are beyond our rational reach, they are not up to us. Examples of the latter are our bodily health, the loss of a child and other things pertaining to the physical world (e.g. wealth or honour). These are not what we should be directing our attention.

The second relates to Epictetus's idea of choice. What we choose to do and how we should act are determined by our own evaluations of what is good. The values of good and evil are not located in the objective and outside world. Instead, good and evil are a reflection of our inner and personal values. In fact, only the inner evaluative approach can serve as the ethical basis of our choices. For instance, he writes:

---

43 This part of the discussion draws heavily on Wehus, "Freedom, Slavery, and Self in Epictetus".
44 Epictetus, *Discourse*, 4.3.7.
45 Some have interpreted that Epictetus's interest in freedom is connected to the fact that he was born a slave, and he has an embodied experience of what it is like to live without freedom.

> No man is master of another's moral purpose [...] In its sphere alone are to be found one's good and evil. It follows, therefore, that no one has power either to procure me good, or to involve me in evil, but I myself alone have authority over myself in these matters.[46]

Bringing these two aspects together, for Epictetus, all evaluative choices are reserved for things that are under our control as human beings. A person's choices are decided by their own value system.[47] This has implications on how we should love, which, in turn, is determined by what we should value.

In *Handbook* as part of *Discourses*, Epictetus reminds us that to love someone or something is to be drawn to the valuable nature of that person or that thing and appreciate them from that nature. Love is not limited to the localised affection and sentiment, but rather should always be directed at the greater value that lies in the nature of persons and things in themselves. However, this does not negate the fact that our love for our families, friends, community and the world is equally real and equally significant and that such love should constitute in part a good life.

In principle, Stoics do not tend to regard emotions as irrational, and hence they do not encourage emotions per se; however, according to Epictetus, loving is a valuable emotional experience in itself and being loving and being affectionate to each other is acting in accordance with reason and with nature and thereby deemed to be right, just and good. For instance, in the context of deepening an emotional bond between families and friends, not being loving and affectionate would be irrational and indifference or disinterest would not be the right thing to do. To love is to value each other as human beings and to love and to be loving is the right way to be and to act as human beings.

Epictetus distinguishes two kinds of affection: love and lust. Love is valuable in itself and should be provided as if a gift, 'free, unrestrained, unhindered'.[48] The quality and intensity of love should not be determined by forces outside of ourselves. By contrast, lust is a desire (for something) that one does not have control over, such as a craving for another person's body and even for their affection in return. When what one lusts for is not available, one can feel 'weak

---

46 Epictetus, *Discourse*, 4.12.8.
47 Also see Asmis, "Choice in Epictetus' Philosophy"; Long, *Epictetus: a Stoic and Socratic Guide to Life*; Taylor, *Sources of the Self: The Making of the Modern Identity*.
48 Epictetus, *Enchiridion*.

slavish, restrained, belonging to others'.[49] Love should be about valuing, not lusting, or desiring. The latter invites unpeaceful experiences. In the words of Epictetus: 'He who fails to obtain the object of his desire is disappointed and he who incurs the object of his aversion wretched.'[50] Likewise, desires as such can be at the root of fears where different negative emotions come to the fore, including jealousy, resentment, possessiveness, shame and even aggression. These are the opposites of virtues.

Despite contrasting love with lust, Stoics do not negate human's needs for physical intimacy. Intercourse between married couples, when considered as part of loving and engaged in moderation and with attentiveness, can be just as valuable. What does matter for the Stoics is not to cling on to our desire, nor the things we love. Instead, it is about holding on our intention to love and the valuable nature of what love seeks out. For example, a rational and detached attitude will keep fears and attachments at bay. On this, Epictetus advises: Never say about anything as if 'I have lost it', but only say 'I have given it back'. This attitude can apply when we lose a child or our beloved. Epictetus rejects being a victim when encountering loss and other uncontrollable situations and assumes an active agency instead.[51]

In summary, Epictetus asks us to focus on what is valuable and suggests that love as valuing be in part cultivating our own virtues and the goodness in those whom we love and those things that we appreciate. In loving, we learn to appreciate the valuable nature of people and things in their own right and in appreciating more of these valuable aspects; we are learning to participate in a virtuous life with one another.

---

49 Ibid.
50 Ibid.
51 Wehus, "Freedom, Slavery, and Self in Epictetus."

Christian Theology on Love as Valuing

[...] in order to make gods of those who were merely human, one who was God made himself human.

—St Augustine, Sermon 192: On Christmas Day

You stir man to take pleasure in praising you, because you have made us for yourself, and our heart is restless until it rests in you.

—Augustine of Hippo, *The Confessions of St. Augustine*

Judaeo-Christian ideas have made love central to religious teaching and placed love at the core of religious way of life. Irving Singer goes as far as to claim that 'only Christianity [...] defines itself as the religion of love. [...] [and] that it alone has made love the dominant principle [...] which God and love are the same'.[52] Singer goes on to maintain that these ideas of love are rooted in ancient Greek thoughts[53] and Christianised by St Augustine, St Thomas and others.

The Christian narrative differs from its ancient Greek counterpart in two aspects. First, it attempts to personify the divine, rendering God personal. Thus God's love is analogous to man's love as illustrated in the Synoptic Gospels: 'the love of a man for his hungry son (Matthew 7:9–11), the love of a shepherd for a single lost sheep (Luke 15.3–7), the love of a father for a wayward child (Luke 15:11–32)'.[54] Second, in Christianity, love as valuing is equated with loving God whose perfect goodness is cherished by man. Hence Christian practice is summarised as the soul's search for the highest good that is God, to whom man can relate and from whom man can seek transcendence. This is akin to idealised Platonic erôs, the energising and generative force of goodness in the world. In this way, love defines the essence of Christian ethics in that love is the supreme value, the source of meaning and the nature of human living and acting.

An important Christian teaching is that it urges each person to value other people as much as oneself. Two significant notions of love are hence

---

52 Singer, *Philosophy of Love: A Partial Summing-Up*, 159.
53 Ibid.
54 Streiker, "The Christian Understanding of Platonic Love A Critique of Anders Nygren's 'Agape and Eros'", 335.

introduced: One is the Jewish/Hebrew idea of *nomos* (a Greek word meaning law), which refers to righteousness, acceptance of God's law and submission to God's will. Nomos can be captured by the central commandment of the Torah whereby love is conceived as a fundamental Christian command summarised for instance in Matthew 22: 37–40:

> You shall love the Lord your God with all your heart and with all your soul and with all your mind. This is the greatest and first commandment. And a second is like it: You shall love your neighbour as yourself.

This command has been varyingly interpreted. For some, it involves self-knowledge and self-love as argued by St Augustine and St Thomas that only by valuing oneself can one love others in a mirroring way. Self-love is a deeper appreciation of human spirit/soul and self-love is constituted in loving God because the self is already a creation of God. Self-love suggests that self-valuing be God-loving, as 'in striving to love God our spirit is striving to love itself. And conversely: in loving ourselves we are also moving towards God'.[55] This one-and-other oneness is reflected in the central message of mutual indwelling, a relational being that we shall further develop in Chapter 3.

The other is the Christian 'agapē' reflected in Martin Luther's theology, a departure from Greco-Christian erôs. Martin Luther challenges the basis of self-love as loving God's creation and, instead, he situates God's love in man's sins. He then proposes Christian agapē, or generous love of all. Love invites virtues and is accompanied by virtues, including empathy, compassion and forgiveness. Thus, Martin Luther writes: 'we are gods through love'.[56] God's agapē divinises love and divinises humans and in doing so, it determines that love is the 'supreme virtue encompassing all others'.[57]

In contrast to classical Greek conception of love which is an aspiration of the lower beings (e.g. humans) towards the higher life (e.g. the life of the gods), Christian divine bestowal indicates a *reversal of movement*,[58] from the holy or the highest good to the common sinner and from the superior to the inferior. In reaching down to the imperfect, God perfects us all. Where the Platonic conception depicts an *ascent* via love's ladder through which humans

---

55 May, *Love: A History*, 88.
56 Ibid, 87.
57 Singer, *Philosophy of Love: A Partial Summing-Up*, 279.
58 CF Scheler, *On Feeling, Knowing, and Valuing*.

can transcend towards the divine, the Christian conception depicts a *descent* first in order for humanity to reach upwards. Humans need God's love for our deliverance highlights our imperfections and hence the need for humility.[59]

***

Augustine of Hippo (354–430): Love as appreciating God's goodness

St Augustine, in his *Confessions*, depicts the loving desire for God as inherent in humans. This is a polemical Christian theological treatise in the form of an autobiography. It describes his life driven by a quest for happiness and meaning, transformed through successive phases of life in which Augustine's views on the substantial nature of happiness are altered. The guiding thread is the longing to love and to be loved. This longing, Augustine believes, is true not just for himself but for everyone – the loving desire for God. He equates God with *being* itself following a neo-platonic doctrine. God's being grounds the ontological structure in all beings and offers a system of order and structure that only exists through participating in God's being.[60]

In *On Christian Doctrine*, Augustine argues that 'some things are to be enjoyed, others to be used and others are to be enjoyed and used, [...] [and] to enjoy something is to cling to it with love for its own sake'.[61] What is important here is to enjoy or value God for no other reason than to love God. To such an extent, loving ourselves and loving others, or neighbourly love, are also aimed at valuing God, albeit indirectly. As humans, we love ourselves and each other for the sake of loving God. In both cases, Augustine explains, our love can be enjoyed and appreciated, not in an instrumental way, but always directed towards the highest value – God. In this process of seeking the highest value, Augustine suggests that love can lead us out of ourselves towards union with God. This might be seen as a form of self-forgetfulness whereby God's purpose becomes our purpose, God's concerns, our concerns, God's will and our will.[62]

Indeed, for Augustine, love is always appreciative attention, a form of valuing. When directed at God's goodness, love can help transcend human

---

59 Nussbaum, *Upheavals of Thought*.
60 Williams, 1968, Chapter Four: Three Forms of Love.
61 Augustine, *On Christian Theology*, 1.3(3).
62 Cf. Rist, *Augustine: Ancient Thought Baptized*.

desire and even love itself. As in Plato's ascent (and the neo-Platonic versions of it), Augustine's ascent of love relies on 'the fundamental kinship of all fine things'.[63] Furthermore, the pathway to the ascent is in many ways similar, though not identical, to the Platonic ascent, with God, in his ultimate goodness, occupying the pinnacle in the place of the beautiful and the good. There are two important aspects of Augustine's account of ascent here.

First, the ascent is unstable. Although for Plato, the attainment of a pure vision of and love for perfect goodness is relatively robust and permanent, for Augustine, by contrast, perfected love and knowledge of the highest good (God) is something one must continually and repeatedly strive for. Love for and the consequent delight in God is constantly torn down and misdirected by longing for mundane things of our earthly and bodily existence, especially by the need for sexual union. To resist and to be consistent in our pursuit of the highest love requires spiritual strength. Hence Augustine's prayer:

> Lord hear my prayer that my soul may not collapse under your discipline ... Bring to me a sweetness surpassing all the seductive delights which I pursued. Enable me to love you with all my strength that I may clasp your hand with all my heart.[64]

Contemplating one's past sinfulness and transgressions can inhibit pure contemplation of and love for God. It may also increase the risk of falling back into sinful bodily loves. Yet, taking responsibility for repenting one's past wrongdoings, a necessary preparation for divine judgment, truly requires it. Moreover, moral development depends on maintaining one's persistent sense of self in time. Continuity in memory of past transgressions is crucial to sustaining this persistent sense of self, integrating earlier wretchedness with gradual moral improvement towards virtues. This integration is key to a coherent sense of a single life, hence a consistent sense of self. For Augustine, this awareness of our past, present and future is in part consisted in the good life and our well-being, which is essentially a sense of moral growth.[65]

According to Augustine, loving desire is an appreciative attention of something one conceives of as good, but it is not within one's power to fully control such desires. Moral ascension is a matter of attaining a correct

---

63 Nussbaum, *Upheavals of Thought*, 532–3.
64 Augustine, *City of God*, I.xv (24).
65 Nussbaum *Upheavals of Thought*, 538–9.

conception and appropriate understanding of what is good (e.g. God) and then retaining or holding fast to such a conception and understanding, despite the attempts and appetites to divert love towards mundane or bodily pleasures. This is an effort that requires God's grace and assistance. Augustine writes that 'my two wills, one old, the other new, one carnal, the other spiritual, were in conflict with one another and their discord robbed my soul of all concentration'.[66] As the ascent is unstable, it thus requires God's reaching down to us which strengthens our spiritual wills to conceive true happiness – the perfect goodness of God.[67]

Second, love's ascent, for Augustine, requires self-knowledge. Kinship between the objects of love is not enough; love also depends on realising that our understanding of these objects must answer to a single common conception of 'properly focal goods'.[68] Our self-knowledge can ensure that loving desire is only directed towards God. This is considered to be an 'ecstatic' conception.[69] It suggests that God alone is love and that only divinity or the perfect goodness is loved. Therefore, when humans love each other, we are loving God and valuing what God represents. The same applies to our love for any being or anything at all – as long as it is love (as valuing), it is always pointing towards God. Therefore as the self-understanding of a single persisting yearning for loving God becomes progressively stronger, the distorting force of the carnal desire will render weaker. It is through desiring the perfect goodness of God that we can self-transcend.

This ascension or transcendence has no limit because God's goodness is boundless. 'Thus, no limit would interrupt growth in the ascent to God, since no limit to the Good can be found nor is the increasing of desire for the Good brought to an end because it is satisfied.'[70] In fact, along with God's limitlessness, by contrast, is human's limitedness in our capacity to fully appreciate God's infinite goodness. Loving desire for the good, through which one may gain a progressively fuller appreciation of God's nature, allows human quality to infinitely move towards the good, as it were, but without ever reaching its destination.

---

66 Augustine, *Confession*, VIII.v (10).
67 Ibid., VIII.vi (15), VIII.x (22). The latter explicitly invokes the same notion, discussed earlier, of punishment for Adam's 'freely chosen sin' appealed to in the *City of God*.
68 Brewer, 2006, 269.
69 In accordance to Brewer's (2006) attribution.
70 Malherbe, et al. *Gregory of Nyssa: The Life of Moses*, sections 238–9.

These two features of love in Augustine's theology highlight that love as valuing God's goodness must be a constant and persistent striving for transcending ourselves towards perfection. This search is at the root of the good life and true happiness. Natural love (for other people and things in the world) alters and changes, but love as valuing God's perfect goodness is the *true* love. Only true love as valuing can allow humans to reach beyond ourselves, an ascension achieved through self-knowledge albeit finite, perfected and transformed by appreciating God's goodness, which is infinite.

***

Thomas Aquinas (1225–1274): Love as desiring the good

In *Summa Theologiae*,[71] St Thomas proposes that faith, hope and love are the three major ways of human's participation in God's nature. Amongst these three, it is love that enables humans to have the possibility of living the *divine* life on earth. Love as valuing sits at the very pinnacle of Thomasian system of virtues.[72]

Similar to Augustine, Thomas also sees love to be our yearning for the good. Because God is the supreme good, then all beings that exist are owed to and are transcended by a loving God. Thomas believes that love is infused into the human soul by God (through grace and divine bestowal). In Thomas's theology, love is conceived as both a cosmic vision (in that God resides in all things in nature because these are God's creation) and an anthropocentric one (in that God resides in all persons who are God's creation). In this sense, love is understood to be animated by God's goodness and embodied by Christ's humanity. Christ symbolises a union of cosmocentric and human-centric visions in Christian metaphysics.

Thomas suggests that an act of love necessarily involves willing some good to someone. There are two aspects towards which such an act of love is directed: (1) the person whose good one appreciates (*amor amicitiae*) and (2) the good which one wills to someone (*amor concupiscentia*). *Amor amicitiae*, or friendship-love, is prior to *amor concupiscentiae*, or passionate desire, and

---

71 According to and edited by Gracia, Reichberg and Schumacher, *The Classics of Western Philosophy: A Reader's Guide*, 'Summa Theologiae' is one of the most influential works of Western literature.
72 Aquinas. *Summa Theologica*, I-II q. 65, a. 3.

provides the focal meaning of love. For Thomas, friendship-love is similar to Aristotelean 'philia', which is love that a person has towards another for their own sake. *Amor concupiscentiae* arises from a sensitive appetite towards or desire for what is good for the other person which one seeks. *Amor concupiscentiae* is akin to the Platonic erôs.

In friendship-love, a person loves another by valuing the good in the other for its own sake. Here the goodness is perceived as absolute goodness. By contrast, in the love of concupiscence, a person loves things that are relatively good, in that their goodness lies in their capacity to benefit the person. Although friendship-love appears to be superior to concupiscence-love, in effect they are two inseparable elements of human love. This is because love entails that a person can value other people's goodness (friendship-love) and at the same time pursues their goodness in recognition that such goodness is beneficial to oneself.[73]

On friendship-love, Thomas goes a step further by referring to Christ's words at the last supper: 'I have called you friends.'[74] This recognition is important to Thomas because by calling those around him friends, Christ establishes that through friendship with him, there is a possibility of friendship-love with God. Here lies the essence of Thomasian theology: a true path to salvation or transcendence is through cultivating friendship-love (*fundari amicitiam*) between humankind and God. Such friendship-love can enable humans to partake in the divine nature of God.

Moreover, according to Thomas, our recognition of the likeness between one's self and another is also a call to love. By seeing others as oneself in that they 'are one thing in the species of humanity',[75] one comprehends other's goodness as the same as one's own goodness. What is good for others is what is good for oneself. However, the likeness in the goodness does not mean it is the human quality that we share with God. Human good has a part-to-whole relation with the divine nature of God. In other words, humans are 'part' of God in that we 'participate in' the divine perfection by assuming a partial and less perfect form of God's goodness.[76] Hence Thomas argues that love of God is the supreme form of love. One must always love God over and above oneself.

---

73 Ibid., I-II, q. 26, a. 4. Cf. Gallagher, "Thomas Aquinas on self-love as the basis for love of others", 26–7.
74 John 15:15.
75 Aquinas, *Summa Theologica* I-II, q. 27, a. 3.
76 Gallagher, "Thomas Aquinas on self-love as the basis for love of others", 36.

For Thomas, loving God over and above one's self does not result in self-forgetting. Following Aristotle, Thomas maintains that love of self is necessarily included in the love of others and in the love of God. Thomas explains why self-love matters as follows: Self-love is fundamental to the human will, the basis for friendship-love with others and vice versa. By being 'affectively united' with others through love,[77] other's goodness can become one's own good, which, in turn, enables one to love the other's good passionately as if one's own. Friendship-love reaches beyond one's self and remains in the other.[78] This outward movement towards others through friendship-love allows love to return to oneself, rendering self-love. Self-love is seemingly a process of self-perfection towards *imago Dei*, in the image of God.

Like the Greek philosophers, Thomas also recognises the importance of knowledge in love as valuing and appreciating the good. He argues that 'no one can love what he does not know'.[79] The good is loved only to the extent that it is known. Thus knowledge is a cause of love – love is always for the known good. Self-love requires self-knowledge which consists of two aspects: (1) knowing that I am (a soul) and (2) knowing what I am.[80] The former is the soul's perception of its own existence; the latter is the soul's awareness of its own essence. The soul's awareness of itself,[81] as Thomas sees it, is fundamental to our contemplation of spiritual beauty and spiritual goodness as the starting point of spiritual love. This suggests that the human soul has a reflexive capacity to (re)turn to itself through rationality and the intellect. Self-knowledge enables soul's understanding of itself by knowing its divine source.

In agreement with Aristotle, Thomas suggests a mutuality in friendship-love which contributes simultaneously to others' and one's own flourishing. However, as a departure from Aristotle's proposal, Thomas suggests that the highest form of flourishing be life in 'caritas' or charity. We will discuss in Chapter 5 how, through moral actions, caritas can allow us to experience 'the closeness of a person to oneself and the nearness of a person to God'.[82] Self-love is included by Thomas in 'caritas' because when one loves oneself for the sake of God, one is engaged in charity.

---

77 Aquinas, *Summa Theologica* I-II, q. 28, a. 1.
78 Ibid. I-II, q. 28, a. 3.
79 Ibid. I-II, q 27, a. 2.
80 Ibid Ia, 1. 87, a. 1.
81 Cf. Cory, *Aquinas on Human Self-Knowledge*.
82 Pakaluk, *Other Selves: Philosophers on Friendship*, 148.

Drawing together these initial expositions on St Thomas's philosophy and metaphysics of love as valuing, we can now see more clearly that from a Thomasian perspective, humans can aspire to a good and virtuous life at different 'levels'. At the first level, love as valuing the good in others, and goodness in God can take us to the good life. This is a moral and ethical pursuit, seeking goodness for its own sake. At the second level, love as valuing can engage our rationality. This is an intellectual pursuit through self-knowledge and the knowledge of what constitutes the good. At the third level, love as valuing perfects our human soul. This is a spiritual pursuit aimed at taking humans ever closer to the divine life. The spiritual life is the highest level of all, which goes beyond Aristotle's contemplative life as the flourishing life.[83] For Thomas, the causes of love are also its objects. In this case, we have seen that the goodness in others, and the goodness of God are both cause and object of love. So everything that is loved is loved as the good. Since God is the highest good, the highest form of love is therefore love of God.

**

Martin Luther (1483–1546): Love as disinterested agapē

The investigation into the nature of love and the place of love in human's pursuit of the good life had been central to Martin Luther's theology. At the core of his inquiry was how humans must love God.

On the nature of love, Martin Luther distinguishes two kinds of love: one is responsive and the other creative.[84] Responsive love is human love, or in Luther's interpretations, Christian erôs. Responsive love is when we find ourselves drawn to the goodness and virtuous qualities in God, thereby responding to the good by loving God. Because God offers Christ to humanity, without any merit on our part, for comfort, redemption, salvation, joy and peace, the nature of God's love is thus unconditional, which does not depend on what humans are or have done. Since God is already perfect and loving, then all humans can do is to respond to God's grace. Creative love is God's love. For Martin Luther, God's love is disinterested Christian agapē. God's

---

83 Aquinas follows Aristotle's view of hierarchical relationship of these first two levels, adding the third sort in addition to them; see Aquinas, *Summa Theologica*, II-II, q. 23, a. 6.
84 Mannermaa, *Two Kinds of Love: Martin Luther's Religious World*.

love is creative because it invites humans to aspire to the greater goodness manifested in all things of God and in God.

These two kinds of love are reflected in the Christian command in that neighbourly love or friendship-love must be the love of God. Thus Martin Luther, in articulating his idea of Christian agapē, contrasts the egocentric self-love that is at the core of both Augustine's and Thomas's theology with a theocentric love of God. According to Swedish Lutheran theologian, Anders Nygren (1890–1978), 'Christian fellowship with God is distinguished from all other kinds by the fact that it depends exclusively on God's agapē'.[85]

Unlike St Augustine and St Thomas, Martin Luther does not insist on human perfection as God's creation. Instead, he highlights human imperfection, such as our sins. By pointing out human imperfection, Martin Luther is able to demonstrate the greater meanings of God's deliverance and God's love as bestowal. He suggests that our fellowship with God be established precisely on the basis of human 'sin, not holiness'.[86] As such, 'sinners are beautiful because they are loved; they are not loved because they are beautiful'.[87] Through the power of God's love, recognising human imperfection can be a starting point of our striving, any progress of which is always superseded by further self-renewal and self-transcendence.

At the core of Martin Luther's teaching is that God's love is provided to people in two expressions: command and promise, or law and gospel. Command sets forth God's will for what people ought to do, a divine vision for human life. Law helps establish social order and a system of righteousness and justice. Command further consolidates God's authority in justification – only God's judgement can determine our freedom. For instance, God's forgiveness and pronouncing humans as righteous can inspire humans to be truly virtuous because it is God's word that shapes the reality. In this sense, commandments or laws are there to guide the good life and right and just living.

By contrast, promise is employed to interpret the Bible and the relevant actions invited by the gospel. That is to say, promise helps people to understand God's word theologically and recognise its application practically. For Martin Luther, 'God does not deal, nor has he ever dealt, with [human beings] other

---

85 Nygren, *Agape and Eros*, 75.
86 Ibid., 648.
87 Mannermaa, *Two Kinds of Love: Martin Luther's Religious World*, 7.

than through the word of promise'.[88] Here is an extended quote from Philipp Melanchthon, one of Martin Luther's students, who articulates how the law and promise integrate towards the right way of living for humans:

> We are justified when, put to death by the law, we are made alive again by the word of grace promised in Christ; the Gospel forgives our sins, and we cling to Christ in faith, not doubting in the least that the righteousness of Christ is our righteousness, that the satisfaction Christ wrought was for our expiation [atonement] and that the resurrection of Christ is ours.[89]

Lutheran theology does stress forgiveness, righteousness and justice. Martin Luther believes that our sin requires forgiveness, and only God can provide such justification and pardon by grace, through faith. Martin Luther argues that 'faith alone makes someone just and fulfils the law. Faith is that which brings the Holy Spirit through the merits of Christ'.[90] Faith, accordingly, is absolute trust and confidence in God's grace, which is the source of meaning and the good life.

Owing to faith, people can willingly and generously love others and do good, not out of self-initiated endeavours but through God who *works* faith in us. Martin Luther proposes that true love be what is revealed in Christ, a selfless love or agapē. In Nygren's interpretation, Christian agapē is characterised by four features. God's love is, first of all, spontaneous and unmotivated, grounded in God's own nature, based on 'what God is like'.[91] Second, the value of God's love, which lies in itself, rather than directed at anything outside itself. This is most significant for Lutheran theology which permits humans or sinners to be loved by God without discrimination. Third, it is God's love that provides humans with dignity and assumes our intrinsic worthwhileness. In this way, agapē is creative love, as it engenders value in humans when we become recipients of God's love. Lastly, God's action that is always primary. Namely, man could not come to God and only God can come to man, and love is 'a

---

88 Martin Luther, 1520, De captivitae babylonica, WA 6:516, 30–33; LW 36:42, quoted in Gregory Walter, 2017, 'Promise in Martin Luther's Thought and Theology' https://oxfordre.com/religion/view/10.1093/acrefore/9780199340378.001.0001/acrefore-9780199340378-e-342

89 Melanchthon, *Basic Theological Doctrines*, quoted in Hagglund, "Melanchthon versus Luther: The Contemporary Struggle".

90 Luther, "An Introduction to St. Paul's Letter to the Romans," 124–5.

91 Nygren, *Agape and Eros*, 76.

way for God to come to man'.[92] All man has to do is to have faith, which is not blind belief, but trust in God's goodness. Faith allows humans to have the right relationship with God.

By establishing the right relationship with God, Martin Luther's reformation succeeded in removing churches' power of dominance and control of salvation. In stressing God's love, the sacrifice of Christ and God's forgiveness of man's sins, Lutheran theocentric philosophy firmly establishes God's power in love and love's power in liberating human from the burden of wrongdoing. God's agapē is the kind of love that only God is capable of bestowing. Agapē is truly 'God's way to man'.[93] Hence according to Luther, Christians are 'conduits' who receive from God all that in Christ and thus are made god-like after being infused with God's love, who in turn offer love to their neighbours.

At the heart of Lutheran theology is the tension between the *hidden* God and the *revealed* God. The hidden God is unknowable to human, although humans can glorify God. The revealed God is perceivable by humans through God's incarnation in Christ. This tension is also known as the tension between theology of glory and theology of cross. The theology of glory is developed in the light of what we expect God to be like, whereas the theology of cross is developed through what is revealed in Christ (hanging on the cross). However, Luther makes no attempt in reconciling command and promise, or law and gospel. Hence the inner man of spirit and the outer man of flesh and desire, the mysterious God who is hidden and the revealed God in Christ, the theology of glory and the theology of the cross, the earthly kingdom governed by law and the church governed by the gospel remain separated.

---

92 Ibid., 80.
93 Ibid., 210.

Love as Valuing in Modernist Thought

Love is nothing but joy accompanied with the idea of an eternal cause.
—Baruch Spinoza, *Ethics*, Part 3

The mind's intellectual love of God is the very love of God by which God loves himself, not insofar as he is infinite, but insofar as he can be explained by the human mind's essence, considered under a species of eternity; that is, the mind's intellectual love of God is part of the infinite love by which God loves himself.
—Baruch Spinoza, *Ethics*, Part 5

During the fourteenth century, humanism had begun to gather momentum. From a humanistic perspective, human beings and our happiness were placed at the centre of our universe. Humanism had encouraged human ingenuity in sciences, arts, literature and education. This was also a time when values and virtues advanced in antiquity were renewed, over Christian teachings, liberating knowledge and learning from religious institutions, and separating science and philosophy from theology. In this context, love as valuing humankind started with the practice of courtly love in the Middle Ages, which was regarded to be *humanising* love.[94] From the Renaissance, love's evolution became oriented more towards perceiving humans as self-created free beings who, through understanding and love, can comprehend and apprehend the world.

This period gave birth to modern Western philosophy (spanning 1600–1800 AD) that focused on exploring the nature of the universe and human's place in it. One of the key characteristics of philosophical investigations at the time concerned freeing human beings from the authority of the Christian institution. Love of human beauty and goodness became itself a celebration of God. Thus, the values in the physical, intellectual and spiritual dimensions of being human merged and fused into a greater 'transcendental unity'.[95] Furthermore, nature was introduced as part of this unity and was equally loved and valued as a source of meaning and goodness. Nature was conceived as part of the divine, or a manifestation of the divine, including human nature, emotionality, rationality and spirituality.

---

[94] Singer, *Philosophy of Love: A Partial Summing-Up*.
[95] de Rougemont, *Love in the Western World*, 134.

From the late eighteenth century to the mid-nineteenth century, Romanticism characterised the Western intellectual orientation through literature, architecture, arts, music and so forth. Romanticism attempted to liberate love from rationality and at the same time alienate love from knowledge. For instance, one of the arguments was that passionate attachment is what makes life worthwhile. This was intended to give rise to the claim that emotional and erotic unity between man and woman be the source of meaning and goodness beyond (rational) appraisal.[96] Love through erotic passion was no longer regarded as a path to transcendence or reaching beyond the human as in the Greek and Christian conception of erôs. Instead, love was understood as valuing the essence of being human. Without divine intervention, humanists argue that persons could seek blessedness and love, creating 'heaven on earth'.[97] The erotic (sexual) became in part the moral and the ethical.[98] The good life involves our mutual recognition of human intrinsic value, including self-love.

So, love as seeking meaningfulness of life continues to flourish but is valued as a pathway to personal happiness and self-actualisation. Instead of for the sake of the divine (e.g. cosmos, or God), love is now pursued as a good in itself, but oriented at multiple ends of love, from satisfying erotic passions to meeting the needs of physical pleasures, from the biological instinct for procreation to the need to sustain stable marriages and society, bringing out the best in both the lover and the beloved.

***

Baruch Spinoza (1632–1677): Love as valuing the totality of existence

In *Ethics*, Spinoza develops his account of love as valuing based on Plato's philosophy.[99] Love is conceived as the most important emotional process which can engender value and inspire virtuous acts. A truly significant contribution

---

96 Cf. Singer *Philosophy of Love: A Partial Summing-Up*, 41–2.
97 See *Tristan*, by Gottfried.
98 This is in spite of the fact that Immanuel Kant consolidates the argument that persons are intrinsically valuable in our own right precisely because we are rational beings whose moral acts are underpinned by reason.
99 Nussbaum, "The Ascent of Love: Plato, Spinoza, Proust".

that Spinoza makes to the understanding of love is the unconditional love directed at God or nature, another person, a good cause, or in sum, the good life. Such love values the intrinsic goodness in God/nature, a person, a project or a way of being and connects one with something greater that is the active power of life and living. In loving or valuing, one can be helped to rise up towards human becoming.

In Part I of *Ethics*, he starts with a unique definition of God – perfect, infinite and eternal being, or even being itself: 'a being absolutely infinite [...] consisting in infinite attributes, of which each expresses eternal and infinite essentiality'. In this sense, only God is truly free, whose existence is solely defined 'by the necessity of its own nature' and whose action is 'determined by itself alone'. Thus in *Short Treatise*, Spinoza maintains that 'God is the cause of all things'.[100]

On the nature of cause, Spinoza distinguishes two kinds of cause: an adequate cause 'through which its effect can be clearly and distinctly perceived' and an inadequate or partial cause 'through which, by itself, its effect cannot be understood'. Spinoza equates God with nature and suggests that God/nature is the ultimate (adequate) cause of everything and, therefore, God or nature is an end in itself. As humans, we partake in God's or nature's being, in both our own existence and in our processes and activities. We are, therefore, constituted in the totality of existence that is God or nature. When we love God, we value the totality of existence.

This claim on the equivalence of God to nature has several significant implications. First, God is not supernatural, and God's being is part of the natural way of things. Therefore, if we are all part of nature and thereby part of God, then God is also an immanent being. Second, as all is determined by God, then our will, our emotions and acts are equally caused by God. This suggests that free will and self-determination may be an illusion. Third, because God as a free cause has no desire nor need, desire and need thus only apply to humans. What implies here is that human's love for God must be truly selfless and cannot be expected to be reciprocated.

According to Spinoza, what humans ought to desire, to strive for, to wish for, to long for, are precisely things that are deemed to be good in their own right as part of the flourishing life. Spinoza further qualifies that what we deem

---

100 Spinoza, *Short Treatise*, I, iii.

to be good are things that can ensure our existence and increase our *power*.[101] This striving for existence and power is what Spinoza calls 'conatus', which is the essence of being human. In other words, the good that expands our being and adds to our power can thereby increase our perfection and enable our continued human-becoming, or becoming better human beings. This is the very desire to live happily and to do well.

For Spinoza, there are two kinds of desire – active and passive, reflecting two kinds of nature, divine and human. God or nature, viewed by Spinoza as active, refers to that which is 'in itself and is conceived through itself', including those attributes of substance that express eternal and infinite essence. In this sense, nature is equivalent to God insofar as nature is similarly a free cause. What he proposes as passive nature is understood to be that which

> follows from the necessity of the nature of God, or of any of the attributes of God, that is, all the modes of the attributes of God, in so far as they are considered as things which are in God and which without God cannot exist or be conceived.[102]

Love as intellectual thoughts is of passive nature because the thoughts are conceived through the attributes of God as in Part III of *Ethics*, VIII, where Spinoza writes that 'Love is nothing else but pleasure accompanied by the idea of an external cause'. He presents passive love as comprising the myriad human emotions in accordance with different kinds of love, from love of God to passionate love, including physical attachment, to love of our children, spouse and others.[103] Emotions thus can be of active or passive nature, depending on their causes. Active emotions, such as love of God/nature, can provide us with an understanding of the true causes of our emotions; whereas passive emotions, such as erotic passion and desire for physical union, can enslave us because we

---

101 McShea, in his 1969 paper "Spinoza on power", points out that Spinoza's notion of power may be understood as both a metaphysical and political concept. As a metaphysical concept, Spinoza defines power as the propensity for a system, such as man, to survive, to realise its essence and to achieve understanding. As a political concept, Spinoza rejects authoritarian, hierarchical and elitist approach to governance, and connects power with democratic engagement.
102 Spinoza, *Ethics*, P15.
103 This conception has been critiqued to be too broad to be of philosophical or even psychological significance, cf. Bicknell, 'An Overlooked Aspect of Love in Spinoza's "Ethics".'

cannot understand them. Humans are constantly subject to this tension between love's activity and passivity which renders us in a continuous striving for power.

For Spinoza, emotions are the modifications of the body, whereby power acts on these modifications either in increased or diminished, aided or constrained, ways. For example, when we feel joy, pleasure and delight of life, we are aware of the increased active power in ourselves. By contrast, when we feel sadness, pain or depression, we can experience a decrease in power. Implicit here is that ordinary love, that is, the emotions motivated by passionate attachments or self-interests, tends to be passive and can be subject to disharmony.

As the ultimate cause of all existence is God or nature itself, love as valuing, according to Spinoza, is an intellectual love and deep appreciation of God or nature, selfless, free from human's will. Spinoza suggests that:

> this kind of knowledge arises pleasure accompanied by the idea of God as cause, that is [...] the love of God; not in so far as we imagine him as present, [...] but in so far as we understand him to be eternal.[104]

He further characterises the love of God as eternal, with no beginning and no end, pursuing all the perfections and goodness appreciated or valued. To some extent, love of God bears little difference from love amongst humans insofar as such love is accompanied by the clear and distinct idea of God as the eternal cause. Spinoza qualifies the perfection of the intellectual love by saying: 'If pleasure consists in the transition to a greater perfection, assuredly blessedness must consist in the mind being endowed with perfection itself.'[105]

Spinoza claims that the highest virtue, which resembles the active power, or highest endeavour of the mind, is to know God and to love God. Such knowing and loving consists in self-conscious awareness of one's own being. To this, Spinoza adds that 'the intellectual love of the mind towards God is part of the infinite love wherewith God loves himself'.[106] This has led Spinoza to conclude that God's love for himself is equivalent to God's love for humans and vice versa: 'Hence it follows that God, in so far as he loves himself, loves man and consequently, that the love of God towards men and the intellectual love of the mind towards God are identical.'[107] It is here that lies a true flourishing life.

---

104 Spinoza, *Ethics*, V. XXXII.
105 Ibid.
106 Spinoza, *Ethics*, V. XXXVI.
107 Ibid.

This is because with intellectual love for God, a person is seldom disturbed in their spirit and by being conscious of one's self and thereby of God and of things in nature, they will never cease to be but always 'possess true acquiescence' of spirit.

The purpose of Spinoza's stressing the primary place of intellectual love seems to elucidate the ways that the human mind can control our emotions because there is 'no more excellent remedy for the emotions than that which consists in true knowledge of them'.[108] According to Spinoza '[t]he more we understand particular things, the more [...] we understand God'.[109]

Spinoza's conception of love as valuing highlights a major point of departure from the cosmos-centric and theocentric visions of love discussed in the preceding sections in the following ways:

First, Spinoza connects God to nature. This has been a tremendous initial step in love's evolution in that God or nature is valued as the totality of existence that encompasses all and in which all can partake. Second, by highlighting the importance of recognising God as the ultimate cause of all, Spinoza accentuates knowledge and reasoning as the way that humans can appreciate and cherish God's or nature's goodness. This emphasis on intellectual love as appreciative and evaluative understanding instead of bestowal subtly introduces a connection between love and power, and the propensity of all things towards thriving. Third, Spinoza recognises the importance of human consciousness in appreciating the perfect goodness of God or nature. This means that the good life and flourishing must include our evaluative understanding of life as a whole. Lastly, Spinoza does not place human love for one another, our love for God, God's love for human and God's love for himself in a hierarchy. Instead, he underlines their equivalence and highlights that being human, including embodying our emotions and intellect, is intrinsically valuable in its own right.

***

Immanuel Kant (1724–1804): Love as valuing the inherent dignity of persons

In his corpus, Kant has put forward ambiguous commentaries on love, most notably, his general division of love into different categories, such as love of

---

108 Bicknell, 'An Overlooked Aspect of Love in Spinoza's "Ethics",' 50.
109 Spinoza, *Ethics*, V. XXIV.

benevolence and love of delight. In doing so, Kant appears to follow the Greek philosophers in recognising the importance of knowledge and reason in love. However, in effect, Kant's contribution to love lies in calling our attention to the non-instrumental nature of human dignity and human emotionality. Love for Kant is both a precondition for and the highest expression of rational morality and virtue. Rationality and virtue, for Kant, are constitutive of the good life.

In attributing to love such a prominent place in the development and full expression of human reason, Kant can be seen as a defender of rationalist humanism, exalting universal reason which resides in each of us and seeing it as the immanent source of human dignity, morality and the good life. Even so, whilst his conception of the nature and imperatives of love are constructed on the basis of pure reason, he maintains that knowledge of God on theoretical grounds is impossible. Instead, he proposes that justification for faith can be based on practical moral grounds. In line with this, he endorses a conception of God as love itself, viewing this divine nature as the 'ground of creation and the moral duties' and our striving for moral perfection as the means by which 'we become worthy of and receive, God's love'.[110]

In *Groundwork of the Metaphysics of Morals*, Kant argues that the supreme principle of morality is a standard of rationality. It is also termed *categorical imperative*, 'an objective, rationally necessary and unconditional principle that we must always follow despite any natural desires or inclinations we may have to the contrary'.[111] An imperative is categorical because it must be followed or acted upon without exception. Kant distinguishes principles of means and ends, which, for our purpose, are referred to as instrumental and non-instrumental values.[112] Things are of instrumental value when their value only lies in attaining goals or utility. Things are of non-instrumental value because their attributes or qualities are meaningful and valuable in their own right. For Kant, humans are of non-instrumental value because we have autonomous rational will. This is where human dignity resides, which allows

---

110 Rinne, "From Self-Preservation to Cosmopolitan Friendship: Kant and the Ascent of Love."
111 Johnson and Cureton, "Kant's Moral Philosophy."
112 Cf Thomson and Gill, *Happiness, Flourishing and the Good Life*; Gill and Thomson, *Understanding Peace Holistically*.

us to determine the laws of morality.[113] It is the presence of this self-governing reason in persons that Kantian thought offers decisive grounds for viewing each person as possessing equal worth and deserving equal respect. Given this, Kant has permitted a person to be treated *both* as a means and as an end but suggests that it be morally wrong to treat a person solely as a means (to achieving end goals). Respecting human dignity as an end in itself forms an essential part of Kantian ethics.

In *Metaphysics of Morals*, Kant recognises that reason is paramount in the moral life. Reason can enable us to examine our feelings and evaluate our motivation or inclinations. Feelings, for Kant, are physiological occurrences (pains and/or pleasures) that are caused by the cognitive faculty, including perception and present experience. The thoughts underlying feelings must be morally evaluated. Kant's moral theory suggests that we should never blindly follow our feelings; nor overcome emotions as mere irrational forces. Instead, we must engage our feelings and emotions when making moral choices and deciding on how to act ethically. This is where Kant's perspectives on love make an important contribution to love's evolution and revolution.

On his conceptions of love as valuing, Kant distinguishes between pathological love and philanthropic love. Pathological love, Kant explains, 'lies in the direction the person's feelings and tender sympathies take'.[114] It is 'a feeling [of] pleasure in the perfection of others'.[115] It is love of delight (pleasure), involving an appreciation of another's physical perfection (i.e. beauty). Philanthropic love, according to Kant, is one of the four moral endowments, which are 'natural predispositions of the mind […] for being affected by concepts of duty'.[116] (The other three moral endowments are: moral feeling, conscience and respect for oneself.) Philanthropic love is a benevolent moral sentiment, constituted by feeling 'satisfaction in the happiness (well-being) of others',[117]

---

113 Kant, *Practical philosophy*, 4:436. For Kant, the notion of autonomy has a special meaning. The autonomous person is not only able to exercise free will and to employ reason but also is able to 'make' or legislate the moral law for herself. The autonomous person is thus not under any external moral authority but is under the authority of her own reason alone. As an autonomous person, such an individual ought to act in accordance with the duties of the moral law as required by reason.
114 Chapter 1, Kant, *Grounding for the Metaphysics of Morals*.
115 Kant, *The Metaphysics of Morals*, 6:449.
116 Ibid., 399.
117 Ibid., 452.

and 'for whom it is well when things go well for every other'.[118] Kant further draws the distinction between benevolence and beneficence: 'Benevolence is satisfaction in the happiness (well-being) of others; but beneficence is the maxim of making others' happiness one's end.'[119] In some ways, this aspect of Kant's understanding of love as valuing echoes that of the Greeks, that is, love as encompassed in the pursuit of the highest good in human life through an ideal of 'a communal notion of perfect happiness proportionate to the perfect virtue of all agents'.[120]

Kant also supports rationality to be a basis of love. For instance, love of delight requires an appraisal and appreciation of beauty that involves reasoning, whereas love of benevolence calls for consideration of prudence. For Kant, rationality is not solely applied when evaluating and appraising qualities in the beloved, but instead, rationality is what uniquely belongs to humans. In this case, love happens only to rational beings who are 'entangled in their rational capacities'.[121] In particular, rationality is also relevant to self-love, which accordingly 'can be divided into love of benevolence and love of delight [...] and both (as is self-evident) must be rational'.[122]

Kant advocates 'the maxim of benevolence, which results in beneficence'[123] and distinguishes between the need for universality of benevolence and the need for active and practical beneficence. It is here, accordingly, that self-love and intimacy with others might present some challenge to our loving and valuing of all human beings. Some people are closer to oneself than others and this, Kant supposes, allows for a corresponding variation in how far one can be expected to actively benefit others. In this situation, it is the maxim of benevolence that helps balance the differentiation.[124] This distinction between

---

118 Ibid., 450.
119 Ibid., 452.
120 Rinne, "From Self-Preservation to Cosmopolitan Friendship: Kant and the Ascent of Love," §III.
121 Rinne, *Kant on Love*, 8.
122 Kant, *The Metaphysics of Morals*, 6:452–5.
123 Ibid., 449.
124 Kant wrestles with this distinction in this quote (Kant, *The Metaphysics of Morals*, 6:451–2):

> Yet one human being is closer to me than another, and in benevolence I am closest to myself. How does this fit in with the precept 'love your *neighbor* (your fellow human being) as yourself'? If one is closer to me than another (in the duty

wishing and acting does not necessarily solve a dilemma confronting all humans: how to maintain universal love for humanity and not to act in ways that privilege those with whom one is intimately connected, such as one's self or one's spouse. According to Kant, the universality of philanthropic love will require a rational account as the basis of love; otherwise one will inevitably privilege those who are closer to us. Thus, Kant proposes that a 'friend of human beings as such (i.e., of the whole race) is one who takes an affective interest in the well-being of all human beings'.[125]

Although Kant devoted thought to intimacy and our tendency to value those closer to oneself more than those who are distant; and given his argument for friendship-love applying to all human beings, Kant strangely expresses repulsion for intimacy or closeness when he discusses the perfect friendship. Perfect friendship is defined as 'the union of two persons through equal mutual love and respect'.[126] Kant describes love and respect as analogous to the natural forces of attraction and repulsion between persons. Thus he writes: 'The principle of mutual love admonishes them constantly to come closer to one another; that of the respect they owe one another, to keep themselves at a distance from one another.'[127] The need to keep distance is to avoid a loss of respect from another. In other words, if a friend benefits from another, they can be regarded as a lesser person or be placed at a less equal position as the friend due to the obligation they owe. Therefore, Kant recommends that acts

---

of benevolence) and I am therefore under obligation to greater benevolence to one than to the other but am admittedly closer to myself (even in accordance with duty) than to any other, then it would seem that I cannot, without contradicting myself, say that I ought to love every human being as myself, since the measure of self-love would allow for no difference in degree. – But it is quite obvious that what is meant here is not merely benevolence in *wishes*, which is, strictly speaking, only taking delight in the well-being of every other and does not require me to contribute to it (everyone for himself, God for us all); what is meant is, rather, active, practical benevolence (beneficence), making the well-being and happiness of others my *end*. For in wishing I can be *equally* benevolent to everyone, whereas in acting I can, without violating the universality of the maxim, vary the degree greatly in accordance with the different object of my love (one of whom concerns me more closely than another).

125 Kant, *The Metaphysics of Morals*, 6:472.
126 Ibid., 469.
127 Ibid., 449.

of beneficence be done anonymously in secret.[128] For Kant, mutual respect in intimate relationship overrides other benefits, such as sharing personal feelings, disclosing one's thoughts and so forth. It is only in the best moral friendship where equally intelligent friends 'share a general outlook on thing' that he thinks can reveal their secret judgements and feelings 'especially those about other human beings [...] [and about] government, religion and so forth'.[129]

This would make Kant's conception of love seem disconcertingly cold and clinical. The severe exclusion of feelings from his analysis of the components of the moral life is in fact more of a heuristic device than a serious recommendation for it to be expunged from meaningful and moral human lives. Even where it allows for intimacy and relationship, due to his insistence that the attractive force of love be tempered and conditioned by the repulsive force of respect. For Kant, love as valuing is a human project which requires caring cultivation and continued moral development. Instead of being awarded union with the divine, or an ascension to the place of beyond the human, Kant's perspective on love as valuing is grounded precisely in human moral progress, but without the assistance of divine deliverance.

***

Arthur Schopenhauer (1788–1860): Love as valuing human intuition

In *The World as Will and Representation*, Schopenhauer establishes that human experiences (e.g. perception and intuition) are conditions of knowledge about the world. This is because 'these conditions and this appearance in a particular place at a particular time, are all that it knows or ever can know'.[130] In this, Schopenhauer highlights the significance of human intuition which all his predecessors tend to ignore. The idea of *the world as will* suggests that all persons are part of the world and thus our experiences and ideas are manifestations of the will. The will underlines the reality of our world, and for Schopenhauer the will is equated to the ceaseless human striving for the good life. In other words, will is what drives us to act, with or without the basis of rational articulation or clear motivation. Will is therefore part of the human subconscious because individuals are only aware of their experiences, representations and ideas but not of the force of the will.

---

128 Ibid., 453.
129 Ibid., 471–2.
130 Schopenhauer, *The World as Will and Representation*, 134.

In this way, Schopenhauer claims that the world as a whole consists of two integral sides: (1) the world as will, unified and as itself; (2) the world as representation, that is, bodies, ideas, objects and appearances. For some commentators, these claims reflect the integral nature of the inner and outer reality.[131] The primary access humans can have to the nature of reality is through our body whereby 'a way from within stands open to us to that real inner nature of things to which we cannot penetrate from without'.[132] In other words, our body is presented to us as representation, whilst the will is a direct inner experience (through our body). Without divine intervention or God's power to transcend, the world as will and as representation, for Schopenhauer, are encompassed by our endless striving.

The force within us activated by love, especially sexual love, is what Schopenhauer calls will-to-life. In *Metaphysics of Sexual Love*, Schopenhauer suggests that in love, a man is principally drawn to a woman's beauty, but he is also guided, in his preference and selection of his loved one, by the perception of 'those perfections which he himself lacks, may be even those imperfections which are the opposite of his own'.[133] As such, love is valuing the beauty and other perfections (exemplary of our manliness or womanliness) out of (biological) instinct, or a highly specialised and individualised form of impulse, which is unconscious. To the person in love, they experience love that is of great significance, worthy of being 'the ultimate goal of almost all human effort', intruding on even the most orderly and sober of pursuits.[134]

For Schopenhauer, love concerns ultimately the 'composition of the next generation' because sexual relations are essential for the continued procreation leading to the preservation of human species. In love, therefore, 'the will of the individual appears at a higher power as the will of the species'.[135] The existence of future generation is conditioned by human sexual impulse in general. It is towards maintaining the 'type of the species' that lovers tend to choose partners whose complimentary 'perfections' or contrary 'imperfections' are in balance with their own, making them suitable to each other directed at the natural aim. Such intuition is channelled through their own wills, to give birth to a new person of a specific nature.[136]

---

131 See, for instance, Wicks, "Arthur Schopenhauer".
132 Schopenhauer, *The World as Will and Representation*, 195.
133 Schopenhauer 1991, 127.
134 Ibid., 122–3.
135 Ibid., 123.
136 Ibid., 126.

Schopenhauer claims that a person's will-to-life is masculine, inherited from the father, whereas the intellect or knowledge is feminine, mostly inherited from the mother. As a feminine aspect of a person, knowledge can be drawn from both woman and man. According to Schopenhauer, knowledge is key to salvation and the kind of knowledge to be sought is knowledge of the world as a whole which affirms the will. Schopenhauer also maintains that the knowledge necessary for salvation is an awareness of life's suffering, of which a woman is more aware than a man. This is because women are more realistic, more down to earth, more matter-of-fact and more present in the here and now than men. Very significantly, Schopenhauer indicates that women are more compassionate, more loving and more sympathetic 'for the unfortunate' than men. In this context, Schopenhauer proposes that feminine virtue of 'loving-kindness' which is primary and the masculine virtue of justice, which is secondary, must complement each other in living out our respective human nature. In this way, humans are driven by an instinct for the good of our species, at the cost of the individuals in love. Anyone who loves another person, as Schopenhauer suggests, does not achieve a sense of meaning or fulfilment as it is for the benefit of the species' continuity. Therefore, it does not come within the individual's conscious awareness of themselves as lovers.[137]

In Schopenhauer's metaphysics, the true nature of reality, which as it occurs in our experience, is a single 'turbulent [w]ill', which manifests in constant 'conflict and struggle'; and as a result, human life is 'essentially suffering, conflict, dissatisfaction and enmity with others'.[138] However, what is important about Schopenhauer's perspective on love's evolution is that it recognises humans as embodied beings and affirms that human life can have meaning despite being torn apart by the will. Equally, it acknowledges the oneness of humanity and the sacrifices people make towards our collective flourishing.

The notion of the primal nature of the will connects Schopenhauer and Nietzsche.[139] Nietzsche takes the idea of will-to-life further and develops his own system of thought, which, for some interpreters, has heralded myriad postmodern conceptions of love.

***

---

137 Ibid.
138 Higgins and Solomon, *The Philosophy of (Erotic) Love*, 121.
139 Dolson, "The Influence of Schopenhauer upon Friedrich Nietzsche."

Friedrich Nietzsche (1844–1900): Amor fati – Love as valuing life

In *Thus Spoke Zarathustra*, Nietzsche challenges the moral ideals imposed by Christianity, especially the ways that religion pre-determines things in the world to be 'good' or 'evil'. (For instance, in contrast to divine love, erotic passions are categorised as antithesis to Christian virtues.) According to Nietzsche, our dependence on rational and metaphysical conceptions of human nature from sources of values beyond the human has resulted in a lack of self-knowledge and self-awareness. Subject to a herd-mentality, people cannot think for themselves, because all moral principles are imposed by Christian teaching. Thus, we can only experience the world in constrained and limited ways. For Nietzsche, the Christian aspiration for transcendence is a form of self-denial because it suggests that human-becoming can only rely on divine intervention to elevate us towards beyond the human. The alternative is therefore to explore how to be human.[140]

Nietzsche highlights the meaningfulness of life in the here-and-now through the words of Zarathustra. These words are life-affirming, including valuing the delights and challenges of life by rejoicing in our authentic experiences in the world.[141]

Nietzsche further develops 'will to power', or human's striving to be who we really are. Power in Nietzsche's thought does not mean control, or strength, rather it refers to an uninhibited self-expression, a form of self-overcoming. The desire for power originates in the fact that many people 'wait all their lives for the opportunity to be good in their way'[142] but are unable to do so because of Christian ideology that has imprisoned people in the above-mentioned herd-mentality. To assume will to power is for each person to find their own path in life.[143] Nietzsche advocates that a person must self-create and determine their own destiny.

Following Schopenhauer, Nietzsche also sees humans as part of nature. Within the natural system, each being is motived by the will, a striving for existence. The truth of this natural system can only be experienced, explored and recognised by persons who are living their lives fully, rather than being

---

140 Nussbaum, "Human Functioning and Social Justice: In Defense of Aristotelian Essentialism."
141 Cf OSHO, 1987.
142 Nietzsche, *Human, All Too Human*, 243.
143 Solomon, 2003.

subject to what Nietzsche calls 'false opposites',[144] such as good vs evil, mind vs body and nature vs human. Accordingly, Nietzsche argues that 'all credibility, all good conscience, all evidence of truth comes only from the senses'.[145] This means our body and embodied feelings and emotions should be at the core of experiencing and expressing our nature as human beings. Feelings and emotions are therefore beyond good and evil. In this way, Nietzsche affirms that the meaningfulness of life lies in the living of it or in becoming what we are. Along with the will to power, including freedom of self-expression, self-creation and self-actualisation, is self-responsibility for our becoming, which for Nietzsche requires self-belief.[146] It is here that Nietzsche proposed *amor fati*.

Amor fati means that to love is to value and to accept the nature of being human, including all its complexities, contradictions and uncertainties. Rather than valuing things and qualities beyond the human, love affirms human realities in their own right. Nietzsche suggests that humans have already those resources to support our capacities to embrace life's challenges. These resources include our '[g]ood nature, friendliness, [...] courtesy of the heart [...] [and] ever-flowing tributaries of the selfless drive'.[147] In the quote below, Nietzsche illustrates the source of love in human vulnerability:

> when the man encounters in another person weakness, a need for help and exuberance all at once, something happens within him as if his soul would overflow: he is in the same instant moved and offended. At this point originates the source of great love.[148]

For humans to live a good life, we must affirm and accept the value of life as such, embracing all its beauties, but also its trials and tests. For Nietzsche, life is where lies our inherent potential for love as valuing, including love of self, love of others and most importantly love of life itself. Hence Nietzsche claims, 'we love life, not because we are used to living but because we are used to loving'.[149] Loving is already constituted in human nature and in loving life, human reality and destiny and all that is involved in being human, we can reject herd-mentality and self-denial and take delight in our full humanity.

---

144 Nietzsche, *The Will to Power*, 371.
145 Nietzsche, *Beyond Good and Evil*, 100.
146 Cf O'Dwyer, "Nietzsche's Reflections on Love".
147 Nietzsche, *Human, All Too Human*, 48.
148 Ibid.
149 Nietzsche, *Thus Spoke Zarathustra*, 68.

Living a human life is the only path to overcome ourselves and our limitations as the result of deceptions and illusions. In accepting life, '[o]ne must have chaos in one, to give birth to a dancing star'.[150]

Therefore, for some, amor fati means that 'life is a continuum of creation and [...] is constructed and reconstructed again and again'[151] from turbulence and confusion. In many ways, Nietzsche's conception of love has helped elevate the natural, embodied and historically situated human over and above the rational, metaphysical, theological and eternal depictions of being human. Through amor fati, for the first time in Western thought, human's life, in all of its fallacies and imperfections, can be truly loved, valued and loveable.

---

150 Ibid., 46.
151 O'Dwyer, "Nietzsche's Reflections on Love", 64.

Post-Modern and Contemporary Conceptions of Love as Valuing

> *If the world is ever to give birth to true companionship and oneness, not marriage, but love will be the parent.*
> —Emma Goldman, *Anarchism and Other Essays*

> *Love alone brings a human being to full awareness of personal existence. For it is in love alone that man finds room enough to be what he is.*
> —Dietrich von Hildebrand, *Man, Woman, and the Meaning of Love*

Following the modern period, Western thought enters into post-modern period.[152] Throughout the nineteenth century, love continues to be valued at three levels. In the words of Kierkegaard, at a 'primary level', it is the most profound, but nonetheless 'hidden' love, which is God's love; at an 'intermediate' level, it is what bridges God's love and human love or the transcendent and the immanent; at a 'human' level; it is the phenomenological experience of intimacy and interdependence.[153] Despite clarifying these three levels, the ambiguity of love prevails – some thinkers lean towards God's love, some focus on the intermediary and others are drawn to human love.

In the post-modern/contemporary Western thought, thinkers (as well as theologians and philosophers) have indulged in love's values in the physical, familial, societal, but also cultural and political, realms. With an interest in the value of the self, in the twentieth century, amidst Freudian attribution to an unconscious sexual drive as a key feature of love, sexual love is regarded as the pursuit of virtue and happiness and thus an end in itself. Also valued are emotionality, individuality and reciprocity.

Amidst these conceptions of love that recognise human individuality and respect for human liberty as an important value, we also find voices of feminist writers and philosophers who invite us to reconsider the place of love in human emancipation, the value of the Other in one's life and how love can embrace human differences and ultimately contribute to a more just and inclusive world.

---

[152] In this book, post-Modern is a term literally referring to the time following the Modern period, rather than a particular school of thought called postmodernism. I will use the words 'post-Modern' and 'contemporary' interchangeably.
[153] Kierkegaard, *The Works of Love*.

The oscillation between redemption/transcendence and passion/immanence continues into the twenty-first century.

***

Emma Goldman (1869–1940): Love as valuing love in its own right

In the same way that Nietzsche challenges Christian doctrine's domination, Emma Goldman, in her writing and in her activism, confronts the society's patriarchal hierarchy as the basis of power domination and class system.[154] She does this by defying the control of religious teaching over people's moral horizons. For Goldman, human freedom is our greatest priority. By human, she does not mean a universalised nature that all humans share; instead, she refers to humans as individuals in myriad attributes that are different from those who are unlike ourselves. This recognition of individual differences, echoing Nietzsche, will join the proceeding contemporary discourses about humans as situated beings in historical, social, cultural, economic and political contexts.

Although not part of the first wave of feminist Suffragette movement, Goldman's philosophy of love encompasses a strong feminist connotation. She recognises that women should be independent and free. For instance, she urges women to 'demand freedom for both sexes, freedom of action, freedom in love and freedom in motherhood'.[155] One of her ideas is for a woman to be able to 'love whomever she pleases', which is progress from a *situation* that both Schopenhauer and Nietzsche have critiqued. That *situation* is where love is a substitute for marriage aimed at breeding a race. Such a situation is where men, women and love itself have all been instrumentalised. In her article, *Marriage and Love*, Goldman points out that men and women submit themselves to marriage, not because of love but because of a convention (similar to Nietzsche's herd-mentality) that most have outgrown of public opinion. Although not denying that some marriages allow love to continue to flourish, Goldman regards marriage as part of the social contract and 'an economic arrangement, an insurance pact'.[156] She likens a woman's investment

---

154 Marshall, *Demanding the Impossible: A History of Anarchism*.
155 Goldman wrote in an article entitled 'Marriage', published in Firebrand, July 1897.
156 Goldman, *Anarchism and Other Essays*, 197–8.

in a marriage to life insurance that 'condemns her to life-long dependency, to parasitism, to complete uselessness, individual as well as social'.[157]

The comparison of marriage to an insurance policy highlights the suppression of women in nineteenth-century Western societies, a phenomenon illustrated in contemporary European literature authored by, for instance, Jane Austin, the Brontë sisters, and Norwegian playwright Henrik Ibsen, amongst others. Marriage is depicted as the most important institution for women. For any woman who is cast out of this institution, life can be profoundly difficult and even miserable both personally and financially. Whereas for those who did find themselves in such an institution, life can be equally depressing, especially in terms of the lack of personal, financial and political freedom.[158] Within such an institution, love is only assumed because for many, it is non-existent. Drawing on statistics on divorce, Goldman reveals 'the barrenness, the monotony, the sordidness [and] the inadequacy of marriage as a factor for harmony and understanding'.[159] Using the story of Ibsen's play *A Doll's House* as an illustration, Goldman suggests that in the marriage institution, men and women merely co-habit. She asks whether there is anything 'more humiliating, more degrading than a life-long proximity between two strangers?'[160] In addition, societal norms tend to regard romantic love, in particular, sex, as immoral and any acknowledgement of such needs would find attitudes of feeling 'shocked, repelled, outraged beyond measure'[161] and hence subtly criminalise the embodied human desires, needs and yearnings. Hence, women were bred and cultivated to serve the marriage institution. According to Goldman, such deprivation represents soul poverty for women, which is inherent in the domination of church and state.

Indeed, Goldman sees the marriage institution as a part of the greater malaise of paternal systems. The first being Christianity and Christian institutions that tend to confine men and women to the doctrine of marriage, family, good and evil. The second being capitalism that places human beings on an 'economic treadmill'.[162] This is as destructive as it is dehumanising because:

---

157 Ibid.
158 Levine, "So Few Prizes and So Many Blanks."
159 Goldman, *Anarchism and Other Essays*, 199.
160 Ibid., 199.
161 Ibid., 200.
162 Ibid., 204.

Love as Valuing 79

> [it] robs man of his birthright, stunts his growth, poisons his body, keeps him in ignorance, in poverty and dependence and then institutes charities that thrive on the last vestige of man's self-respect [...] [It] makes a parasite of woman, an absolute dependent [...] [and] incapacitates her for life's struggle, annihilates her social consciousness, paralyzes her imagination and then imposes its gracious protection, which is in reality a snare, a travesty on human character.[163]

Instrumentalisation (and thus dehumanisation) has been the prevailing characterisation of capitalist economy in Western societies since the industrial revolution. Goldman's analysis, which poses sharp criticism of capitalism, remains relevant today in the twenty-first century. It is within such a context that Goldman identifies the narrowness of the first wave of feminist movement in the late nineteenth century that called for respect of women's rights to vote and their other civil rights, including the legitimacy of their employment and financial and political independence. In *The Tragedy of Women's Emancipation*, Goldman writes: 'emancipation should make it possible for woman to be human in the truest sense',[164] and not in such a way that posits women as the opposite or the enemy of men. That means it 'will have to do away with the absurd notion of the dualism of the sexes, or that man and woman represent two antagonistic worlds'.[165]

Thus Goldman's view is more radical than those who have inspired her thoughts in that she separates marriage from love and in doing so, she establishes the value of love in its own right. In contrast to the previous accounts, Goldman proposes that the value of love lies in *loving*, not so much *what* one loves, nor *whom* one loves. Goldman then argues that true emancipation 'begins in woman's soul', an 'inner regeneration', because 'after all, the most vital right is the right to love and to be loved'.[166] Hence Goldman conceives love as valuing to be 'the strongest and deepest element in all life, the harbinger of hope, of joy, of ecstasy; [...] the defier of all laws, of all conventions; [...] the freest, the most powerful moulder of human destiny'.[167] With this conception, like her predecessors (i.e. Schopenhauer and Nietzsche), she not only affirms the value of human life itself but also highlights love as the greatest anchor of human life

---

163 Ibid., 204.
164 Ibid., 187.
165 Ibid., 196.
166 Ibid., 195.
167 Ibid., 205.

and the only pathway towards true emancipation, for all humankind, men and women.

Goldman advocates 'free love', a life in love that 'lives itself unreservedly, abundantly, completely'.[168] Note here, Goldman doesn't say who is doing the loving in this way, because the meaningfulness of love lies precisely in itself or loving for loving's sake. Only in this way, can love beget love, in the example where women love freely and the children born in love will equally be loved freely and abundantly. Goldman points out that 'love in freedom is the only condition of a beautiful life'.[169] Goldman thus highlights a human future where love is the true source of meaningfulness and the good life.

Emma Goldman's vision assumes love's intrinsic value (i.e. being valuable in itself), rather than as a means to an end, however noble these ends may be. She sees love as antithetical to the rigid (instrumental) formality of an institution. For Goldman, emancipation starts from recognising the value of love in itself. By valuing the value of love as the foundation of human life, men and women can liberate our souls and seek true flourishing together.

***

Dietrich von Hildebrand (1889–1977): Love as value-response

Dietrich von Hildebrand takes a similar view as Goldman and believes that love's value truly lies in loving and being loved and in witnessing other's being loving. In *The Arts of Living*, he proposes that when one loves a person, love is a value-response. In other words, love is our only (appropriate or adequate) response to the intrinsic value of the other person as a whole being.

In *Nature of Love*, he explains that this is because love is intrinsically valuable, where the value of love is itself and when we love someone, we respond to their intrinsic value, or preciousness and nobleness in its own right. This is in contrast to love as a means to personal gain. However, love's response is not uniform, but in accordance with the position of preciousness in the hierarchy of values.[170] For instance, our response to material or inanimate things, such as beauty in a work of art, our response to other sentient beings, such as birds and animals in nature, and our response to another human being must be

---

168 von Hildebrand, *The Arts of Loving*, 205.
169 Ibid., 206.
170 von Hildebrad, *Nature of Love*

appropriate to the weight we attach to each of the beloved. Our love for the human person must not be instrumental because persons are bearers of values and being persons is intrinsically valuable and are ends in themselves.

For von Hildebrand, love as valuing is a *gift* and once received, the beloved can feel affirmed and become more aware of their own intrinsic value or their intrinsic preciousness. In this regard, the act of loving is constituted in our good life and in turn contributes to our happiness and well-being. In a similar vein, other people whom we love are likewise comprised in our good life and happiness and by loving them, they become in part our well-being, and they further enrich our happiness.

Von Hildebrand outlines two aspects of love: one is moving beyond our self-interest (and directing our love at something of value in its own right), or 'transcendence', and the other is taking delight in what is right through the participation of the heart. In doing what is right, love can help liberate us of the confines of our reality, or 'immanence'. According to von Hildebrand, instead of disinterested love, love as *intentio unionis* is our deep appreciation of the preciousness of the beloved such that love moves us close to them. Whereas love as *intentio benevolentia* concerns a recognition of one's best interest as the best interest of the beloved. Thus by loving, the lover and the beloved can enter into each other's subjectivity.

For von Hildebrand, the heart's attachments are important for love. Hence he considers *ordo amoris* or the appropriate ordering of our heart's attachments. What should our heart be attached to? And what should our heart be attached more? Here von Hildebrand introduces the notion of loving objectively. Evaluating the value of the object of love requires objective factors so that a person can discern how to attach the heart and to what extent to attach the heart. In this sense, von Hildebrand's conception of love is not independent of reason. Although love's response is an emotional one, reason remains necessary to evaluate our attachment.

So *ordo amoris* or the ordering of our heart is given, such as people in our family where parents tend to be more attached to their children than those of strangers. We can also be more attached to our spouse and our close friends more than others. These attachments, for von Hildebrand, are as if 'being ordered', and, in each case, we assume a particular kind of affinity with some people, stronger or weaker.

Hildebrand's philosophy on love as valuing also highlights its verb form and regards it as a practical attitude. In other words, our beloved is not valued, admired and affirmed; our love also inspires our acting upon our loving attitude, such as by providing what the loved ones would need to live a flourishing life. This is termed as 'effective affirmation', that is, affirming the values or the goods of the other person firstly for their sake and secondly for the goodness in the world.

These are just a few brief examples of how von Hildebrand discusses love as a value-response. The central tenet of his argument is that love as valuing does not instrumentalise another person to meet our own physical or emotional needs. Love is acting on the recognition of the intrinsic value of the other person as a whole being and on the appreciation of the beauty and goodness of the other in their own right. This does not imply that we shall idealise the beloved without realising their limitation; nor does it mean that we emphasise on the importance of the other person through our own pride. Love as a value-response means that when we love, we also invite the valuable aspects in the other person who in turn would bring the potentiality into actuality. In short, according to von Hildebrand, as love is a value-response, when we love someone, we *give* of ourselves to them. It is both self-donation and self-gifting.

***

Simone de Beauvoir (1908–1986): Love as integrating transcendence and immanence

De Beauvoir provides an important voice in the development of existentialism. Her philosophical thoughts have continuously been reinterpreted, and new insights about her ideas are still emerging. Joining other philosophers such as Nietzsche and feminist writers, de Beauvoir rejects the moral laws devised in the name of cosmic meaning, God or human nature.

In *Ethics of Ambiguity*, she maintains that the greatest domination of religion and (divine) humanity lies in their being treated as the absolute source of meaning and hence causes of our action.[171] In doing so, although faith and beliefs allow us to seek transcendence from our existential struggles, they can, at the same time, allow humans to escape from our responsibilities for creating and partaking in the conditions that have shaped our existential experiences. Both the kingdom of God and human utopia encourage us to forego the present for the sake of future, as if our current life in the here and now is a mere sacrifice or a means to an end (i.e. salvation and redemption).

---

171 De Beauvoir, *Ethics of Ambiguity*.

In the absence of God and universally conceptualised humanity, de Beauvoir recognises the inherent dignity of all persons but not in an abstract and cosmically prescribed sense. It is rather in a sense that my life is valuable in its particularities already intertwined with others' life. In this case, the values of my life must be appreciated by others for it to be valuable. Accordingly, an ethical life consists in the choices that we make in the situations we find ourselves. Freedom, for de Beauvoir, is always situated because as persons, we are already embedded in the world and therefore find ourselves inescapably related to others. For instance, de Beauvoir argues that each person's freedom resides in their capacity to make choices but every choice we make affects the choices of others. Therefore it is necessary that we accept our responsibilities for other people's lives. Thus, the other and their choice become intertwined with and mutually constituted in that of our own. To seek justice and to live ethically, we must take into account others' interests, form a political alliance with other people and challenge the structural conditions that limit our respective freedom.[172] Thus de Beauvoir concludes: it is impossible to value our own freedom without valuing the freedom of others. In other words and putting it positively, to will our own freedom is also to will others' freedom.

In *The Second Sex*, de Beauvoir examines the nature of love. She contrasts the experiences of love between men and women in a patriarchal society (e.g. structurally dominated by Christian doctrines and similar moral laws) and points out that women have been objectified sexually and instrumentalised by men to fulfil men's desires and help men pursue their interests. For men, love is part of their salvation, but for women, it is subordination to men to ensure men's transcendence. In this context, men are deified as if they are god-like, hence women's devotion to and vocation in loving men. Indeed, de Beauvoir calls our attention to the fact that the defining value of women has been measured by their love or effective devotion to men through, for example, marriage, motherhood and servitude. To such an extent, a woman in love would be entirely subservient to her beloved by reading the books he reads, enjoying the pictures and music he likes, being fascinated by the views he sets his eyes on, marvelling at the ideas he thinks, adopting his friends and foes and, above all, dreaming to be identified as valuable in his consciousness.[173] What de Beauvoir has unfolded here is that women's oppression is not only actualised by institutions, such as marriage and family and the overall societal

---

172 Ibid.
173 De Beauvoir, *The Second Sex*, Part II, Chapter 12, "The Woman in Love".

and cultural norms and practices, it is also internalised by women themselves to such an extent, it becomes 'intrinsic to women's identity and thus be embraced, not resisted, by women'.[174]

However, these oppressive institutions also present themselves as controversial in terms of men's part in them. For instance, de Beauvoir reflects on the paradox of marriage where men play the role of God and at the same time engage in carnal bestiality of sexual encounter and questions men's power and control over women:

> The paradox of marriage is that it brings into play an erotic function as well as a social one: this ambivalence is reflected in the figure the husband presents to the young wife. He is a demigod endowed with virile prestige and destined to replace her father: protector, overseer, tutor, guide; the wife has to thrive in his shadow, he is the holder of values, the guarantor of truth, the ethical justification of the couple. But he is also a male with whom she must share an experience often shameful, bizarre, disgusting, or upsetting and in any case, contingent; he invites his wife to wallow with him in bestiality while directing her with a strong hand towards the ideal.[175]

Both portrayals together form a powerful critique of a patriarchal system, where men are holders of values and judges of morality, and women are subordinate part of men and followers of ideals set by men. Equally, it challenges the social, political and religious categories used to justify women's inferior status. It highlights the ambiguity of transcendence. She writes:

> Every subject posits itself as a transcendence concretely, through projects; it accomplishes its freedom only by perpetual surpassing towards other freedoms; there is no other justification for present existence than its expansion towards an indefinitely open future.[176]

Transcendence is regarded predominantly as men's pursuit, as if only 'an indefinite need to transcend' justifies the meaningfulness of their existence.[177] In pursuing transcendence, women and men, for that matter, have been treated as objects and instrumentalised. At a more general level, transcendence

---

174 Atkinson, "The Descent from Radical Feminism to Postmodernism," 1.
175 De Beauvoir, *The Second Sex*, Part II, Chapter 5.
176 Ibid., 16.
177 Ibid., 17.

seems to instrumentalise the lived human experience – it requires scarifying immanence for the sake of transcendence. In this process, men treat women as the 'other', who in turn assume themselves as the other and since women's own transcendence 'will be forever transcended by another essential and sovereign consciousness', they find themselves deemed to be inessential. Clearly, this violates human dignity and renders such love unethical.

According to de Beauvoir, ethical love values the dignity of both partners equally. Such love enables loved ones to mutually identify each other as worthy and valuable. Hence ethical love encompasses reciprocity and equilibrium. Love should not only be limited to women as their vocation, as a form of their dedication to men and men's projects; through love, women should also have the freedom to seek becoming, to transcend and to go beyond their present conditions and such intentions ought to be supported by men in the same way that women have done for men. When conceived as such, love can become a joint project whereby men and women integrate transcendence and immanence to pursue authentic love for themselves and for each other. Authentic love is therefore the pathway to true individual freedom. Here we find self-giving without the self-sacrificing (from which women tend to suffer); equal devotion without the subordination in which women tend to be placed and mutual engagement without the alienation of the women.

For de Beauvoir, ethical love can truly liberate women from two battles: in the former, a battle of the 'feminine', women who attempt to reduce men to their sexual prey, confine them in their 'carnal passivity', entrap men with womanly charm and beauty and imprison them in the women's immanence. In doing so, women would have furthered themselves as objects, and their salvation is situated in her passivity and alienation. In the latter, a battle of the 'emancipated' women, who demand to be dominant as much as men, to be active and powerful as men and reject the passivity and docility that men have imposed. However, in this process, women can inadvertently adopt masculine values, and they begin to work, think and act on the same basis as their male counterparts, as if the only legitimate status is that of men and the only way for women to be equal is to become men. In this battle, women's sovereignty resides in men's accepting it.

From de Beauvoir's perspective, a woman who fights such battles 'assumes herself as both self and other',[178] by using her vulnerability and her strength at the same time. 'The conflict will last as long as men and women do not

---

178 De Beauvoir, *The Second Sex*, Conclusion.

recognise each other as peers, that is, as long as femininity is perpetuated as such' and a vicious circle of confrontation will perpetuate 'because each sex is victim both of the other and of itself'.[179] Instead, seeing ethical love as mutual valuing can help defuse the tension between the two adversaries, that is, the masculine and the feminine who tend to battle against each other in the pursuit of personal freedom. This is because, as de Beauvoir highlights, 'each camp is its enemy's accomplice'.[180]

Ethical love must be genuine love which:

> ought to be founded on the mutual recognition of two liberties; the lovers would then experience themselves as both self and other; neither would give up transcendence, neither would be mutilated; together they would manifest values and aims in the world.[181]

Women do not need to depend on men for affirming their values and worth, nor for suggesting path towards self-transcendence. Instead, each woman can be her own source of liberation and salvation. In her own authenticity, a woman discovers and embraces her strength, where although confined in a feminine universe, she can become free. In light of women's new-found transcendence, de Beauvoir proposes that instead of fighting a battle on the ground of transcendence, men and women should form partnership and collaborate with each other in the pursuit of a flourishing life together.

Clearly ethical love is an invitation for men to rise to action and become genuine partners of women. For de Beauvoir, this mutual recognition of human value and our inherent worthiness can only be possible when such values are embraced and lived in our day-to-day action, where transcendence is achieved through immanence and liberation is engaged by men and women in equal partnership.

Simone de Beauvoir has anticipated the risk of women's liberation movement where, by emphasising the differences between men and women, the gulf between people is widening and the chance of such bifurcation of humans can result in 'every individual [...] pitted against every other'.[182] She argues that 'humanity is something other than a species: it is an historical

---

179 Ibid.
180 De Beauvoir, *The Second Sex*, 185.
181 Ibid., 667.
182 Atkinson, "The Descent from Radical Feminism to Postmodernism," 4.

becoming; [...] [and] it is taken for granted that in the timeless heaven of Ideas a battle rages between these uncertain essences: the Eternal Feminine and the Eternal Masculine',[183] as if there were two different forms on earth, corresponding to different historical moments.

> Simone de Beauvoir's conception of ethical love might have been the greatest and most radical contribution to human's endeavour to seek transformation and to overcome our individual and collective limitations: by integrating transcendence and immanence, as well as the masculine and the feminine.

---

183 De Beauvoir, 1949, Conclusion.

Conclusions: The Supreme Values of Love

In this chapter, I gathered some accounts of love to demonstrate how thinkers in the different epochs of Western history have supported the thesis that love's value lies in the quest for the good life. Although the conceptions of love have evolved over time, the quest for the good life through love is unceasing, rather than finite. In this way, love as valuing offers us a glance at human's journey towards transformation. Without such a quest, exploration of and contemplation upon all things beautiful and valuable, such as cosmos, God, nature, humanity and life itself, can remain trivial.

The inquiry into the values of love starts with claims that love lies at the core of the universal essence, and ends with accounts that articulate the particularities of love manifested in human life. This includes persons as rational beings, their emotionality, the potential for social, economic and political reciprocity, passionate pursuits and equality. Such an investigation may be considered to be an ontological quest to understand *being* itself.[184] It stresses that love as a source of meaning and the good life has an 'eudaimonistic' value, reflecting what is non-instrumentally valuable.[185]

The classical Greek cosmocentric conception regards love as seeking values in divine qualities, such as beauty and goodness, the sorts of essence found in all things. To love in this case involves appreciating (or appraising) and evaluating these essential qualities. Christian theocentric arguments maintain that human's deepest spiritual inspiration derives from love of God, whose eternal goodness can be bestowed upon humanity so that love of man is possible. As these sketches illustrate, Greek love as valuing the timeless essence of divine beauty and goodness and Christian love as celebrating God's perfection can somewhat undermine the value of love between persons, especially our valuing the transient particularities of humans. Both reflect the yearning of human soul for the realm of the sacred, the divine, but in doing so, human beings (and human life in the here and now) are not valued as who we are as ourselves. It is as if in pursuing divine qualities and God's virtues, transcendent love appreciates less the non-instrumental values of being human in their own right.[186] Humans have been recognised as beings who can attain divine qualities only by ascending with love's ladder and God's grace. It might

---

184 Tillich, 1955.
185 Nussbaum, *Upheavals of Thought*, 49.
186 May, *Love: A History*.

even be argued that both Greek love and Christian love tend to undermine humanity, according to Augustine, to achieve transcendence. 'Thus, for the sake of the lover's own flourishing, it ends up drawing the truest love from the personal to the impersonal, from the individual to the general and from the human to the – literally – inhuman.'[187]

This ascending in reaching for the divine and likewise the divine descending in order to help deliver humanity from our sin have been the two features that have been targeted by modern conceptions of love. Clearly, human striving to surpass ourselves doesn't mean that being human and living the life as human being is less meaningful, but instead, an awareness of the sacredness of love can help root love in our being human as we seek to rise above the human as a form of self-transformation, progress and learning. The latter is the thesis put forward by the modernist and post-modern conceptions of love.

Indeed, as the brief reviews in this chapter illustrate, from the seventeenth century, humans as the beloved subjects have been endowed as valuable (as good and beautiful) who could be pursued as the end of love. Love amongst persons has hence been understood to be both moral and ethical and love as valuing applies to persons whose nature is thence animated, perfected and transcended by no other means than love itself. These accounts truly mark the continued evolution and revolution of love in which both the human and nature are revered without the need to rise above them or to reach beyond them. That is to say, the ethical life lies precisely in the beauty and goodness of living a human life naturally.

---

187 Ibid., 51.

CHAPTER 4

LOVE AS RELATIONING

Love as relationing has been an evolving idea in Western thought. Earlier thinkers have argued that humans, by our very nature, are already in union with one another, as demonstrated in our oneness, the harmony of cosmos and God's Trinity. As relational beings, humans regard love as a perpetual yearning for a deeper bond. What is more, a relational conception of love affirms mutuality without which, there cannot be said to be a lover and a beloved. By contrast, later proposals identify that satisfying desire should be at the core of human happiness, such as the utilitarian view advocated by Bentham, and regard love's relationality to be rooted in the pursuit of pleasure, especially in meeting our biological and psychological needs for the sake of a happy life. Then enters the 'free market' of love, as Erich Fromm notes, where the desire for union and closeness are satisfied through the consumption of 'love', in films, books, MTVs and pornographic sites. In the Western capitalist regime, longing for packaged and commercialised 'love' directs people away from genuine relationships with others and with the world. It is assumed that people's needs and wants can be met instantaneously by producing, selling and buying 'love'. This awareness of how humans have responded to the characteristics of the passing epochs and to the demands engendered by the Western socio-economic systems is important for our understanding the evolution in love's relationality.

At first glance, these evolving Western conceptions of love as relationing seem to follow a similar pattern as those proposing *love as valuing*. That is to say, they shift from an emphasis on a yearning for a connection with the divine, to the recognition of love's centrality in human's relationships, personal, social and political, covering a whole range of ideas. Some contemporary thinkers revisit, review and reflect on earlier conceptions. In doing so, they offer novel interpretations of previous propositions and understandings on love's relationality. For instance, through reinterpretations, the relational feature of love has been reconsidered. On this, twentieth-century French philosopher

Gabriel Marcel suggests that love be a verb, 'being' loving, being in relationship, or relationing, rather than 'having' love, or having loving relationships. Love is understood as an act. Others explore the spaces within which love as relationing is invited, enriched and sustained, such as Luce Irigaray's recount of Diotima wisdom on love as holding our in-between-ness. Just like in music, it is the space in between the notes, not the notes themselves, that provides the opportunities for music to articulate meaning and engage the listener's active appreciation, Irigaray recognises the significance of spaces within which a relational matrix can unfold, in our personal, socio-economic and political lives. The notion of the space can help us understand that there are no boundaries separating one person from another, humans from the divine beings, or one kind of life from another, one way of being human from another.

Similar to Chapter 3, this chapter will examine these themes conceived in the different historical and conceptual orientations that have given rise to meanings of a good life, including the cosmological, religious, modernist and more contemporary views.

Classical Greek Conceptions of Love as Relationing

> *Every heart sings a song, incomplete, until another heart whispers back. Those who wish to sing always find a song. At the touch of love everyone becomes a poet.*
>
> —Plato, *Symposium*

Classical Greek thinkers highlight love's relationality by stressing the importance of unity, bondedness and mutuality. Plato, in *Symposium*, although suggesting love as always directed at beauty and goodness, also describes love as taking place within a space amongst persons and between humans and the gods. By placing the nexus of love in relations, Plato avoids reducing love to mere self-interest, or as a means to an end, however noble such an end might be. For instance, in Symposium, in the allegory presented by Aristophanes, the lovers' initial separation has determined a perpetual yearning for (re) union with the loved ones. This seems to be the foundation for romantic love but without the necessity of sexual desire. Another example is Socrates's argument, in advancing the wisdom of Diotima, that effectively proposes two ideas: one is that erôs is relational as it is directed at another person and is, at the same time, self-involved as it is aimed at self-transformation through possessing the good and beauty. The other idea is that love's relationality precisely lies in its being an intermediary, providing an in-between space and serving as an energising force that is creative, inviting beauty and goodness in those who are being brought together into the space and partaking in sustaining the in-between-ness.

For Aristotle, philia and agapē characterise love's relationality but in different ways. In the perfect philia or friendship-love, Aristotle outlines mutuality and non-instrumentality as the main features underpinning the relationship between friends and that such friendship-love is constituted in our flourishing life. By contrast, according to Aristotle, agapē or love for humanity in general, including love for strangers, does not require mutuality, and it can be extended to beyond the human, including divine missions and the greater good.

In all these cases, love is necessarily relational. In some way, classical Greek conceptions of love have laid down the foundational arguments that later generations of philosophers may elucidate, reinterpret, expand and expound on love's relationality, thus ensuring love's evolution and continuity.

***

Aristophanes (c. 450–388 BC): Love as perpetual yearning for union with the beloved

In *Symposium*, Socrates's summary of love is preceded by a number of other presentations amongst which is the myth put forward by Aristophanes. The myth that Aristophanes presented has been influential in the way some have romanticised love.

Aristophanes recalls a myth that portrays primordial humans as spherical, with two sets of limbs, two identical faces upon a circular neck allowing the head to turn in all directions. According to this myth, early humans were strong, powerful and at times aggressive. They were perceived as a threat to the gods. As a result, the gods decided to punish them but not destroy them completely so as to retain them for the sake of sacrifices. This meant to weaken humans' strength and reduce their power. The gods' solution was to divide every single early human into two entities. In this way, each new human being would only have one set of limbs and one forward-facing head. Feeling vulnerable and incomplete, each severed, divided now seemingly half human yearned and sought to reunite with their other half.

Through this allegory, Aristophanes presents a vision of early humans as relational beings by their prior state of oneness, thereby wholeness. Their longing for union is deepened by the present state of separation. This yearning is regarded as love or desiring for relationing and returning to the original wholeness. Love is a way of restoring humans' oneness. In this sense, as interpreted by many, Aristophanes offers a conception of love as sustaining relational wholeness.

From this perspective, it may be suggested that in Aristophanes's account and in Plato's philosophy, love and sexual desire are fundamentally different. The myth articulates a non-sexual yearning for oneness.[1] Instead of sexual attraction, love as relationing orients towards union or wholeness, a goodness where meaningfulness of life resides.

With the wholeness in mind, Aristophanes suggests love to be a relational force, an effort to overcome individualism, separation and alienation. Love seeks a mutual embrace and a fusion of those who are disconnected from each other. Love is beyond a mere physical union and is not sexual contentment.

---

[1] Here is a point that Singer (*Philosophy of Love: A Partial Summing-Up*) suggests that Freud has missed: that human sexual instinct is only derived from the need for restoring to wholeness.

Instead, love's relationality reconfigures the physical distances between one and another through a deeper yearning for restoring the whole. What is more, the wholeness, according to Aristophanes's allegory, pre-determines the lovers' interconnection or interrelatedness, and each lover seeks a specific other with whom they were once conjoined.

A very ancient allegory, it offers at least four significant characterisations of love:

First, it can be interpreted that love is not only to desire something *good* in the other, but in effect, love desires something good in the other which a person does not only recognise as good but which they also seek as part of their well-being. Contrary to the standard interpretation that love involves a subject (the lover) and an object (the beloved), Aristophanes's myth of human oneness and wholeness gives rise to a relational conception of love as between co-subjects. Love embodies an intersubjective relationship. Identifying lovers as co-subjects is an acknowledgement that the other is already constituted in our life, or our well-being. Our deep relational connection with them is in part our shared eudaemonia or flourishing. The co-subjects in turn complete the union, through which lovers become a 'we'. Second, the urge to return to the beloved, restore the whole and achieve the (re)union with our co-subject suggests that the oneness or wholeness is constituted in the goodness. Hence love is believed to a driving force for the good. The relational bond resumed through union is seen to be able to extend the good. Third, a connected point, the allegory highlights that the separation is a form of woundedness, a brokenness, which requires healing, repairing and restoring. Love restores the wholeness which has become the popular contemporary definition of healing. Lastly, this myth implies that love cannot be mere random coupling for pleasure. Instead, love inspires us to unite with the right person.

Although Aristophanes's contribution to *Symposium* is brief, the allegory is nevertheless an important one. This is because both the notion of humans as integrated relational beings and the idea that love holds our wholeness seem to have offered a foundational understanding of love's relationality.

***

Diotima of Mantinea (c. 440 BC): Love as a daemon (in-between)

Given her absence in *Symposium*, Diotima of Mantinea, the Priestess, offers wisdom of love through Socrates's recounting a dialogue between Diotima and himself. In Chapter 3, I outlined Diotima's conception of love as valuing the qualities in things good and beautiful, from the body to the soul, from words to deeds and to goodness and beauty in themselves. This constitutes love's ladder which symbolises an ascent, arising from the physical to the immaterial and to the eternal. It highlights love's potency in sustaining a consistent process of becoming. In this section, I will focus on Diotima's conception of love as sutaining an in-between space – a relational definition.

In Socrates's recount, Diotima offers the allegory of Erôs as the child of Poros and Penia. Poros is the son of Resource, a god, whereas Penia, the daughter of Poverty, is not a divine being. Therefore, all the qualities that the parents can offer to the child Erôs tend to be opposite in nature. Erôs finds himself a being of the in-between: neither a god nor a non-god, neither a being in plenitude (i.e. with infinite resource) nor in poverty (i.e. being needy and lacking), neither good nor bad, neither beautiful nor ugly, neither wise nor ignorant. Erôs is always in-between these opposites.

According to Diotima, Erôs is a great *daemon*, also spelt as *daimon*, which means a spirit who is in-between a deity and a human. In effect, 'everything daemonic is between divine and mortal'.[2] By nature, Erôs is an intermediate and his raison-d'être is 'interpreting and transporting human things to the gods and divine things to men; entreaties and sacrifices from below and ordinances and requitals from above [...]'.[3] In mediating and intermediating, Erôs draws what is good from both the human world and the divine realm. Erôs is the desire for procreation to reach the ultimate goal – from begetting of children to begetting of the soul, in the union of the finite with the infinite, in the appreciation of the good and the beautiful and in enriching and divinising the soul.

What is highlighted in this allegory is that love as relationing sustains an in-between-ness. As a daemon, Erôs knows his potential because his father would show him the divine qualities already abundantly present in himself. At the same time, Erôs also recognises what is lacking in himself through the perspectives of his mother. Mediating between the divine and the embodied mortal, love enables human beings to partake in divine qualities. In doing so, love lifts humans to a higher state of being. Therefore, love can be interpreted as an enlivening and inspiring force – a generative energy. (Indeed, this generative power of love as told by Diotima, recounted by Socrates, is already

---

2 Plato, *Symposium*, 202d–e.
3 Ibid., 202e.

reviewed in Chapter 3 about love as valuing, e.g. by valuing, love is begetting more goodness, more beauty, more wisdom and more enlightened soul where truly happiness dwells.)

According to Diotima, as a medium, an intermediate and a mediator, love facilitates the meeting of the opposites. This meeting is important because, in this case, love as relationing does not insist upon transcendence. Instead, through relationing, love helps integrate transcendence and immanence in that the encounter 'permits the meeting and transmutation or transvaluation between the two'.[4] Thus Diotima points out four key components vividly present in this in-between space: the immanence, or the here-and-now, which love appreciates, the two poles of opposite qualities, which love invites and integrates and the direction of striving, of going beyond, or transcendence.

Through relationing, love inspires human-becoming by enriching those qualities (e.g. goodness, beauty and wisdom) already present. Thus transcendence is simultaneously consisted in immanence. In this way, love itself enables a continuous perpetual shift, to-and-fro progress, indefinitely. Therefore, 'love is complementary to gods and to men in such a way as to join everything with itself'.[5]

***

Aristotle: Friendship-love in a flourishing life

The ancient Greek concept of philia is much wider than our modern concept of friendship. It applies not only to intimate relationships such as between spouses, between other family members or between friends, but also involves relationships between, for instance, colleagues or business partners, with customers and amongst fellow citizens.[6] As we have seen in Chapter 3, in keeping with the diverse conceptions of love that Aristotle employs, he distinguishes three major forms of loving friendship, namely *character* friendship, *pleasure* friendship and *advantage* friendship. All three forms of friendship-love, to Aristotle, are genuine forms of love as relationing, and they all have important ethical and political parts to play in the good life.

---

4 Irigaray, "Sorcerer Love: A Reading of Plato's Symposium, Diotima's Speech," 33.
5 Ibid., 34.
6 Cooper, *Reason and Emotion*.

According to Aristotle, friendship-love hinges on how the friends/lovers act in pursuit of their friend's good for its own sake. He lays emphasis on the 'practical and active element' in friendship, including 'wanting for someone what one thinks good for his sake and not for one's own and being inclined, so far as one can, to do such things for him'.[7] This is because each friendship-love depicts not only a particular kind of relational bond but also the way that such relationality unfolds.

One important difference between character friendship and the other two forms of friendship featured in Aristotle's conception, for example, pleasure friendship and advantage/utility friendship, concerns their relative stability.[8] According to Aristotle, in character friendship there presents a high degree of stability and permanence since the good character, being an actualisation of a person's essential nature, tends to be a stable and enduring state of that person. Pleasure and advantage/utility friendships, by contrast, do not enjoy such stability and endurance, because they are contingent on a person's self-interest. Indeed, the qualities of a friend that one finds pleasurable or advantageous or useful to oneself matter to one purely because they answer to one's desires or needs without which one would no longer receive any pleasure from or take advantage of one's friend. The longevity of pleasure and advantage/utility friendships, therefore, is subject to chance and circumstance, and these friendships tend to be less stable and less enduring.

Another difference amongst these friendships lies in their relational depth. Character friendship, through profound knowledge about one's friend and deep appreciation of the friend's good moral character and qualities, tends to cement deep union and intense relational intimacy amongst the friends. Whereas friendships founded on self-interests and conceived as means to an end, be it pleasure or advantage or utility, cannot yield meaningful human bond as will character friendship.

The third difference amongst these forms of friendship is mutuality. Character friendship is developed upon prolonged mutual knowledge, and mutuality in turn sustains the longevity of the friendship. In contrast, pleasure and advantage friendships are not necessarily mutual – one's wants and desires do not always correspond to those of one's friends. In other words, self-interests are seldom shared. In fact, self-interest is a form of egoism and accordingly, friendship intended to instrumentalise cannot prevail.

---

7 Aristotle, *Rhetoric* II 4, 1380b35-1381a2.
8 Cooper, *Reason and Emotion*.

For Aristotle, philia, or character friendship, entails deep and mutual love. Wishing what is good for the friend's sake and taking delight in things and activities with the friend, love as relationing stresses that the friend is comprised in our well-being and flourishing. Instead of needing the friend for the sake of our own happiness, the good life consists in having friendship-love and friends with whom we experience friendship-love. Self-interest tends to instrumentalise both love and friends. By contrast, when our friends are already constituted in the good life, we love our friends in a non-instrumental way. Friendship-love and friends are intrinsic to our flourishing.

Therefore, philia is non-instrumental. Aristotle emphasises two important relational aspects of philia:

The first is a deep self-other connection. In *Nicomachean Ethic*, Aristotle points out that 'a friend is another self'.[9] To recognise the friend as one's 'other self', according to Aristotle, one must first have a good self-knowledge and a strong self-relationship. Indeed, Aristotle suggests 'an extreme degree of friendship resembles one's friendship to oneself'.[10] An explanation about this is that one loves the friend and their good character for their own sake because one finds similar goodness in one's self, goodness that one intentionally cultivates as part of the good life.

The second aspect is that to have virtuous friends is to share a good life with them. Once again, self-awareness is a quality of a virtuous person, whose close friendship with others determines that one yearns for living an intertwined life with one's friends. For Aristotle, living together entails spending time on things that bring mutual delight, partaking in activities that are mutually enriching, sharing words and thoughts and experiencing the other's feelings and emotions as if one's own. Aristotle concludes that 'this would seem to be the meaning of living together when said of human beings'.[11] Aristotle further articulates that the greatest happiness or flourishing is to share a contemplative life with friends. Such a life is 'more than human', a life that is closer to the life of the gods or the divine life.[12] By seeking the perfect philia, love as relationing can transcend our life and make human life closer to living in the divine realm.

Aristotle's understanding of these forms of friendship is central to his political philosophy, concerning ethics. For Aristotle, humans by nature are

---

9 Aristotle, *Nicomachean Ethics*, 1169b6.
10 Ibid., 1166bl.
11 Ibid., 1170b.10.
12 Ibid., 1177b.25.

social and thus our relational life is already constituted in our life in the polis or political community. He argues that polis proceeds the individual and their family and involves our duties and responsibilities for one another and for our flourishing life together. Accordingly, he writes that it is friendship-love that 'seems to keep cities together and lawgivers seem to pay more attention to it than to justice'.[13] Love as relationing lays the true foundation of collective human flourishing through shared political life.

***

Epictetus: Love as both self-belonging and other-belonging

For the Stoics, human affection towards oneself and for each other originates from our natural tendency towards the good. Included in these goods is self-love. This tendency of self-love is so strong that, according to Epictetus, '[w]hatever, then, seems to it to stand in the way of this, whether brother, father, child, beloved or lover, it hates it, accuses it and curses it. For by nature it loves nothing as much as its own benefit'.[14] This self-regarding nature is *oikeiosis*, which, in Stoic ethics, means affinity, appropriation or 'a dispositional impulse every animal has to care for an object that, in some way or other, it views as *oikeion*, i.e., as 'belonging to itself'.[15] It is self-love for its own sake. Oikeoisis might appear to be egoistic and self-serving, however, self-loving, according to Epictetus, does not contradict love's other-regarding nature, nor love's altruistic or social tendencies. This is because the Stoics believe that human beings also have an oikeiosis to our fellow beings, and it is this belonging-to-other's feeling that can enable us to love others for their own sake. In this sense, a personal oikeiosis is simultaneously a social oikeiosis. This is to say that humans can be both self-belonging and other-belonging.

When understanding oikeiosis in this way, 'doing everything for its own sake is no longer asocial', affirms Epictetus.[16] This is because, as Epictetus explains, love and our inherent tendency for procreation are first manifested as a relational force in our love for our children who are *other* to ourselves.

---

13 Ibid., 1155a22-24.
14 Epictetus, *Discourses*, I.19.11-5.
15 Magrin, 'Nature and Utopia in Epictetus' Theory of Oikeiōsis', 293.
16 Epictetus, *Discourses*, I.19.11-5.

Love's relationality is then extended to loving our siblings, as well as loving our parents. Such relationing is further broadened to loving friends and others in the community. Given this other-regarding orientation to love, according to Epictetus, where tensions between the need for loving oneself and need for loving others arise, self-love always takes priority because without self-benefiting and self-relating, one cannot extend love to others.

Given this assumed priority of self-love, some have proposed that the Stoics do not really see a tension between our inclination to love ourselves and our inclination to love others.[17] Instead, these two inclinations indicate that the Stoics would feel unhappy if one is only pursuing self-interest against that of others.[18] A good life, for the Stoics, must therefore contain both self-loving and other-loving which together allow a person to contribute to the common good benefiting oneself and others at the same time.

Epictetus further suggests that humans naturally have a sense of dignity (and shame) through our access to the rational principles that govern our soul. Likewise, humans 'have some natural reliability, a natural affection, a natural benevolence, a natural patience with one other'.[19] These qualities, broadly placed under love, constitute the greatness of the human soul, marked by our nobility and freedom and are what make humans truly relational beings. According to the Stoics, our virtues direct our relational inclinations and determine the choices we make and the ways we act relationally in the community.

Epictetus further elaborates on this mutuality as follows:

> Therefore, if I am there, where choice is, only then will I be a friend of the sort one ought to be, a son and a father. For this will benefit me, to preserve the reliable man, the man without shame, the patient man, the abstinent man, the cooperative man and to guard my relations [...].[20]

This elaboration is important as it highlights that human's other-regarding quality is not merely acting on our instinct for procreation and spices preservation. Rather, it is a rational choice, an intentional act to love and to

---

17 Klein, 'The Stoic Argument from Oikeiōsis'. Mentioned in Magrin, 'Nature and Utopia in Epictetus' Theory of Oikeiōsis'.
18 Ibid.
19 Epictetus, *Discourses*, II.10.22-3.
20 Ibid., II.22.19-21.

benefit others as part of our personal oikeiosis or self-love. When choosing to be the kind of person that virtues denote one to be, one is living out the good life. For Epictetus, each person's well-being is always bound up with the well-being of others, and loving others is therefore a rational choice of loving one's self. Others are already constituted in one's own well-being.

Living out our virtues in a life of well-being is a feature of our political community, or the cosmopolis, a city constituted by human beings and gods, held together by the law of reason.[21] Life in the polis is where personal ethics and relational ethics merge into one. That is to say, for virtuous persons, there is no such separation between self-regard interest or self-love and other-regard interest or other-love within a political community. Epictetus makes an analogy that each person is part of the polis in the same way that one's foot is part of one's body – it is not part-whole relationship, that is, a community being made up of a collection of individuals, nor the common good as an accumulation of individuals' interests. The foot-body analogy stresses that all persons are relationally integral to the unity of the whole.

---

21 Ibid., III.24.9-11.

Christian Conceptions of Love's Relationality

> *Beloved, let us love one another, because love is from God; everyone who loves is born of God and knows God. Whoever does not love does not know God, for God is love. God's love was revealed among us in this way: God sent his only Son into the world so that we might live through him. [...] Beloved, since God loves us so much, we also ought to love one another [...] God is love and those who abide in love abide in God and God abides in them.*
>
> —1 John 4:7–11 and 16[22]

> *There is neither Jew nor Greek, there is neither slave nor free, there is neither male nor female; for you are all one in Christ Jesus.*
>
> —Paul, Galatians 3:28

In Judaeo-Christian theology, love as relationing is not only being conceived but also further deepened in the logos (i.e. through rational argument) that love amongst humans is only possible through the grace of God. In contrast with what Aristotle identifies as the just nature of love and the deservedness of love, Christian conception of divine bestowal is supposedly unconditional, like a mother's love for her child. As highlighted in Chapter 3, this conception suggests that agapē or caritas, God's love, may involve a feminine principle, even only implicitly.

Christian love stresses human relationships as unconditional, altruistic/ selfless and humble. True human relations must mirror God's relations with mankind (which has love as its foundation). It is through love that we become God-like, and we are able to take part in the divine relationship. Love defines the union, communion and fellowship between God and the human soul but also Church and human community.

Love as relationing is particularly highlighted by St Augustine and St Thomas because their philosophies have explored the metaphysical nature of our being as being-in-relation, or as relational being. This is found in their interpretations and articulations of two important Christian notions – *mutual indwelling* and *mutual redemption*. Both are situated within a doctrine of Trinity, an inherent reality of God as relational being.[23]

Although the differences in Augustinian and Thomasian conceptions of love are subtle, these differences are nevertheless significant. For Augustine,

---

22 Quoted in Simon May, *History of Love*, 85.
23 See Burns, *St. Thomas Aquinas's Philosophy of Love*.

God *is* love, embodied in the 'whole Christ', a holistic presence. By loving God and loving our neighbour, humankind can become Christ-like and thereby aspire for the qualities of the divine being. St Augustine recognises God as trinitarian relational being and believes that love, through our relationship with Christ and other human beings, is instrumental to human's ascension towards God. Whereas Thomas, who equally identifies God's being as already relational through God's own Trinity, suggests that in participating in God's love, the divine qualities are realised through humans actively experiencing ourselves and each other as relational being. As already touched upon in Chapter 3, this is the beginning when we see the turn from the ascending view of transcendence to a descending view whereby God comes to humans in order to help humanity to rise up towards closer to divine state of being.

***

Augustine of Hippo: Love as fellowship with God

St Augustine argues that caritas or eternal charity begins with one's affection towards our fellow human beings, and it is in our mundane and ordinary love for each other that our love for God is found and actualised. This theological argument forms an important aspect of the Christian ways of being. Love determines how we should relate to each other, a mirroring of God's love for humans. Augustinian love already assumes the relational nature of our being and recognises that love enlightens human paths towards living out this relational nature in our everyday personal life, social life, political life and, above all, our life in communion with God.

Augustine distinguishes between two kinds of love or desiring/longing: *cupiditas* and *caritas*. Cupiditas is appetitive longing for pleasures found in the world, including the pleasure we experience in our relationship with things and with other people. Because cupiditas is aimed at satisfying one's own appetite and desire, it is effectively selfish love. Without applying human will, cupiditas can mean that a person wants to possess what they find desirable for themselves and thereby succumb to lust. In this way, selfish love can chain a person to what brings them selfish pleasure, who in turn becomes attached to the pursuit of self-centred pleasure. When the person misidentifies pleasure as *happiness*, they can then be locked in such self-interests. Hence by pursuing and desiring pleasure from outside of oneself, a person can become separated from their soul and such desire may result in self-alienation.

By contrast, caritas is the purest love for God and the opposite of appetitive craving for pleasure. Caritas seeks true delight and deep enchantment (rather than mere pleasure) in the union with God. In caritas, love's object is eternity and through love, mankind can have the opportunity to acquire a learned capacity to transcend our limitation and transform ourselves into unperishable being. Caritas is a closeness or communion with God. It is God's absolute power internalised in the will of persons who can then strive to assume God-like qualities.[24]

According to Augustine, in pursuing cupiditas or pleasure from outside of oneself, a person can experience a separation not only from their soul, their self, but equally from things, nature and other people in the world. To shift from this separation to relational integration, it requires caritas, love of God. This means that through loving God, we can love our self appropriately, other people, the world and our life in the world. When we love God and when the lover becomes one with God and when the love for the lover is united with God's love, we can return to self-love. When love for God is the foundation of human's love for other people and the world, we become one with fellow humans and with the world.

In this distinction, Augustinian love seems to involve two mutually constituted aspects: on the one hand is the movement of coming out of one's self or being drawn out of one's self by our love for others and for the world. In Chapter 3, we discussed this as a form of self-forgetfulness. Thus, from Augustine's perspective, love is primarily ecstatic, compelling and propelling. Love enables one's self to be thrusted towards and into the other (including the divine Other) and towards and into the world. However, when we seek what is outside of our self, for example, when we are attached and drawn to pleasures caused by things and people outside of the self and even when one is searching for God, such desire and search will always be empty because it is devoid of will and self-knowledge. This is the risk of cupiditas. Only caritas allows us to turn inward and inspires us to be truly united with the other and even become the other, an identification with and transformation into the other, as in 'I am you'. To love is to become *one* with the other. Here the other can be a person, beings in nature and God.

Augustine's conception of love as relationing or communing lays the foundation for an understanding of humans as relational beings. Our

---

[24] Similar reading of the differences between cupiditas and caritas can be found in Hanna Arendt's 1996 book *Love and Saint Augustine*.

relational being is achieved through love, which consists in becoming part of God's being, being like God and being one with God. In and through love of God, our relational being is further realised in our being one with each other, being one with the world. Love as relationing depicts a beautiful Christian notion, *mutua inhaesio* or mutual indwelling, which is located in both God and humanity, a holy communion.

The origin of this idea of mutual indwelling derives from the relational concept of God's Trinity. God's Trinity presupposes that the three Persons constituting God are equal in their greatness: the greatness of the Father and the greatness of the Holy Spirit equals the greatness of the Son. No one's greatness is more than that of another or the sum of the other two together. The three Persons are not the same and neither are they separate. Augustine writes: 'The Father is God, the Son God, the Holy Spirit God […] yet there are not three Gods – but one God – the Trinity Itself.'[25] The very nature they share is love. Indeed, Augustine explains God's Trinity through love's relationality: the Person that loves, the Person that is loved and the Person who is love itself.

As God's creatures, humans are persons in ourselves only insofar as we are consciously aware of our relation with God. Augustine maintains that God, in creating humans in his own image, has already permitted human relationship in the Trinity and hence the possibility of close union with the divine Persons through love. Love's relationality allows humans to mirror God's trinitarian qualities in the three pre-requisites (i.e. memory, intellect and will) of our ability to contemplate the eternal forms, to know God and the world. These three qualities distinguish humankind from other creatures in the world, such as animals. They also determine human action of remembering, understanding and committing to the love of God. Furthermore, these capacities presume that humans should live relationally, with God, with each other, with all that is in the world.

Moreover, it is these relational qualities that enable us to respond to God's call to love. Hence Augustine claims: 'My love is my weight; wheresoever I go, it is my love that takes me there.'[26] Love directs and guides our volition. When we fail to act on this call to love, we can end up in self-alienation and separation as in the case of pursuing Cubiditas. Alienation and separation are against our relational nature and therefore our failure to return the call to love is equivalent to self-destruction. This human telos is also interpreted as

---

25 Augustine, *On the Trinity*, 8:10.
26 Augustine, *Confession*.

existential participation,[27] which determines that persons are to be drawn to one another in their union with God and in doing so, each person will embark on a journey of personalised self-perfection or self-transcendence in and through such a relational bond.

In this way, love as relationing does not need to be over-identifying with others, nor to be over-obsessed with one's self. It is, instead, in the relational process that each person may further develop their personhood and become more fully human. According to Augustine, there is no such distinction between love of mankind and love of God – there is only love (which is love of God).

God's trinitarian qualities are in turn reflected in the human soul, or our self-conscious awareness of our self. In other words, our self-knowledge through love is manifested in our conscious awareness that I am an 'I'. For Augustine, without self-knowledge, there cannot be love because '[t]he mind cannot love itself unless it also knows itself'.[28] Self-knowledge is integral to the love of the self (as Chapter 3 illustrates) and hence a trinitarian interconnection amongst the mind, self-knowledge and self-love. All three elements, also termed as will, memory and understanding, although appearing to be distinguishable, are mutually constituted and therefore inseparable. Augustine concludes on the relational triad in the following passage:

> Now this triad of memory, understanding and will, are not three lives, but one; not three minds but one. It follows that they are not three substances but one substance [...] one essence [...] Therefore, since all are covered by one another, singly and as wholes, the whole of each is equal to the whole of each and the whole of each to the whole together. And these three constitute one thing, one life, one mind, one essence.[29]

These interdependent trinitarian qualities and dynamics are illustrations that human life and human world are at best a reflection of God's relationality and God's relational being. For Augustine, to live a flourishing life is to live justly, and to live justly involves the right relationships.[30] The right relationships characterise the right order of the cosmos. Given humans are created in the image of God and because humans are instilled the threefold God-like

---

27 See Vacek, *Love, Human and Divine: The Heart of Christian Ethics*.
28 Augustine, *On the Trinity*, 9.3.
29 Ibid., 10.18.
30 Ibid., VIII.7.10.

capacities and trinitarian qualities, we are not placed in an inferior place within the right order. Instead, humans are already in fellowship with God.

Additionally, Augustine suggests that justice (or right relationships) be reflected in the 'rightly ordered love'.[31] Here we find love of God to be the highest, most intense and most devoted love. Next is our love for each other and our love for things in the world. Such love must be applied appropriately and to the right degrees. Love of God defines ethical relationships where 'all men are to be loved equally'.[32] The same doctrine lays the Christian foundation of recognising and upholding the fundamental equal worth of all human persons. For Augustine, the Christian interpretation of justice facilitates and sustains the right relations based on our common fellowship. Hence, in *St. Augustine: A Harmonious Union*, Torchia proposes that '[the] relational dimension to Augustine's understanding of human personhood [...] raises the bar of human affectivity to a higher plane'.[33]

***

Thomas Aquinas: Love as mutual indwelling

Love as relationing is central to St Thomas's philosophy and theology. There are three key arguments that we may relate to here as a way to understand how Thomas supports this thesis. The first is very similar to Augustine's claim that God's Trinity already determines our nature as relational, in 'mutua inhaesio' or mutual indwelling; the second is that love itself is a form of relational being or being-in relationships; the third is that, in loving, we find the perfect life as *via redamationis*, where friends love mutually and redemptively without self-sacrifice.

In *Summa Theologiae*, instead of beginning with the role of Father, Son and Spirit in the history of salvation as specified in the Scripture, Thomas discusses the divine essence, or the inner life of God, as the 'immanent Trinity', 'the mutual relations these processions imply' and the 'persons that the relations constitute'.[34] In the Trinity, the Father and the Son are known and loved by each other, and the love that ensues from that relationship is the Holy Spirit,

---

31 Augustine, *City of God*, 15.22.
32 Augustine, *On Christian Doctrine*, I.28.29.
33 Torchia, *Exploring Personhood*, 19.
34 Kerr, *Thomas Aquinas: A Very Short Introduction*, 49.

which in turn is the loving relationship between God's self-knowledge and God Himself. According to Thomas, another way of describing the three-part God is as follows: The Father is God as known to God, the Son is the self-knowledge or self-awareness that proceeds from the Father, and the Holy Spirit is love proceeding from the relationship between God and God's self-knowledge. Love, as the movement of the will, is an internal process that originates and proceeds from God who loves or wills.[35] Here Thomas summarises: 'Therefore God's being by way of love in His will is not accidental being, as in us, but essential being. Consequently, God considered as existing in His will is truly and substantially God.'[36]

For Thomas, God is *Being* itself, not a state but a verb, which means to be, or the act of being. God is existence itself. This is important as it distinguishes God from all other beings who are created, or who belong to some genus. As the essence of being, or the essence of existence, it allows God to be [in] dwelling in all creatures or all that is created. Whilst in God's creatures, there is a distinction between their nature and their existence, such a distinction does not apply to God. For Thomas, 'finite beings are relational because they depend on one another, they lack so much but also because they have a certain innate drive to self-communication, to enrich others'.[37] The metaphysical essence of humans' being becomes therefore sustaining and enriching the webs of relations containing all things created.

According to Thomas, love is the 'primary *passion* of the soul'.[38] Passion or *passio* originates in *patior*, meaning to suffer or to be affected by something other than one's self, including other people and things encountered in the world. As we are always affected by others, passions or emotions are already constituted in our daily ebbs and flows. Thomas distinguishes 11 basic passions, 5 of which are opposites, including love–hatred, desire–aversion, hope–despair, fear–daring, joy–sadness, and the 11th being anger. Clearly, all these emotions are in part connected to others, if not directed at others. Therefore passions are already rooted in relations.

To love is to be moved by what is beautiful and good in things beyond one's self and to be drawn to what is beautiful and good. Here Thomas takes love as relationing to a another level, from union to *mutua inhaesio*, mutual indwelling.

---

35 Thomas, *Summa Theologiae*, q. 37 a1 ad 2m.
36 Ibid., SCG IV, cap.19.
37 Kerr, *Thomas Aquinas: A Very Short Introduction*, 119.
38 Thomas, *Summa Theologiae*, q.25 a2.

Love is not a mere passion, but rather, love is the cause of all human passions. It starts with coming-together (communion), a substantial and affective union or becoming one with the beloved. Coming-together is the condition of further intimacy, followed by going-inwardly (mutual indwelling) and moving-outwardly (ecstasy), each step deepening the relational bonds through emotional connections, into all human actions (everything that the lover does). What kind of love can cause all these effects? Thomas answers: 'Here we are speaking of love in a general sense, inasmuch as it includes intellectual, rational, animal and natural love.'[39]

Thomas argues that love has both apprehensive and appetitive power. He describes the apprehensive power in a sense of truly capturing 'for that I have you in my heart'. This captivating force is not superficial but requiring an intimate knowledge of the beloved, until it can penetrate the human soul because it allows one to 'searcheth all things [...] the deep things of God'.[40] Love's apprehensive power can envelope and encapsulate the beloved in the intimacy of profound knowing. At the same time, love's appetitive power allows the lover to take delight in the beloved, towards beauty and goodness which the lover wills to the beloved 'because the complacency in the beloved is rooted in the lover's heart'.[41] Complacency is *complacentia*, a fundamental disposition of uncritical affinity, a recognition of the beauty and goodness in others in ways that resonates through the whole of one's being.[42] With these two powers, the lover and the beloved are drawn to each other, become closer to such an extent that the lover is *in* the beloved and vice versa. This is the essence of mutual indwelling. Using friendship as an example, Thomas illustrates that such union cannot be superficial possession or external enjoyment of the beloved, rather it seeks to take delight in the beloved fully and perfectly. This effect of friendship-love resembles Aristotelean 'philia' in that the lover or friend wills the beauty and the good for the beloved or friend's own sake and vice versa, but the Thomist love goes deeper and more intimate. Love enables not only mutual indwelling but also mutual identification of each person as both the container of the other's love and the content of the other's love.

Hence Thomas summarises that love is a 'unitive and concretive power', which inspires 'caritas' in us towards those who are less fortunate, moves us

---

39 Ibid., q.28, a6.
40 Ibid., q. 28, a2.
41 Ibid., q. 28, a2.
42 Schindler, 2017.

into 'communicative relationship with each other' and enables us to turn towards better things.[43] Love is at the core of our well-being as Thomas affirms: 'For when we love a thing, by desiring it, we apprehend it as belonging to our well-being.'[44]

Thomas's theory of love as relationing suggests that humans seek union with God and only by loving can we become united with God. Thus love 'extends to all the activities of human life by commanding them, not by eliciting immediately all acts of virtue'.[45] In many ways, according to Thomas, God's relationship with man through communion has laid the foundation for an affective relationship of man to man.[46] Thomas's philosophy of love, especially in his conception of mutual indwelling as an act and an effect of love allows the lover and the beloved to join in union as simultaneously one and two who mutually contain and are contained by each other. As Thomas suggests, this is the closest we can understand God as love.[47]

**

Michel de Montaigne (1533–1592): Love as fusion of souls

French writer and philosopher, Michel de Montaigne,[48] drew his understanding of love mainly from two sources: classical Greek thought and Christian theology on ethics and love and his personal experiences of profound friend-ship-love, especially with Etienne de la Boétie.

In *On Friendship*, Montaigne suggests that amongst the different kinds of love, including natural, social, hospitable and passionate/erotic, what is of highest significance is friendship-love.[49] This proposition is akin to that which

---

43 Ibid., d10.
44 Ibid., q.28, a1.
45 Ibid., q. 23, a4, ad2.
46 Streiker, 'The Christian Understanding of Platonic Love A Critique of Anders Nygren's "Agape and Eros",' 335.
47 Burns, '*St. Thomas Aquinas's Philosophy of Love.*'
48 There have been doubts from commentators such as Comte-Bonville who explains in his book *Dictionary of Love by Montaigne* that it is not clear whether Montaigne's philosophy of love is completely rooted in Christian teaching or Christian theology. Nevertheless, I have decided to place Montaigne under Christian thinkers purely because he is Christian himself.
49 Montaigne, *On Friendship*

is put forward by Aristotle concerning philia. For Montaigne, friendship-love is perfect love because it is an end in itself – love for love's sake. Friendship-love embodies and inspires equality, mutuality, symmetry, justice and freedom. Here love's gifts are abundant and immeasurable. By contrast, the other kinds of love listed are not so perfect because they are always subject to personal, social, economic and political needs and demands. For instance, Montaigne observes that matrimonial love can be either intended for an economic exchange or towards an underlying political partnership. Love, in such a case, tends to require a certain measure of fairness and reciprocity. Additionally, the union of heterosexual couples will necessarily serve to satisfy personal needs and to meet the social purpose of reproduction. Hence these kinds of love are imperfect. They are imperfect because they are treated as a means and are appraised by the instrumental values they bring.

As the title of his essay suggests, Montaigne's experiences of intense friendship-love have convinced him of its perfection in contrast to the imperfection of passionate love. Echoing Aristotle, Montaigne sees that friendship-love is first and foremost a dimension of the human condition, as pointed out by André Comte-Sponville in his book *Montaigne's Dictionary of Love* (the French title is *Dictionnaire amoureux de Montaigne*). For Montaigne, goods such as beauty and grace can attract people to one another, but only as a starting point. Such an attraction opens the door to much deeper relational processes through which the friends/lovers can explore and discover each other's qualities that can be enriched and enhanced by love. Despite the attraction and affection, according to Montaigne, friendship-love cannot be defined, nor such affection explained. He writes, 'why I loved him, cannot be expressed'.[50] Love as relationing does not require an articulation, as he further affirms: 'because it was he, because it was I'.

Friendship-love happens because:

> our souls had drawn so unanimously together, they had considered each other with so ardent an affection and with the like affection laid open the very bottom of our hearts to one another's view, that I not only knew his as well as my own; but should certainly in any concern of mine have trusted my interest much more willingly with him, than with myself.[51]

---

50 Montaigne, *The Complete Works of Montaigne*, 169.
51 Ibid.

Friendship-love connects people in a spiritual relatedness, characterised not by a lack, want or desire (which seeks to be satisfied), but by a joyous and intense affection. Indeed, friendship-love prompts a fusion of souls whereby the friends/lovers fuse themselves into one until 'there is no more sign of the seam by which they were first conjoined'. Fusion of souls is to be rejoiced and the two friends/lovers are elevated to a spiritual realm as if two bodies are united by one soul. Through friendship-love, one can no longer feel separated from the other. This means that true friends/lovers are few because for such friendship-love to be so enveloping that it conjoins the whole soul, it can only be, in Montaigne's own words, 'by some secret appointment of heaven'.

The fusion, however, does not erase the *other*ness in the friends but maintains the self-other dynamic in an interconnected way. Love enables a person to self-identify with the other who shares and partakes similar ethical goods, such as beauty and graciousness. This involves an openness and appreciation of one's own otherness, or aspects of oneself that one is not familiar, or still discovering. Elizabeth Guild, in her entry in the *Oxford Handbook of Montaigne*, evokes that 'the gift of love is to [be able to] lose oneself in the other, "I" and "you" transformed into a "we" that is not a plural'.[52]

Moreover, Montaigne does not regard the self and the other in friendship-love as separate entities, nor does he see them as opposites. For instance, when talking about his awareness of de la Boétie's qualities, Montaigne says that the other is an ideal self. Therefore, the relatedness is already present which love further deepens. Love transcends the self-other distinction into interconnection. Continuing referring to his friendship-love with de la Boétie, Montaigne highlights the significance of non-egoistic good-will in the relational dynamic:

> Not merely do I prefer to do him good than to have him do good to me, I would even prefer that he did good to himself rather than to me: it is when he does good to himself that he does most good to me.[53]

Here lies the mutuality of love – what is good for one friend/lover is good for the other friend/lover and vice versa. Love unfolds into a closeness and mutual participation in a common life together 'for neither of us reserved anything for himself, nor was anything either his or mine'.[54] Love as relationing is integral

---

52 Guild, "Montaigne on Love", 635.
53 Montaigne, *The Complete Essays*, 1105.
54 Montaigne, *The Complete Works of Montaigne*, 170.

to a flourishing life for both friends/lovers. In fact, love not only constitutes each friend/lover's well-being but also sustains the friend/lover's flourishing. For example, Montaigne has taken delight in the friendship-love for a lifetime, even after de la Boétie's death.

Located in a flourishing life, love's soulful union is therefore not abstract. It is embodied, passionate and intensely human in the here-and-now. On this, Montaigne reflects on his own corporal being and that he rejoices 'unapologetically' in his body, his corporeality. The immanent beauty of life is found in the integration of body and soul, intuition and reason, the worldly and other worldly. To love is to embody and live out our spiritual relatedness by participating in each other's realities more fully, more purely and more delightfully. Thus, Elizabeth Guild proposes that 'in the end, what attaches Montaigne to life is perhaps less other human beings than love of interrelatedness per se'.[55]

The inclusion of Montaigne in the exploration of Christian conceptions of love is really interesting. In some ways, Montaigne's philosophy of love has modern tendencies. Although he recognises the power of love in lifting humans towards a higher state of being, his exploration of friendship-love provides a more integral view of human-becoming – it is through living love's relationality that we may seek to go beyond our personal limits. Embedded here is the recognition of persons as individuals and our embodied humanity matters as much as more enlightened qualities we should aspire.

---

55 Guild, "Montaigne on Love", 647.

Love as Relationing in Modernist Humanism

When one has once fully entered the realm of love, the world – no matter how imperfect – becomes rich and beautiful, it consists solely of opportunities for love.

[...] the cure is precisely to learn all over again the most important thing, to understand oneself in one's longing for community [...]

—Kierkegaard, *Works of Love*

With the progress in science and technology, since the Enlightenment, Western thinkers have concerned themselves with ideas such as human subjectivity, our place in the world and our relationship with each other and with the world. This later becomes a *science* of the self, or more precisely, the science of self-consciousness. Amidst the exploration of the self, Western thinkers also wrestled with two incompatible notions: a relational connection or emotional affinity between people on the one hand and the absolute rational subjectivity of mankind on the other. A further tension is between the individualistic nature of being human and the relational nature of our common life found in our ways of being as a part of family, community and society.

This was a process whereby the modern subject became self-defining. Instead of in relation to a cosmic order, or a divine image, what was advanced in this time was an atomic psychological and political subject, individualistic self who could singularly make up the society. As the self-defining subject came to the fore, the world itself became external, neutral, knowable and contingent. Man could now *understand* the world and even *control* it, especially through the advancement in modern science and technology. However, progress also led to 'disenchantment', in the words of Max Weber, highlighting our view of the world during modernity as reducible to observable categories of causal relations, devoid of myths and mysticism.

A significant milestone of this 'progress' was marked by the work of French philosopher René Descartes (1596–1650) who meditated upon and investigated the thinking self (as if a disembodied being). According to Descartes, the thinking being seemingly could seek the truth of the existence of their own consciousness, including the innate ideas one might consciously hold, such as mathematical truth, or the truth of God. In fact, Cartesian meditation has established in the Western philosophy, human's relationship with our thoughts and objects of our thoughts (i.e. things in the world). s Descartes defended the distinct separation between the non-materialistic thinking mind (which is spiritual) and the physical body (i.e. the brain) that does the thinking. Also established is the relationship between the subject (who does the thinking and observing) and the object (that is being reflected upon and observed). Hence arrived the recognition of scientific method as the principal way of knowledge. The mind-body dualism further served as the foundation for rationalism and empiricism over the values of cosmos and God, thus advancing individual freedom.

Parallel to the advancement of scientific methods, during modernist period, love's relationality was initially a break-away from a cosmocentric and theocentric ontology. This shift was often attributed to the introducing of nature as a cause. In this case, human's relationship with nature, our lives in nature and more importantly our lives within societies in their multifarious complexities have become the focus of philosophical reflection. As early as the fifteenth century, this particular relational dimension of love already began to shift, first to the renaissance's courtly love conditional on the worthiness of the beloved for the sake of their virtues and then to the intimate romantic bonds free from moral constraints, allowing the lovers to regard the relationship itself as an end. In this transition, many thinkers have become interested in the natural state of human's being.

The investigation into human nature was reflected in a number of philosophers' discussions on the state of nature, that is, the hypothesised natural state of human's existence before society came into being and the structure of human society in accordance with the state of nature. Notably, such thoughts were put forward by Thomas Hobbes, John Locke and Jean-Jacques Rousseau. Together with their contemporaries, Adam Smith and Fredrich Hegel, they proposed the principles of liberty and rationality of the Enlightenment. As Robert Nozick suggests in *Anarchy, State and Utopia*, an inquiry into the state of nature can serve the explanatory purpose in that it helps articulate the *non-political* as foundational to understanding the realm of the *political*. These thoughts have been highly influential at the time and have paved the way for societies to conceive what should be at the core of human relationship. These explorations were also meaningful in enabling us to understand what relations are constituted in political lives and how governance, laws and social institutions support these relationships. These will be discussed in Chapter 5.

Below I briefly examine each of these ideas on the natural state of being. They can serve as contexts within which different conceptions of love as relationing are rooted and developed.

In *Leviathan*, English philosopher Thomas Hobbes (1588–1679) argues that human's natural state is one of fear, selfishness and thus war. In such a state, humans tend to be 'solitary', 'poor', 'nasty', 'brutish' and 'short'.[56] From this

---

56 Hobbes, *Leviathan*, Chapters XIII–XIV.

view of human nature, Hobbes proposes that as selfish and self-serving people, humans would underpin our relationships with self-interest, mutual suspicion, violence and instrumentalisation. This also means that human relations would either be perpetually warring, fighting for scarce resources, or calculated cooperation based on mutual benefit. Thus, human's political life would involve a submission to sovereign authority whose role is to regulate human desires and interests to ensure mutual survival. It equally requires policing to defuse tensions from escalating into wars.

For John Locke (1632–1704), a Scottish philosopher, human's state of nature is more optimistic than that which was depicted by Hobbes. Deriving his philosophy from Christian thought, Locke, in *Two Treatises of Government*, argues that humans are governed by the law of nature by which people tend to abide in the prudent ways they act, distribute resources and relate to each other. As rational beings, people would not harm one another and instead, they respect each other's liberty and property and are free to pursue their interests and aspirations. Human relationships would thus be characterised by peace, good-will, as well as mutual support and mutual preservation. Any violation of this natural law would be deemed to be wrong and therefore punishable.[57]

French philosopher Jean-Jacques Rousseau conceived the pre-societal state of nature as the 'golden age', where persons, although solitary, are found in a state of dignity by self-identifying as being of intrinsic value. In this state of nature, people have compassion for each other. The phrase 'noble savage' has been used to interpret Rousseau's vision of this natural state of being. However, in this idyllic state, the individuals are weak and require society (i.e. through collaboration and mutual support) to ensure human flourishing. Rousseau warns that when the circumstances change, such as growing population, increased productivity and shrinking resource, there would inevitably be competition, envy and exploitation of the vulnerable. In this case, a social contract would be necessary to cohere human interests.

Against such conceptual backgrounds, Adam Smith and Fredrich Hegel are powerful voices in affirming human goodness in love, but, more importantly, they also outline how love defines and underpins our relationship with one another and with the world, as well as our political life in communities and nations.

***

---

57 Locke, *Two Treatises of Government*.

Baruch Spinoza: Love as a pathway to flourishing

In Chapter 3 of this book, I briefly outlined Spinoza's conception of love's potency as giving rise to the values of human consciousness through which we can truly appreciate our desire for love of God. In this chapter, I will focus the discussion on Spinoza's ideal of love as relationing. Indeed, Spinoza places love within a conception of the good life which is constituted by our consciously recognising and appreciating our place in the whole of existence with God as the ultimate cause. In other words, for Spinoza, love is the pathway to greater human flourishing. At the heart of human flourishing, according to Spinoza, lies our relationship with an 'other'.

In Part III of *Ethics*, Spinoza focuses his investigation on *Origin and Nature of the Emotions*. He claims at the opening of Part III that 'no one [...] has defined the nature and strength of the emotions and the power of the mind against them for their restraint'. As already touched upon in Chapter 3, Spinoza defines emotions as modifications of the body (or the effects on the body) by which the body can experience either an increase or decrease of its 'active power'. Spinoza argues that emotions, such as pleasure, joy and delight, tend to involve greater active power. By contrast, emotions, including pain, sorrow and displeasure, involve lesser power.

He then adds that when a person is aware clearly and distinctly that they themselves are the adequate cause of any of these bodily modifications, their emotion becomes in effect an activity. Whereas when a person is not the cause of the bodily modifications, then the emotion becomes a passion 'wherein the mind is passive'. This distinction allows Spinoza to put forward what he terms as 'high-mindedness', which is the well-reasoned desire whereby a person endeavours to unite with other people in friendship and to support others aimed at the good of others. Examples Spinoza provides as demonstrating high-mindedness include courage, courtesy, mercy and so forth.

Spinoza regards love's emotionality and relationality as 'elation accompanied by the idea of an external cause'.[58] When one loves another person, the other can become a cause of one's own joy and delight. Because the cause of this emotion is external to one's self, one's relationship to this kind of love tends to be passive. Passivity means that one attributes to an *other* the responsibility for one's own happiness and becomes dependent on others. This kind of love prioritises the place of another person or other people in one's own

---

58 Spinoza, *Ethics*, III, d.VI.

life. Relationship between people emerged for revering other is dynamic. At the same time, like any emotion, such relationship is also unstable.

In the light of one's ongoing and historical interactions with the beloved, the lover comes to be associated with all emotions, including those one might not wish to dwell on, such as guilt, jealousy and fear. As such, Spinoza suggests that the lover can be infinitely bound up with the beloved, emotionally. For instance:

> If we conceive that anything pleasurably affects some object of our love, we shall be affected with love towards that thing. Contrariwise, if we conceive that it affects an object of our love painfully, we shall be affected with hatred towards it.[59]

In this way, overtime, love can become associated with emotions that the beloved tends to cause, which include not only elation and pleasure but also dejection and pain. The resulting vacillation can erode and eventually destroy this kind of love. Dynamic emotional life tends to characterise human's relational experience. However, according to Amélie Rorty's reading, in Spinoza's view, there is a superior form of love, which should be cultivated as part of our flourishing life.[60] On this, Spinoza highlights three ideas about love as relationing:

The first concerns the cause of one's happiness. For Spinoza, one needs to realise that the beloved idol is not the sufficient cause of our genuine elation or delight. Instead, the joy derives from the fact that the qualities in the beloved correspond to those of one's own. Hence the propensities for one to be affected by the beloved. In other words, elation, delight or happiness are jointly caused by the beloved's qualities which are reflected in those of the lover.[61] Furthermore, the nature and qualities of both the beloved and the lover are bound up by their historical and psychological relatedness. Indeed, physical qualities, from Spinoza's perspective, are the result of our genetic inheritance and environmental circumstances, whereas psychological qualities are the fruit of our upbringing and wider social relations. These contextual relations are dynamic and ongoing and include the past interactions and continuous relational bond between the lover and

---

59 Ibid., xxii.
60 Rorty, "Spinoza on the Pathos of Idolatrous Love and the Hilarity of True Love."
61 Rorty, "The Two Faces of Spinoza."

the beloved. Therefore, it is necessary to be aware of one's beloved as already constituted in these webs of relations, including relations to one's self. Such an awareness is the basis for recognising that the other is in part already constituted by one's self and that one's self is in part the cause of one's elation in a more robust sense than one previously acknowledged.[62] Love as relationing in this first case is about the intertwined nature of our relations which combine to cause our delight and happiness.

The second idea that Spinoza explores is about one's place in nature. According to Spinoza, one can gain a more proper scientific grasp of how every individual is constituted by their place in the complex system of nature. In fact, Spinoza always speaks of 'nature of God', identifying the two at the same time. This awareness of one's place in nature heightens a sense of one's self. A person participates in the complex nexus of conceptual and causal relations of nature, as a being both constituted by and constituting other beings or things by virtue of one's (more or less direct and mediated) relations and interactions with them.[63] As both a physical and psychological being, the lover correctly views herself as 'composed of adequate ideas of the properties common to every part of extension, she does not conceive of anything falling outside her boundaries, her nature'.[64] This point stresses the mutually constituted aspect of our being in nature and as part of nature. Rather than love as being passively caused in one by something external, one sees love as issuing forth from one's own essential nature as part of an all-encompassing nature. Love becomes active.

The third idea is about how our understanding of nature determines our understanding of love. For Spinoza, it is possible to come to recognise nature itself as having an integrity and unity that makes it an *individual* in its own right. Nature as an *individual* is thus composed of every other individual, just as a living organism is an individual in its own right which is composed of individual cells, molecules or atoms.[65] Once achieving this view of nature, it follows that when one loves, one loves another individual 'as-a-particular-expression-of-the-vast-network-of-individuals that have affected him'.[66] Conceived so, by loving

---

62 Ibid., 305; Thomson and Gill, *Happiness, Flourishing and the Good Life*.
63 Rorty, "The Two Faces of Spinoza," 2009.
64 Rorty, "Spinoza on the Pathos of Idolatrous Love and the Hilarity of True Love," 363–4.
65 Ibid., 367.
66 Ibid., 367.

someone, the lover 'loves all that has made him [...] In loving him, she loves herself'.[67] According to Rorty's interpretation, this is a superior form of love and is truthful love. Loving oneself and indeed loving the whole of nature is inextricably bound up with truly and actively loving an 'other'. Such truthful lovers are not only more joyous but also more effective and beneficent than unenlightened lovers. Rorty suggests that truthful love, according to Spinoza, can generate the desire 'to act on behalf of a common good. Promoting the real [...] welfare of an extended self properly arises from a [...] recognition of interdependence'.[68]

By contrast, idolatrous love, because it is passive and due to its connections with dejection and varieties of hate, jealousy, anger, vengefulness and so on, is a form of bondage, of being *ruled* by one's passions or emotions. It can be regarded as a form of enslavement. The only way to be rid of such bondage is to disperse love from an exclusive focus on an individual conceived as bounded off from the rest of nature. The lover thus actively pursues the qualities of the other as an extension to the whole nexus of nature itself, of which both the lover and the beloved are part. In doing so, the wholesome relationality can transform the enslavement of idolatrous love.

In Chapter 3 of this book, we have learned that one way to transcend and transform these passive and destructive emotions is through knowledge. For instance, Spinoza argues that the more we understand why we are experiencing hatred towards or anger at someone, or feeling jealous about someone, the more we can cease to be hateful, angry or jealous. In doing so, we can experience the ideal of love. By approaching love as relationing in this way, the lover is able to free themselves from myriad forms of suffering or dejection. Spinoza suggests that understanding is an important pathway towards being loving and becoming loving truthfully, which is already constituted in a flourishing life. Above all, Spinoza has introduced the interconnection between one's qualities as an individual and one's qualities as already constituted in the extended qualities of nature which contains all individuals. The most important point implied here is that what holds such interconnection is love as relationing – by loving, we experience such interconnection and mutual intertwining.

***

67 Ibid., 264.
68 Ibid., 364.

Jean-Jacques Rousseau (1712–1778): Harmonising amour-de-soi and amour-propre

The central tenet of Rousseau's philosophy is located in the argument that human beings are good in their natural state of being but become corrupt by society.[69]

In *Discourse on Inequality*, an essay written in 1754, Rousseau suggests that when we examine human society with a 'disinterested eye', we are immediately met with violence of the powerful and the oppression of the vulnerable. These external relations seem to dominate human society and determine the working of human institutions. It is therefore important to peel through these relational layers so that we can truly understand how human's 'natural faculties' impact our 'successive development'.[70] Thus Rousseau's investigation aims to separate the constitution of things and their effects.

According to Rousseau, the primitive human is solitary and physically weak, but with all the necessary faculties for each one to be self-preserving and self-sufficient.[71] In the primitive, pre-social state, individuals are separated and do not exercise complex reasoning. Instead, they act largely from instinctive passion. However, metaphysically speaking, in the state of nature, humans can have choices and are thus not merely bound by their instincts. This presupposes human's free-will, which means that we are not strict followers of rules prescribed by nature. Awareness of this liberty and self-conscious awareness of one's self as an autonomous being reflect the spirituality of the human soul. In this state, humans not only have the potential to achieve rationality and morality but can also have the capacity to self-improve and self-perfect. According to Rousseau, it is precisely human's capacity to learn, to improve and to perfect ourselves that in time:

> draws man out of his original state, in which he would have spent his days insensibly in peace and innocence; that it is this faculty, which, successively producing in different ages his discoveries and his errors, his vices and his virtues, makes him at length a tyrant both over himself and over nature.[72]

---

69 Bertram, 2010.
70 Rousseau, *Discourse on the Origins of Inequality*.
71 Ibid. In Rousseau's imagination, the state of nature that the savage or primitive humans find themselves is similar to many contemporary 'indigenous' communities at the time, such as those in the Caribs, and others in Africa.
72 Rousseau, *Discourse* 1, 14.

Rousseau argues that it is through human passions, wants and desires (e.g. for food, sex and rest) that our knowledge and reason become improved, for greater good or great ill. This is because our capacities to overcome nature's limits can drive us to seek betterment in human conditions. He notes that human primitive passions are the basis for compassion, a disposition that belongs to beings who are weak and subject to all kinds of aversity. For Rousseau, compassion comes before rationality, or reflection. In such a natural state, moral deprivation is almost impossible and it is in this pure emotion of nature (i.e. pity and empathy) that puts one in the place of those who are suffering. Humans ought to be able to offer compassion to others and by moderating the *violence* of self-love and self-preservation, compassion can allow humans to love each other and to preserve humanity as a whole.

Objecting the Hobbesian view of human nature, Rousseau proposes that human natural propensity is compassion (rather than rationality), which is the root of humans' success in the world. Friendships and other more complex relationships are effects of compassion. Human's innate drive for self-improvement and self-perfection mentioned above also prompts us to communicate and cooperate with each other. At the same time, it is precisely these qualities that 'are more likely to condemn them to a social world of deception, dissimulation, dependence, oppression and domination'.[73] Hence Rousseau begins his book *The Social Contract* with his much-quoted observation: 'Man is born free; and everywhere he is in chains. One thinks himself the master of others and still remains a greater slave than they.'[74]

How did this change come about? Rousseau sets out to answer this question and notes that civilisation is also the beginning of inequality. He stresses two kinds of inequality: (1) natural or physical inequality which is 'established by nature and consists in a difference of age, health, bodily strength and the qualities of the mind or of the soul' and (2) moral or political inequality 'because it depends on a kind of convention, [...] is established, or at least authorised by the consent of men' and 'consists of the different privileges, which some men enjoy to the prejudice of others'.[75] Notwithstanding these two kinds of inequality, Rousseau maintains that 'the fruits of the earth belong to us all and the earth itself to nobody'[76] and condemns private ownership of

---

73 Bertram, 2010, 5.
74 Rousseau, *The Social Contract*.
75 Rousseau, *Discourse on the Origins of Inequality*, Preface.
76 Ibid., *Discourse 2*.

our earthly commons. For Rousseau, human's natural goodness (as described in the Discourse) can become 'wicked' due to the unjust institutions' allowing private ownership of properties and unfair distribution of resources. Inequality determines the way humans go about self-interested love.

In *Emile*, Rousseau develops his philosophy of love and distinguishes two pathways to love as relationing: 'amour-de-soi', original approach to self-love in human's natural state, and *amour-propre*, an altered mode of self-love as the result of societal influences. When the natural man is motivated by the instinct of self-preservation, they pursue amour-de-soi. Amour-de-soi propels the natural human to meet their biological needs, such as gathering food and seeking shelter. In addition to self-preservation and serving self-interest, the natural human also experiences a relational emotion, *pitié* or compassion, directed at relieving the suffering of others. According to Rousseau, pitié (or pity) is both an original drive alongside *amour de soi* and a development of amour-de-soi. It is 'the source of our passions, the origin and principle of all others, the only [sentiment] that man is born with which never leaves him as long as he lives'.[77] This also warrants humans to be repugnant from inflicting harm upon another human being not only due to their being rational but more importantly because they are sentient beings like oneself and partake similar qualities as oneself.[78]

At the same time, all other sentiments and emotions are modifications of the self-love caused by forces alien to nature. The further one's self is removed from amour-de-soi in the modifications, the more one experiences contradictions in one's emotions. One such contradiction is amour-propre, pride, vanity or self-alienation caused by sociability. It is here that one begins to fall into the trap of the double illusion of amour-propre: by allowing one's action to be judged and defined by others and otherwise by becoming self-sacrificing.[79]

---

77 Rousseau, *Emile*, Part IV. My translation. The original text is: La source de nos passions, l'origine et le principe de toutes les autres, la seule qui nait avec l'homme et ne le quitte jamais tant qu'il vit est l'amour de soi; passion primitive, innée, antérieure a toute autre et dont toutes les autres ne sont en un sens que des modifications. En ce sens toutes si l'on veut sont naturelles. Mais la plupart de ces modifications ont des causes étrangères sans lesquelles elles n'auraient jamais lieu, et ces mêmes modifications loin de nous êtres avantageuses nous sont nuisibles, elles changent le premier object et vont contre leur principe; c'est alors que l'homme se trouve hors de la nature et se met en contradiction avec soi.
78 Rousseau, *Discourse on the Origins of Inequality*.
79 Rousseau, *Complete Work*, I. On se fait la règle de tout, et voilà précisément ou nous attend la double illusion de l'amour-propre; soit en prêtant faussement a ceux que nous

No longer a natural man, the social man, seeks amour-propre, to affirm one's worthiness in comparison with others.[80] In turn, the social man depends on other's acknowledgement and approval of their worthiness. The desire for things to satisfy a self-concern aimed at proving to others one's worthwhileness can imprison the social man to other's demands. These demands tend to include ownership of things, wealth and social status to represent assumed worthiness and respectfulness. In contrast to amour-de-soi, amour-proper is a negative passion and hence a source of evil, according to Rousseau, because pride and vanity can allow people to seek and feel that they are superior to others.

For Rousseau, amour-propre, rooted in sexual competition and comparison, is linked to the rise of civilisation, society and commerce.[81] Amour-propre can alter the natural state of humanity because social conventions and political regimes are in place to stimulate competitiveness and narcissistic desires in humans. Thus, amour-propre becomes more toxic when combined with the emergence of private ownership of properties and inequality. Superfluity and the rise of leisure class further shape the contour of human desire, resulting in self-absorbed amour-propre, which necessarily encourages selfishness and egotism. In such a society, human relations tend to be situated in a measurement of self-worth tied to the level of materialistic comfort, ownership of assets and access to power. All of these require self-assessment, or amour-propre, a recognition from others about one's own social advantages. Amour-propre prompts one to compare (and compete) with others for wealth and political domination based on social convention and consent through political institutions.[82]

However, as a relational notion, amour-propre can lead to both degenerative and generative relations.[83] When amour-propre is a zero-sum game, imprisoning people in pride and vanity, our relationship with others is degenerative and can result in instrumentalising one's self and one's work for solely wealth and status, relinquishing one's true worthwhileness and dignity to materialistic advantages relative to others. Likewise, amour-propre

---

jugeons les motifs qui nous auraient fait agir à leur place; soit dans cette supposition même, en nous abusant sur nos propres motifs, faute de savoir nous transporter assez dans une autre situation que celle nous sommes.
80 Kolodny, "The Explanation of Amour-Propre."
81 Pignol, 2010.
82 Kolodny, "The Explanation of Amour-Propre."
83 See Gergen, *Relational Being,*.

can subjugate people to the measure of these advantages, treating those without advantages as less worthy. Rousseau highlights this to be the root of dehumanisation. When amour-propre is driven by seeking advantages and superiority over others to justify one's worthiness of respect, it is inflamed.[84]

In spite of all the above, amour-propre can be a meaningful generative idea especially when it is understood as '(a) desire to have and to be evaluated by others as having a certain value, albeit in comparison with others'.[85] In this case, it can be regarded as a healthy sense of self-love, underpinned by the desire for non-instrumental self-dignity and for an equal worthiness in relation to others, hence contributing to generative relations.

The distinction between these two kinds of self-love (i.e. amour-de-soi and amour-propre) determines the way that Rousseau analyses institutional relations, such as oppression, or caring, develops the idea of social contract, advances his ideal of human community and underpins his views on commerce and economy. Written over 20 years before the French revolution, Rousseau's analysis points to the importance of interconnection between ethics and politics. Ethics here refers to the nature of human relations constituted in the good life within a society. By pointing out the self-contradiction prompted by amour-propre, Rousseau invites a reflection on how social institutions and public policies can be dehumanising. He uses slavery as an example to illustrate the misplaced values concerning human relationships as a cause of humanity's downfall. In doing so, he also creates an opportunity for us to consider the promise of redemption, for instance, from the enslavement of others. Indeed, the promise might pivot on two aspects of the non-political relational fundamentals identified by Rousseau: on the one hand is amour-de-soi that inspires not only compassionate human relationships but also our interest in freedom through intuition and our propensity for self-transcendence/self-perfection; on the other hand, it is amour-propre that is founded on humans' rational capacities and self-identification as equal social beings, including our recognition of our mutual interdependence and our interests in cooperating with one another relationally and acting justly towards each other. These form the relational foundation of a flourishing life.

***

---

84 See Dent and O'Hagan, "Rousseau on Amour-Propre", and Kolondny, "The Explanation of Amour-Propre."
85 Kolodny, "The Explanation of Amour-Propre," 169.

Adam Smith (1723–1790): Love as relationing at the core of our well-being

A contemporary of Jean-Jacques Rousseau, Adam Smith's conception of human nature is similarly idealised. In *The Theory of Moral Sentiments* (first written in 1759), Smith spells out his reflection on love which tends out to be the focus of a lifelong inquiry.[86] To this end, he explores human's capacity for loving each other and the relational orientation of human life in both the personal and political domains. Unlike Rousseau, Smith articulates that self-love itself is not enough.

In the opening lines of his book, Smith proposes that some principles in human nature are present in all moral sentiments, such as our interest in other's (mis)fortune and in their happiness for their own sake. Amongst human's natural (moral) sentiments is particularly:

> pity or compassion, the emotion which we feel for the misery of others, when we either see it, or are made to conceive it in a very lively manner. That we often derive sorrow from the sorrow of others, [...] for this sentiment, like all the other original passions of human nature, is by no means confined to the virtuous and humane, though they perhaps may feel it with the most exquisite sensibility.[87]

This insight is central to Smith's own thinking about humanity, our economic activities, social institutions and political systems. Similarly to Rousseau, Smith draws on the state of nature as the basis for his argument and suggests that humans be empathetic by nature, and we have the (innate) capacity to feel compassion, especially when confronted with the sufferings of others. Being empathetic and compassionate is not necessarily cultivated or learned, but instead, such qualities can be present even in the most violent persons.

For Smith, humans have the inherent capacity to partake in other's feelings and emotions, through empathy and compassion. He describes humanity as constituted in the exquisite fellow-feeling which enables us to grieve for others' sufferings and to rejoice at their happiness. It is from this fellow-feeling that arises mutual empathy and sympathy. This sets the relational connection

---

86 Adam Smith's first book was *The Theory of Moral Sentiment*, which he revised before his death. Hence a lifelong inquiry.
87 Adam Smith, *The Theory of Moral Sentiments*, Chapter 1.

between persons as naturally non-instrumental. Likewise, Smith recognises the central place of human relationships in our well-being and happiness.

The core tenet of *The Theory of Moral Sentiments* is love, and Smith discusses love as relationing systematically.

To begin, Smith argues that love is an important moral sentiment in the dual dimensions in that '[m]an naturally desires, not only to be loved, but to be lovely'.[88] In other words, on the one hand, humans need love, love of the self, from which arises our natural yearning to pursue proper object of love; at the same time, humans also aspire to be such a proper object of love. Both appreciation and evaluation of our own qualities and our praise-worthiness/love-worthiness require a relational lens in that we can 'view them with the eyes of other people'.[89] As Smith points out, a person can only be loved if they are considered as lovely by others and that others' appreciation of their love-worthiness corresponds to and is echoed by their own self-evaluation as such. This may seem to reflect the Christian doctrine whereby we desire the goodness in ourselves that we would like to see in others and vice versa, but it goes beyond this reciprocity. Smith postulates that the mutuality of other's affirmation for one's love-worthwhileness and one's own recognition of one's love-worthiness is truly love's relationality, which is constituted in our happiness and well-being.

According to Smith, it is in human's nature that we are inspired by the desire to please our fellow beings and discouraged by the aversion to offend them. More importantly, nature affords humans the capacity to love and cherish each o ther's qualities f or their own sake. That is, love motivates us to seek, approve or desire good qualities for their intrinsic values. This is akin to an Aristotelean notion of friendship-love whereby friends are drawn to each other out of admiration and appreciation of each other's qualities from a non-instrumental perspective. As much, because we are so inspired by our love for good qualities or virtues that we can be deterred by a real abhorrence of vice. To reject and refuse evil refers to the real courage and strength of humans. It is this disapprobation of vice, such as vanity, violence and so forth, that prompts humans to seek forgiveness and atonement, essential for being relieved from hatred and resentment. The mere possibility of this deliverance from guilt or disgrace, for Smith, can bring happiness and peace.

---

88 Ibid.
89 Ibid., Chapter 2.

The nurturance of our moral sentiments, according to Smith, requires a *third* voice, the viewpoint of, what he calls, the 'impartial spectator' that can enable us to perceive the other:

> neither from our own place nor yet from his, neither with our own eyes nor yet with his, but from the place and with the eyes of a third person, who has no particular connexion with either and who judges with impartiality between us.[90]

Imagining a disaster that happened to millions of strangers in a distant land, Smith underlines the voice of a man/person of humanity, 'who shows us the propriety of generosity and the deformity of injustice; the propriety of resigning the greatest interests of our own, for the yet greater interests of others'.[91] This voice of humanity is not the voice of Christians advocating love of our neighbour, nor is it the voice of classic Greek promoting universal love of agapē. Instead, Smith argues, 'it is a stronger love, a more powerful affection, […] the love of what is honourable and noble, of the grandeur and dignity and superiority of our own characters'.[92]

This stronger love could have easily been conceived as the appreciation of human qualities as intrinsically valuable in their own right such as that which we discussed in Chapter 2. In this context, Smith suggests that this stronger love will render any selfishness, self-interest and disregard of the plight of others 'the proper object of the contempt and indignation of our brethren'.[93] Accordingly, persons of humanity must take a relational view of ourselves through the perspectives of *other* citizens of the world. The more we empathise with other people's sorrow and partake in their joy, the more we are able to cultivate self-command and desist selfishness, jealousy and aggression towards others.

In contrast with Rousseau's natural man whose empathy for other's suffering originates in their feelings of fear, vulnerability and pain, stronger love, in Smith's vision, is grounded in the recognition of love as relationing which is central to human well-being. It is this relational nature of love, being and well-being that determines our desiring to be virtuous, our acting decently towards each other, our regarding each other with empathy and compassion

---

90 Ibid., Chapter 3.
91 Ibid., Chapter 3.
92 Ibid., Chapter 3.
93 Ibid., Chapter 3.

and respecting each other as beings of intrinsic worthwhileness. In this sense, any such self-awareness is already juxtaposed with our awareness of others and our consciousness of the third voice, or the perspectives of the impartial spectator. Thus, Smith proposes that those who act 'according to the rules of perfect prudence, of strict justice and of proper benevolence, may be said to be perfectly virtuous'.[94]

Indeed, for Smith, it is love's relationality that can inspire the virtues of prudence, justice and benevolence. By prudence, Smith means the care directed at what are essential for our happiness and well-being, such as health, wealth, status and reputation. Here, Smith encourages moderation in bodily desires and sees the pursuit of wealth in itself as corrosive and considers seeking status and fame as destroyer of characters' serenity and peace.[95] When combined with virtues such as humanity, generosity and compassion, prudence consists in the noblest of human character. True prudence thus involves those acts that are wise and judicious, directed at greater and nobler purposes in addition to personal well-being.

Justice, according to Smith, consists in negative and positive virtues. As a negative virtue, justice is what restrains us from making someone else worse off, or from hurting others. It marks 'the boundary beyond which no individual's pursuit of self-interest can extend'.[96] Whilst all free societies require justice,[97] negative justice can mean that we are sitting still and doing nothing despite the world's violence and oppression. By contrast, the positive justice is beneficence, which, for Smith, means taking positive and proactive actions to help improve other people's lives. Examples of beneficence are kindness, generosity, friendship and self-sacrifice for the greater good. Hence Smith writes, 'the wise and virtuous man is at all times willing that his own private interest should be sacrificed to the public interest of his own particular order or society'.[98]

By benevolence, Smith refers to our affection that reaches beyond ourselves, to include our children, parents, relatives, friends, others and even strangers whom we may love and revere. We love those who are endeared to us, not due to selfishness, but owing to our personal/private benevolent affection.

---

94 Ibid., 418.
95 Roberts, *How Adam Smith Can Change Your Life: An Unexpected Guide to Human Nature and Happiness*.
96 Campbell, 1967, 574.
97 Ibid.
98 Adam Smith, *The Theory of Moral Sentiments*, Chapter 3.

Such affection can be extended publicly to others who are distant from us and even nation states whose societies bear greater noble characters. Such public benevolent affection is likened to the fellow-feeling that one can have towards humanity at large.

These three virtues further illustrate that Smith's relational orientation to love has personal, societal and political implications. For instance, Smith highlights that love can play a central part in laying a humane foundation to a society. In any given society, people are simultaneously in need of mutual affection and assistance and exposed to mutual injuries. 'Where the necessary assistance is reciprocally afforded from love, from gratitude, from friendship and esteem, the society flourishes and is happy […].'[99]

When such ethics is applied to economic activities and commerce, the implication can be profound. It is when humans appeal to one another's self-love or our inherent dignity that we are also attending to our innermost self-consciousness, a third voice, or the perspective of the impartial spectator. Only then, can we be inspired to be sympathetic towards the 'resulting mutual gains from trade of both parties'.[100] In this context, Smith wrote in his infamous and much-misinterpreted passage in his book *The Wealth of Nations*:

> It is not from the benevolence of the butcher, the brewer or the baker that we expect our dinner, but from their regard to their own interest. We address ourselves not to their humanity but to their self-love and never talk to them of our own necessities but of their advantages.[101]

It has been suggested that 'appealing to another's self-love can evoke sympathies on two accounts'.[102] First, appealing to the butcher, the brewer or the baker's self-love in mutual exchange of the fruit of our own work (in the form of product or commodity) is morally superior to pursuing self-love by demanding other's benevolence, such as their charity. Second, appealing to the butcher, the brewer or the baker's self-love is more practical and more efficient than merely appealing to their benevolence/charity because it allows us to offer something meaningful in return. Therefore, economic activities based on love's relationality can invite people to recognise the dignity in our being/well-being

---

99 Ibid., Chapter 1.
100 Black, "What Did Adam Smith Say About Self-Love?" 21.
101 Smith, *The Wealth of Nations*, 14.
102 Black, "What Did Adam Smith Say About Self-Love?" 21.

and in our work and to see all mercantile exchange as directed firstly at our own well-being, through simultaneously meeting the well-being needs of others. Work, as illustrated in Chapter 2, is thus constituted in a person's well-being. It meets well-being needs of one's self and others, strengthens our dignity through self-love, provides service to the community at large and enriches relational connections with others in the community.

***

Friedrich Hegel (1770–1831): Love as mutual participation in generative relations

The development of Hegel's thought on love tends to be located in his earliest texts. According to Charles Taylor, the philosophical climate of the era when Hegel was actively developing his thoughts was marked by inquiries into the nature of human subjectivity and its relation to the world, uniting two seemingly indispensable images of man, deep affinities with each other and utter incompatibility with each other.[103] Like most of his contemporaries, Hegel's philosophical development was first influenced by Kantian conceptions of freedom, morality and human dignity. However, as soon as Hegel started to explore the nature of love, or the nature of God, which is love,[104] he moved away from Kantian thoughts to develop his own philosophy.

In 1797–1798, Hegel wrote *The Fragment on Love*,[105] which was a prelude to his book *The Spirit of Christianity*. His later writings, although appearing to be a departure from his earlier interests in theology, continued to hold love as one of the central threads. To such an extent, some have argued that love remains to be a key theme throughout the entirety of Hegel's work.[106] Accordingly, his overall conception of love occurs within a context of a cosmological conception of meaning, often interpreted as understanding human's proper place in the whole of nature. Such an understanding in turn offers insights into our personal and social life in nature as full expressions of our self-consciousness.

In *The Fragment on Love*, Hegel wrestles with human difference and human identity and the reconciliation of these two, setting the ground for a lifelong

---

103 Charles Taylor, *Hegel*, 3.
104 Bjerke, "Hegel and the Love of the Concept."
105 Hegel, "The Fragment on Love" in *Early Theological Writings*, 302–8.
106 Bjerke, "Hegel and the Love of the Concept."

interest in dialectics.[107] Hegel argues that love exists only between equal beings because it involves lovers perceiving their beloved as 'living beings from every point of view'.[108] This statement involves a recognition that one's own nature as a living being in all essential respects is likewise present in the nature of the other. This mutual recognition as the basis of love is crucial for Hegel because it renders no one being superior nor inferior.[109]

Hegel is initially concerned with love as the deepest unity of the subject and the object. He claims at the opening of *The Fragment on Love*: 'There is no living union between the individual and his world; the object, severed from the subject, is dead; and the only love possible is a sort of relationship [...].'[110] With such a passage, Hegel already establishes the importance of human subjectivity or our innermost nature through which the material worlds are rendered meaningful. He points out that there appears to be a separation between a person and their world; however, the world, although external, is 'never absent' because God is always present, mediating and compensating for any disruption and loss of connection.[111] This may be seen as Hegel's attempt to develop a philosophy of love that critiques Kant's logical categories and the impossible unity of life's 'vagaries and determinations'.[112] Hegel goes on to suggest the mutually constitutive relationship be already present in us because each person is conditioning and being conditioned by what one is opposed to (e.g. the world and other people). In other words, there is no determinant without the determined and vice versa.

This mutual conditioning and mutual determination are extended to being itself as 'nothing is unconditioned; nothing carries the root of its own being in itself'.[113] Thus, Hegel argues for our mutual-constituted-ness, highlighting that each person is always already relationally situated and through love, all opposites can be reconciled and transcended. Hegel terms this an *absolute* unity that involves relations amongst subjects who are not only their own objects but also objects of other subjects. In this case, unity is not an immediate relation in love or self-consciousness as abstraction, but instead, the unity is only realised

---

107 *Nohl*, 1907, 378–82.
108 Hegel, "The Fragment on Love" in *Early Theological Writings*, 302.
109 Hegel, *The Phenomenology of Spirit*.
110 Hegel, "The Fragment on Love", 302.
111 Ibid.
112 Bjerke, "Hegel and the Love of the Concept," 77.
113 All quotes in this paragraph are from the first page of Hegel's "The Fragment on Love", , 302.

through the lived and dynamic life and social processes. This suggests that even at this early stage of his thought, Hegel already began to see the connection between love and the good life, setting the scene for his later developing the idea of love as a relational bond in human communities.

The words that Hegel uses to describe love include genuine love, true union and love proper. Love for Hegel is fundamental to life. He maintains that love is more than understanding because reason can leave the manifold meanings of related terms as distinct and therefore separate; and rationality keeps the determining and the determined in opposite. Instead, love, Hegel argues, is feeling, or sensing, but not the kind of affect that purely belongs to an isolated individual. Rather, love is the process that transcends the separation and the opposite. Despite this unifying force, according to Hegel, love does not erase difference, which remains as 'something united and no longer as something separate'. In this sense, love presides in a living whole.

If lovers insist on their independence, the relationship would most likely be antagonistic and incomplete. Protecting independence is as if holding back oneself as a private property and resisting union. Hegel considers such a sense of an exclusive individuality as shame. Shame is not an effect of love as it arises from rage (as the result of the need to defend one's right and property). Accordingly, any such hostile encounter between people necessarily renders human relationship loveless. Hegel suggests that shame be a characteristic of tyrants, or anyone who instrumentalises others, including those who instrumentalise themselves, such as using one's charm to attract money. Instead, love must be situated within a recognition of love's intrinsic value.

Hegel contrasts fear with love and points out that our fear of mortality and of losing that which is our own can vanish when love, an act mutual giving and receiving, cancels the separation and the opposites. Hegel proposes that love's gift be a mutually enriching life through our exchange of thoughts and participation in diverse inner experiences. This non-instrumental orientation to love as relationing further strengthens the whole. According to Hegel:

> [...] it seeks out difference and devises unifications ad infinitum; it turns to the whole manifold of nature in order to drink love out of every life. What in the first instance is most the individual's own is united into the whole in the lovers' touch and contact; consciousness of a separate self disappears and all distinction between the lovers is annulled.[114]

---

114 Hegel, *Early Theological Writings*, 307.

Notwithstanding his optimism that love can bridge separations, in this earlier short text *The Fragment on Love,* Hegel recognises love's dilemma which concerns the subject-object, intuition-reason and self-world divides. In his later writings, he continues to explore the necessary presence of difference and separation for love's unification and reconciliation to be meaningful. For instance, throughout Hegel's writing, he discusses the ways that love invites ethical bond between people (i.e. families, communities and societies).[115] At the same time, Hegel's deliberately leaving love's dilemma unresolved also illustrates his maintaining an openness to the other, to difference and to the yearning for union due to the separation. It might be said that Hegel insists on non-sameness as the basis of love and on human relationship as situated in one's encountering the other as an 'other' whose difference touches one, moves one, shakes one and transforms one.

Hegel thus points to the limit of moral law as set out in Kantian morality. According to McGowan's interpretation,[116] love inspires and enacts reconciliation with the other, whereby the world out there enters one and therefore ceases to be external and objective. Love seeks to connect, to reconcile, to make whole and to heal and according to Hegel, love transforms the Kantian conception of duty into a Christian idea of intertwining. Love enables us to identify with the other in all their difference, without reducing or eliminating that difference. By identifying with the difference in the other, love holds and sustains differentiation and contradiction, which necessarily 'animates love rather than destroying it. [...] Love is able to succeed at exactly the point where duty fails'.[117]

Later, in his book *The Phenomenology of the Spirit,* Hegel argues that self-consciousness, a constitutive aspect of love, is developed through participating in the life of an 'other' and that self-completion is only achieved through the power of difference where the lover's self-surrender is the basis of greater self-realisation for the other. By self-negating, the lovers enhance each other's self-determination. This does not fully address love's dilemma, but it does introduce a promising pathway towards resolving it. In further developing his thought, Hegel proposes that love is connected to an absolute and all-encompassing self-consciousness, or the *Geist.*[118] Hegel equates Geist, or spirit, to reason and truth itself. He argues that the 'pure unity of the I and of being, of being-for-itself and

---

115 See Hegel's lectures on right, and political sciences.
116 McGowan, "Hegel in Love".
117 Ibid., 14.
118 Hegel, *The phenomenology of spirit.*

being-in-itself, is determined as the in-itself, or as being and the consciousness of reason finds the unity'.[119] The unity is a unity of the intuitive, or unconscious and the rational in existing-in-and-for-itself. Hegel concludes: 'The essence existing-in-and-for-itself (which as consciousness is at the same time actual and which represents itself to itself) is spirit.'[120] Accordingly, 'spirit is ethical actuality',[121] and spirit is conscious of itself 'as its world and of the world as itself'.[122] Here Hegel likens the process of the spirit's being and becoming to the plant's growth and development, from the seed to the fruit:

> [...] the result of this whole movement [...] is what I call, in abstract terms, 'being/or self'. This is man's self-confrontation, the self-consciousness of the spirit. [...] The spirit alone is truly aware of, or 'for', itself, identical with itself ... It is in the spirit alone that by being for another it has being for itself. It makes its potentiality an object to itself and so is its own object, it and its object are one. Thus the spirit is alone with itself in its object, in its other. What it produces, its object, is itself; in its other, it comes to itself. The development of the spirit is its outgoing and dispersal, its self-differentiation, and at the same time its homecoming.[123]

For Hegel, our *true spirit* is manifested in the myriad ways in which love, friendship and justice embody the relational structure of our self-conscious lives as always in a community with others. Atomised individual cannot flourish precisely because they are alone. Instead, it is through our relational bond with others that we each become more fully human. Love invites mutual participation in purposive activities in purposive community where we recognise ourselves as an 'I' through our being part of the 'we'. In Hegel's words, 'for the ethical is in itself universal and this natural relationship is essentially just one spirit and only as spiritual essence is it ethical'.[124]

Hegel claims that our mutual recognition as human beings is an expression of love. It is this mutual recognition that determines humans as relational beings. In Hegel's vision, it is through love that persons, our purposive activities, relational process, communities and political structure are constitutive of the

---

119 Ibid., Chapter VI. Spirit, #437.
120 Ibid., Chapter VI. Spirit, #437.
121 Ibid., Chapter VI. Spirit, #438.
122 Ibid., Chapter VI. Spirit, #437.
123 Hegel, *Introduction to the Lectures on the History of Philosophy*, 78–9.
124 Hegel, *The phenomenology of spirit*, Chapter VI. Spirit, #450.

greater whole. Within the whole, all mutually nourish each other towards co-flourishing in the world and with the world (rather than apart from the world). Hegel suggests that the more we engage in purposive activities, the more we become conscious of our place in the world and our relationships with the world and the more we grow in our consciousness. Being human, in this sense, is to be embedded in an ethical community of love, bound by our responsibility for each other.

In this way, Hegel was able to place his vision of the spirit within a political structure, such as a nation state, which he imagines as an enlargement of family and purposive community, or civil society. In the myriad relational process and flow is always love. It is love that compels us towards purposive living through meaningful activities and actions.

***

Frederick Nietzsche: Love as a relational force

In Chapter 3, we examined Nietzsche's conception of love as 'amor fati' or in his own words 'the formula for human greatness'.[125] This is also stressed in his book *Will to Power* where he suggests love as relationing be the highest state that a philosopher can attain as long as we:

> cross to a Dionysian affirmation of the world as it is, without subtraction, exception or selection [...] The highest state a philosopher can attain: to stand in a Dionysian relationship to existence [...]

What is a Dionysian affirmation of the world? Dionysus is introduced by Nietzsche in his first book *The Birth of Tragedy* alongside Apollo, where he offers a way to get out of the dichotomy between reason and intuition. It articulates the interconnection of transcendence and immanence. Nietzsche explores the confluence of these two sets of conceptions in the context of aesthetics through which he provides a basis for love's insistence on ethical relations amongst people.

To do so, Nietzsche borrows, from Greek mythology, two mystical figures, Apollo and Dionysus, each embodying a particular conceptual and artistic origin and characteristics and together they represent two radically dissimilar

---

125 Nietzsche, *Esso Homo*, 238.

realms of art. Apollo is a god, who represents the form of things and who, from the perspectives of Schopenhauer, also stands for 'principium individuationis' or the principle of individuation. It symbolises the dream world where 'the wondrous forms of the deities first appeared before the souls of men',[126] from which poets draw their inspirations. However, the moment when man 'suddenly loses his way amidst the cognitive forms of appearance, because the principle of sufficient reason, in one of its forms, seems suspended [...] the blissful ecstasy'[127] is also the moment when he rises up from man's 'innermost core' and from nature. In a state of ecstasy, the world of Dionysus is open to humans, a world of wine and intoxication where 'subjectivity becomes the complete forgetting of one self'.[128] Nietzsche describes vividly that, under the Dionysiac force, in the singing and dancing, 'man expresses himself as a member of a higher community [...] [and] each man feels himself not only united, reconciled and at one with his neighbour, but one with him'.[129] For Nietzsche, this oneness reflects the Apolline and Dionysiac reconciliation.

Indeed, Apollo and Dionysus have been regarded as coming from separate art worlds: Apollo is the god of light, the creator of 'beautiful illusion of the inner fantasy world'.[130] It represents the 'higher truth', 'the perfection' and is symbolic of arts in which 'all the delight, wisdom and beauty of "illusion" speak to us',[131] and through which life becomes possible and worthwhile. Dionysus, by contrast, is the child of Zeus and a mortal and is the god of wine. He is without form and is intuitive and instinctual. The potency of Dionysiac magic lies in engendering the bonding between humans and connecting those who are alienated, experiencing hostility from the gods and from each other. Dionysus unites and connects people through the reconciliatory power of singing and dancing. In reconciliation, the enslaved are liberated, the boundaries between people dissolve, harmony and oneness ensue. According to Nietzsche, Dionysiac powers are rooted in nature itself, 'without the mediation of the human artist and in which nature's artistic urges are immediately and directly satisfied'.[132] Apollo embodies the transcendent potential in the individual's

---

126 Nietzsche, *The Birth of Tragedy*, 1.
127 Ibid., 1.
128 Ibid., 1.
129 Ibid., 1.
130 Ibid., 1.
131 Ibid., 1.
132 Ibid., 2.

becoming, where the illusion of redemption is broken by Dionysus, opening the doors to the hearts that are moved and moved again by the flow of jubilation and ecstasy.

On the first page of *The Birth of Tragedy*, Nietzsche introduces these two gods and their mythical characters (e.g. their opposition) but also highlights their integration in the way arts are conceived:

> To the two gods of art, Apollo and Dionysus, we owe our recognition that in the Greek world there is a tremendous opposition, as regards both origins and aims, between the Apolline art of the sculptor and the non-visual, Dionysiac art of music. These two very different tendencies walk side by side, usually in violent opposition to one another, inciting one another to ever more powerful births, perpetuating the struggle of the opposition only apparently bridged by the word 'art'; until, finally, by a metaphysical miracle of the Hellenic 'will', the two seem to be coupled and in this coupling they seem at last to beget the work of art that is as Dionysiac as it is Apolline – Attic tragedy.[133]

This passage captures Nietzsche's entire thesis – coupling or integrating the rational and the intuitive. For Nietzsche, it is this relational flow between reason and passion that dissolves the individual self, creating a bridge that draws people closer to each other into unity through chorus, or singing en masse. The integration of the two hitherto strengthens our experience of community and belonging, drawing together life's gifts that are both optimistic (i.e. dream-like illusion in the Apollonian art) and chaotic, painful and tragic (i.e. our everyday lived realities in the Dionysian music). Amidst the coupling, there lies love, a ceaseless yearning for life's possibility and an animating and energising force that sustains all generative bonds towards oneness.

From the classical Greeks, until the Enlightenment scholarship, few philosophers have been distracted from the potency of rationality and associated virtues as human's moral anchor. In writing *The Birth of Tragedy*, Nietzsche invites us to move away from the purely rational and the abstract and contemplate on life's suffering in and through art. This is because, as Nietzsche argues, (Greek) tragedy as sung by the chorus can allow us to witness, partake and experience together life's pains in a most intense manner. Nietzsche argues that (Greek) tragedy can transform the audience from spectators into participants and pain

---

133 Ibid., 1.

into joy. Thus life's meaningfulness is not only analysed and conceptualised but also experienced, mutually witnessed and co-participated. At the heart of Nietzsche's proposition here is the recognition of the relational as fundamental to bridging the gap left by the rational principle of individuation and the compassionate identification with human suffering beyond the individual.

For Nietzsche, tragedy is both a cognitive affair (e.g. our understanding of the pain and loss in life itself and our awareness of the imperative to act morally in supporting those in need) and a heart-wrenching force (e.g. a direct experience and collective witnessing of the sorrows and suffering, as much as joy and delight, achieved in the sung chorus). Merely having faith in reason and rationality, as opposed to intuition mediated through music, we could lose our hope for genuine appreciation of life as lived. Here Nietzsche discusses the difference between an abstract listening and the embodied listening by using Wagner's opera *Tristan and Isolde* as an example. Given the force in Nietzsche's words, this passage can only be quoted in full below:

> I should like to ask these genuine musicians whether they can imagine a man who could perceive the third act of Tristan and Isolde, unaided by word and image, simply as a tremendous symphonic movement, without expiring at the convulsive spreading of their souls' wings? How could such a man, having laid his ear against the heart of the universal will and felt the tumultuous lust for life as a thundering torrent or as a tiny, misty brook flowing into all the world's veins, fail to shatter into pieces all of a sudden? How can he bear, in the wretched bell-jar of human individuality, to hear the echo of innumerable cries of delight and woe from a 'wide space of the world's night', without inexorably fleeing to his primal home amidst the piping of the pastoral metaphysical dance? But if such a work can be perceived in its entirety without negating the existence of the individual, if such a creation can come into being without destroying its creator – where should we seek the resolution of such a contradiction?[134]

In this passage, Nietzsche invites us to allow ourselves to be carried away by Dionysiac force in the music with an Apolline analysis. Implied is that these two contradicting forces, that is, the rational and the emotive, are at the root of human ethical development. In particular, Nietzsche insists on the importance of the presence of the *other*, the one that is different and even opposite, in one's

---

134 Nietzsche, *The Birth of Tragedy*, "Attempt at Self Criticism," 2.

own transformation. For instance, elsewhere, Nietzsche has suggested that to love is not to desire love, but to seek more.[135] The 'more' refers to growth, but growth cannot happen without the need for others. Love introduces the relational nature of human transformation, rooted in the lived realities of life. This indicates that Nietzsche did not set out to address the reconciliation of science or rationality with intuition through arts, but rather, he was aiming to explore 'art under the lens of life',[136] and more importantly, what, under the lens of life, 'is the meaning of morality?'[137]

In this effort, as a very first book, Nietzsche already challenged religion and rationality as an imposed transcendent vision for life and affirmed the meaningfulness of life in the rich day-to-day lived realities. Nietzsche calls this inquiry into Greek tragedy to be one that aims at 'understanding the Dionysiac-Apolline genius and its works of art, [and] gaining a sense of the mystery of that union'.[138] Without going into the details here, for our interest, I draw on Nietzsche's conclusion on the nature of this 'duality' in Greek tragedy, that is, 'the expression of two interwoven artistic impulses, the Apolline and the Dionysiac'.[139] According to Nietzsche, this duality is where Dionysus speaks with the voice of Apollo and Apollo speaks with that of Dionysus. In a similar vein, gods, men, choristers and spectators collaborate in order to achieve the full tragic experience.

So, what does Nietzsche's *The Birth of Tragedy* (and its articulation on the integration of the Apolline and Dionysiac arts) have anything to do with love as relationing? There are at least three significant implications:

First, Nietzsche's discussion of the Apolline-Dionysiac oneness points to love's relationality as beyond being a mere emotional connection. The Apolline-Dionysiac integration makes love as relationing an energising force that holds everyone in the music hall, the Greek theatre, and everything in nature into bonding, into oneness. In this process, the boundaries between rationality and intuition are dissolved. Love encourages our active engagement in both at the same time. In this case, love insists on the presence of an 'other', someone different, who is beyond one's self and who always has an important

---

135 Nietzsche, *Thus Spoke Zarathustra*.
136 Nietzsche, *The Birth of Tragedy*, "Attempt at Self Criticism," 2.
137 Ibid., 4.
138 Ibid., 5.
139 Ibid., 12.

place in one's life. So important the other is in one's own life, it seems that without them, our life would have little meaning. In *Thus Spoke Zarathustra*, Nietzsche writes:

> one morning he [Zarathustra] rose with the dawn, stepped before the sun, and spoke to him thus: 'You mighty star! What would your happiness be if you did not have those for whom you shine!'

The recognition of the presence of the other and their place in one's own happiness is also to affirm love's relationality. This relational dimension of our being is a key to human flourishing.

Second, Nietzsche illustrates that love lies in the affirmation of life's meaningfulness in itself and not beyond. In other words, to love is to engage intensely with all that is constituted in life, rather than dismissing life's contents in the lived realities including all their chaotic complexities, such as joy and pain, ecstatic pleasure and profound suffering. Love is not a state of being, nor an emotion, but rather, love is an action. Love is our active relationing with all that is in life, in our singing, dancing and rejoicing. In other words, love is acting out our relatedness.

Third, Nietzsche uses Greek tragedy to stress the importance of the co-creative and collaborative process as a key to engendering the good life. Once again here is where love's relationality applies. In fact, it is through love's relationality that one becomes empathetic towards the other's traumatic experiences and opens themselves to the other's lived realities. In mutual listening, mutual witnessing, mutual presencing and mutual partaking in the singing and dancing, love transcends the suffering, helps heal the wounds and brings the community into deeper bond.

Love's Relationality in Post-Modernist Thought

> *Love is not primarily a relationship to a specific person; it is an attitude, an orientation of character which determines the relatedness of a person to the world as a whole, not toward one 'object' of love. If a person loves only one other person and is indifferent to the rest of his fellow men, his love is not love but a symbiotic attachment, or an enlarged egotism.*
>
> —Erich Fromm, *The Art of Loving*

Recognising the harms to human lives and societies resulted from dehumanising approaches to economic growth, work and relationships, in the twentieth and twenty-first centuries, there have been renewed interests in understanding human nature, but not in a universal sense as explored by modernist thinkers. Instead, post-modernist thought gives rise to an interest in the individual self, an interest that seems to bring forward conceptions of personhood in opposite directions.

At one end is the preoccupation with the idea of the person as a singular, separate and unique entity. Moving away from modernist obsession with the natural man, post-modernist thinkers ask questions about what constitutes the self, individual subjectivity and personal identity, not in a general sense, but in a person's myriad particularities, such as class, ethnicity, language, sexuality, gender, physical ability, body image and the list goes on. An atomic conception of the person individualises love, and makes love's relationality almost impossible due to its situating love within an egoistic orientation. At the other end, it is the emergent relational view of the self, or the conscious 'I', the subject, or subjecthood/selfhood and the object or the things in themselves are not separate but interrelated as a person-in-(and-with)-the-world. Replacing the Kantian transcendental ego/self, the post-modernist self resides in a higher realm that transcends ordinary knowledge and experiences as opposed to an empirical self. It is also termed the phenomenological self, for instance, recognised in the work of Martin Heidegger and Merleau-Ponty. This relational view of self and of human nature stresses a *with*-ness, acknowledging that being human is being in relationship with each other, with the world and in the world. Alongside the claim of the self as a being-in-and-with-the-world is a shift from the unifying view of the natural man who partakes in a common humanity, to the necessary interdependent view of the self, other and the world where one's self-awareness is intimately connected with that of the other and of the world. Introduced here is a recognition of multiplicity, not just the multiplicity of identities, or the multiplicity of positions and dispositions that we inhabit and embody, but also the multiplicity of worlds. Hence being persons is further reflected in our experiences of ourselves as beings who move in between the multiple *worlds*.

From atomically situated self to relational self, post-modernist explorations bring the inquiry closer to the questions including what it means to be loving and how love embodies the relationality amongst persons, other beings and the world(s). To this end, some contemporary philosophers have reclaimed love's relationality as necessarily non-instrumental, motivated by love only, in the words of C. S. Lewis and Gabriel Marcel. Others, such as Luce Irigaray, even propose to return to the classical Greek conception of love as sustaining the spaces in-between oneself and others. In this way, love as relationing defines our being as being-with: with each other, with the world and with all that is sacred. As Nussbaum confirms, love is truly 'a mystery and depth, a tremendous power, without which life would be impoverished, lacking, perhaps, in the strongest sources of benevolence itself'.[140]

***

Gabriel Marcel (1889–1973): Radical love

Since industrial revolution, humanity begins to suffer from growing alienation, from oneself, from others, from nature and from the divine. Gabriel Marcel, the French philosopher, dramatist and writer observes, in his book, *The Mystery of Being*, that in such a world, human's yearning for transcendence, meaning, coherence and truths is amiss.[141] Therefore, Marcel calls this world a 'broken world'.[142] In a broken world, people tend to be treated as cogs in machines, and each person also risks considering themselves and being considered by others as 'an agglomeration of function', social, biological and psychological. In this context, Marcel argues that people tend to attempt to know and to relate to each other in ways akin to solving a puzzle. Identifying a person as

---

140 Nussbaum, "The Ascent of Love: Plato, Spinoza, Proust," 928.
141 Marcel, *The Mystery of Being, Vol. I: Reflection and Mystery*.
142 In one of his plays, 'The Broken Heart', Marcel describes the broken world as a human world whose heart has stopped beating: 'Don't you have the sense that we are living … if you can call that living … in a broken world. Yes, broken like a watch that has stopped. Its mainspring no longer works. To all appearances nothing has changed. Everything is in place. But if you put the watch to your ear … you hear nothing. Remember, the world, or what we used to call the world, the human world … before, it must have had a heart. But it seems that heart has stopped beating.'

problem is turning them into something knowable, for example, by breaking a person down to the parts or roles they play (e.g. occupation, or function in an institution) as if an object. The other person and their features become some *things* that one talks about. Here lies an 'I–It' relation, in the words of Martin Buber.[143] The risk of such an identification is that over time, one begins to self-identify (unconsciously) with these occupations or functions. The more one so self-identifies, the more one becomes an assemblage of these labels, such as our utilities, functions or roles.[144] When one self-identifies through the lenses of utilities and functionalities, one sees oneself as a means to an end and is thus instrumentalised and denied as a subject. Also instrumentalised is our life as a person.

For Marcel, titles and roles (and similarly one's other identity categories) are things that one can have, or they are identifiable items that a person can own, rather than who and what we are. The way we relate to each other in this case 'comes down to the distinction between what we have and what we are'.[145] According to Marcel, having suggests possessing. To define a person through the personal artefacts that one possesses implies that such knowledge about the person is outside the intense fabric of life. This perception of another person is likely to be motivated by assimilation, absorbing the other into one's self. Thus, assimilation offers no access to an understanding of an 'other'. Rather, in assimilating the other, the other ceases to be a person but ends up becoming a collection of roles and identifiable labels. Applying functions and other identity categories to perceiving the other tends to reduce the other to one's own scheme of references (with which one can in turn use to solve the puzzle, or the other). When people are treated as puzzles, their existence is further objectified by what Marcel calls the primary reflection(or thinking about and analysing things in isolation), resulting in abstract generalisations. Assimilation and objective abstraction of the other are both part of the primary, consisting in forms of instrumentalisation or dehumanisation, Indeed

---

143 Buber, *I and Thou*.
144 Marcel is more concerned with this person's losing the sense of wonder and the need for the transcendent, thus rendering their being in the world more technical rather than spiritual. This is an ontological concern rather than an epistemological one, which however, does allow us to seek the knowledge of the Other through a recognition of their place in the world/cosmos. Marcel's own view is that this ontological concern must be beyond a mere concern for a person's psychological state, mood, attitude, to include the wholeness of their being, including their spirit and the aspiration for the transcendent.
145 Marcel, *Being and Having*, 155.

it is dehumanisation that denote our present broken-ness where each person is divided into discrete multiplicities in a disparate world.[146] Some treat abstract differences with misunderstanding, or fear; others can treat differences with contempt, discrimination and even violence.

Marcel suggests that instead of categorisation, or dehumanisation, human beings must be perceived as a mystery (rather than as a bundle of their artefacts). Hence our encounter with each other as humans can only take place at the level of being. As a mystery, human's being involves each person's presence. In presencing, we participate in the material world, such as through experiences and work. As a mystery, a person's being also entails in our presencing and participating in the lives of others through being a part of family, friendships with others and belonging to a community, Our being is further comprised in our presence and participation in the metaphysical world through faith, hope and love. Being is simultaneously a presence and a participation. Therefore, at the level of being, presence and participation allow an access to other people and their lived realities which are ontologically higher and phenomenologically richer.

That is to say, the other and their otherness can only be known, understood and experienced as an enveloping force, a mystery, in and through our presence, participation and engagement with them in an encounter. For Marcel, an encounter with the other thus has deep spiritual significance because it is neither a chance, shared interest, taste (in things, places), nor a common affliction that has led to such an encounter. It is the meeting amongst (human) beings whose nature is characterised by the very mystery we share. As already mentioned, a mystery cannot be resolved nor understood rationally as a case or a problematique.

Using an example of being told of the misfortune with which one is demanded to sympathise, Marcel elucidates the significance of regarding the other as a mystery: a rational response in this situation is that one can imagine the sufferers' realities, accept that they deserve sympathy and believe that it is only logical to respond to the sufferings with sympathy and it is in one's duty to offer such sympathy. Clearly a rational and logical response tends to treat the sufferer, or the other, as a case in front of us, an object, and when acting on duty, one is not bringing oneself into a (spiritual) presence in the other's experience. In this case, there is no encounter, as such. By contrast, to truly encounter is to enter into the other's being as a co-subject. In this case, one

---

146 Marcel, *Le Monde Cassé Suivi de Position Et Approches Concrètes du Mystère Ontologique.*

becomes a presence in the sufferers' life. Such presence can 'only be invoked or evoked' and the evocation must be 'fundamentally and essentially magical'.[147]

An encounter between persons should be transcendent, which means that it must be situated within their experiences of each other but at the same time go beyond what is external, for example, from the perspectives of role functions and identity labels. The transcendence will include self-transcendence where one self-identifies equally beyond the perspectives of categories. It is transcendent in both cases (self and other transcendence) because human's being as mystery already implies a person's intrinsic value, which applies to one's self and so too equally to other people. Insofar as we encounter each other as beings of intrinsic value, there is ethical interpersonal relationship. Hence Marcel proposes that the most important way to nurture (ethical) relationship in everyday situations be through (radical) love.

In Marcel's conception, love as relationing is constituted in a form of openness, availability and communion with the other. Love thus conceived is central to his philosophical thought. Marcel proposes that presence assumes love which becomes a binding force for one and the other. For instance, the more the other becomes a presence, a spiritual co-esse, to me, the more the other reveals me to myself. This is because love applies to the whole being, and the presence of the other invites me to return to my self and participate in my self as a whole being. In this way, 'I' and 'Thou' become two co-subjects of love in mutual presence.

In Marcel's writings, there are a few intertwined aspects of love through *disponibilité*, or availing.

First, love implies an affective element. It is not objective knowledge, duty and obligation that bind persons together, nor is it the romantic sentiment (which necessarily involves the ego) that draws people close to one another. Instead, it is the pains and delights, sorrows and joys that are comprised in the human bond. It is precisely by availing oneself in these affects and emotions (instead of duties or obligations) that one finds the impetus to stand in solidarity with the other. A fulfilment of an obligation contre-coeur is devoid of love and is not enduring.[148]

Second, love is embodied, or making ourselves a presence in the lived experience amongst whole beings. This means that each person is present in their human wholeness and participates in the other's realities as a whole

---

147 Marcel, *The Mystery of Being, Vol. I: Reflection and Mystery*, 208.
148 Marcel, 1962, xxii.

being. Thus, the beloved cannot be perceived as having abstract elements, (e.g. good characters, beauty), nor general features such as humanity. Love concerns what is present in the wholeness where the beloved is more than an assemblage of wonderful items. Love of humanity is only an extension and expansion of love for the whole human being. It is in this sense that love directs our recognition of the other as real, whole and irreducible to parts.

Third, love is oriented towards goodness and invites the good in oneself and in the other. The sole focus of love is the beloved,[149] the other and their whole being and well-being, all of which are intrinsically valuable and require our presence. It assumes that value and goodness are inherent in the mystery of being, and by availing oneself to the other's well-being, one experiences well-being.

Fourth, love transcends. Love is the encounter between co-subjects, each of who is a 'thou' to the other. It is in the realm of the I-thou, or the 'we' that is where and how love is experienced. Marcel sees that 'love posits the beloved as transcending all explanation and all reduction'.[150] The two co-subjects avail themselves and are presence to each other, thereby transcending each other in love. Love through presencing and availing is love without possessing the other, nor losing oneself. Hence love does not allow for domination nor slavery. Instead, love is relational mediation and as we shall see, it is also a gift to one another.

All these interlocking aspects are encompassed in Marcel's core ideas of presence and availing (disponibilité) and together they suggest that love has the potential to restore the broken world and heal the human relationships fragmented and shattered by instrumentality and dehumanisation. In fact, Marcel makes significant claims towards this potential of love. For instance, in Marcel's philosophy, love is akin to promise-keeping, which is dialogical and involves one's commitment to and dedicated care for the other. The commitment is a response to the other as a mystery and as already seen, it is different from fulfilling one's obligation which overtime will be devoid of love and its durability. Instead, a commitment to love in Marcel's case is a gift/bequest to the other, which does not depend on the other's characters, virtues or acts, nor does it rely on one's absolute consistence. It is rooted in faith, belief, or trust in the other and is creative because it allows one to draw strength from something that is beyond oneself, something greater, or the transcendent.

---

149 See also Thomson and Gill, *Happiness, Flourishing and the Good Life*.
150 Marcel, *Metaphysical Journal*, 62.

However, for Marcel, love is not unconditional in an absolute sense. Rather, love 'implies an ardent and mutual questioning', which is not blind faith.[151] Marcel explains that to love the other is to inspire something from them and to inspire something from them is equivalent to gift-giving. In other words, to love the other is to offer them the opportunity to expand their self, which is the gift. On this point, C. S. Lewis echoes Marcel's view. To a certain extent, it is implicit in Marcel's proposition that natural love is itself limited and we must return to God's love, or gift-love, for love to truly envelop human relationship.

Marcel concludes that love as relationing allows us to appreciate the other without comprehending the other nor absorbing them into ourselves. Likewise, love recognises the other's otherness and invites hermeneutical endeavour as a pathway to dialogue with the other. In this way, love is a human calling that defines the ethical nature of our being and relating.

***

Luce Irigaray (1930): Love as horizontal transcendence

Luce Irigaray has written and continues to write extensively on the subject of love within the arenas of philosophy, linguistics and psychoanalysis and has proposed several highly influential ideas on love within the sphere of feminist thought. Her overarching and mutually constituted projects extending across her oeuvre include deconstructing and disrupting historically male-dominated, patricentric metaphysics, philosophies and discourses. In her early works, Irigaray has sought to demonstrate how women are effectively de-subjectified, excluded and otherwise othered within theory and praxis. According to Irigaray, within Western philosophical and psychoanalytic traditions, the singular, mono-logical subjectivity constructed by language and materialised in culture is not merely sexless and abstract, but effectively a cultivated reflection of the male subject. As such, *sexuate* difference (i.e. the existence of two, essentially distinct, gendered subjects) is not yet manifest nor recognised. In this sense, there is no neutral subject, there is only the veiled representation of the male subject. Thus, the female non-subject takes the form as man's other.

Irigaray's conception of love is co-constituted in her conception of sexual difference, which serves as the basis for her mutually interpenetrating ethics

---

151 Marcel, 1962, 249.

and relational ontology. Within her thought, love has played a critical role as a relational ideal and a transformative agent for true personal, interpersonal, societal, political and even broader systemic changes to human consciousness. For instance, in an article entitled 'Introducing: Love between Us', Irigaray suggests that negotiating with and overcoming the exploitation between the sexes and developing new ethical relationality between men and women as the gateway towards furthering human history are part of generating novel existential horizons by facilitating and cultivating love as relationing in all levels of the society.[152]

For Irigaray, woman and man are not dichotomised opposites, but are different. This difference is not an essential, ontic distinction dictated by nature, but rather an ontological difference pertaining to the meaning of being in the Heideggerian sense.[153] Being for Irigaray is constructed and mediated by language and culture and their evolution over time and as such is concerned with becoming.[154] Subjectivity, or more broadly, being and becoming, is not to be understood to be one, but to be two, which she proposes, as distinguished in sexual difference.[155] In *An Ethics of Sexual Difference*, Irigaray asks, 'If sexual difference is to be overcome is it not imperative first of all to find a sexual ethics? If one day we are to be one must we not now be two?'.[156] Thus sexual difference has been a key notion to Irigaray's re-conceptualisation of the Other, central to her relational ontology. She criticises Levinas's concept of radical alterity which, in Irigaray's perspectives, tends to propose a disembodied, intangible and abstract otherness, unknowable and infinitely distanced. Instead, she suggests that men and woman are radical Other to one another, precisely owing to their sexual difference.

Irigaray's ethics of love are characterised by openness and dynamic fluidity; just as femininity and masculinity are not bound, atemporal and unchanging, neither are person's modes of being-in the world and being-with each other. The constant fluctuations in our ways of being must be received with an open embrace and attentiveness.[157] In order to recognise an 'other'

---

152 Irigaray, 'Introducing: Love between Us,' 181.
153 Jones, 'The Future of Sexuate Difference: Irigaray, Heidegger, Ontology, and Ethics.'
154 Ibid.
155 Ibid.
156 Irigaray, *An Ethics of Sexual Difference*, 179.
157 Gingrich-Philbrook, 'Love's Excluded Subjects: Staging Irigaray's Heteronormative Essentialism,' 227.

as a subject, the perceived subject has to be understood not only in the initial instance of encounter as irreducibly other (in her words, 'other as other'),[158] but also as dynamically changeable over time and within different spaces. This shift constitutes our mutual becoming. Irigarayan love and ethics can therefore be characterised as ever-continuous *relational* process, not as a singular event of comprehension.[159] Only when the other is not subsumed into preconceived categories of comprehension can they be mobilised into a perpetual process of understanding - perceiving *you* as 'always other and non-appropriable by *I*'.[160]

Irigaray makes a distinction between projective love of the same and genuine love as encounter with the radical other.[161] Love of the same can be compatible with historical conceptions of love as the fusion of two subjects into a singular identity, such as that espoused by Aristophanes in Plato's *Symposium*. For Irigaray, love as fusion wherein Otherness is overcome by sameness is a fallacy rooted in the projection of preconceived categories. Instead she proposes that the Other must be preserved and that an irreducible Otherness rooted in sexual difference is in itself the site of wonder, respect and appreciation, from which love can be cultivated. Irigarayan love for the Other goes beyond a subject-object relation which reduces the other to an egocentric projection as a known object. She conceives of love as relational mutuality between two irreducibly other subjects, such that desire in love is not desire *for* but rather desire *with*. Subject-object is reconfigured as subject-subject which transcends a binary category, by presenting a co-subjective simultaneity.

Irigaray proposes the phrase 'I love to you' (as if love is a bridge that holds the 'I' and the 'you') in order to demonstrate the 'site of the non-reduction of the person to the object'.[162] Ethical, loving relationships of all kinds can thus be characterised in terms of mutual directionality, rather than assimilation/fusion or radical alterity. This site of non-reduction can be understood in Irigaray's post-Hegelian terms as 'the negative'.[163] Becoming a subject and being in the world requires recognition. However, this process of transformative becoming is not that of being accorded a subjectivity such as in a Hegelian master-slave dialectic, but rather becoming and being involves having one's radical and

---

158 Irigaray, *Between East and West*, 124.
159 Irigaray, *Sharing the World*, 1.
160 Irigaray, *Between East and West*, 124.
161 Irigaray, *An Ethics*, 97–115.
162 Irigaray & Martin, *I Love to You*, 110.
163 Bostic, 'Introduction: The Recent Work of Luce Irigaray,' 4.

irreducible difference recognised and consequently the negative (the distance between) maintained. The negative allows (co)subjects to simultaneously develop and actualise their subjectivity, while mobilising two (co)subjects towards a dual universal relationality in a perpetual state of transcending.[164] As such, Irigarayan love can be characterised as becoming – a process of harmonious and creative indeterminacy facilitated by the negative of positive difference. Self-transcendence as a requisite foundation of ethical relations is reconfigured from a hermetic process of actualisation as an exclusive spiritual capital of men into a relational process facilitated uniquely by loving encounter with the irreducible Other.

An important concept that Irigaray proposes is 'horizontal transcendence', challenging the hierarchical verticality of top-down relations within politics and religion, both institutional and personal.[165] The transcendent and spiritual is not ordained by an external arbiter but comes into being within the dynamic, negative in-between-ness. Thus, horizontal transcendence is availed through immanence mediated by love.

This relational ontology is not limited to the erotic and intimate but is crucial in all forms of sociality, especially within the realm of politics, governance and leadership.[166] For example, while an authoritarian/dictatorial regime enforces categorical boundaries upon citizens as objects, democracy strives towards an ideal of mutually constituted relationality, facilitated by dialogue with others and commitment to subject-subject relations. Irigaray has stressed the bidirectional mediation of the systemic and local/intimate in terms of love. At the same time, for Irigaray, the potentialities for loving as relationing can be limited by political, social, economic and cultural power dynamics and narratives, often framed in terms of the appropriation/renunciation of women's existential horizons imposed by historically entrenched, mono-logical, male subjectivity. Indeed, the systemic, institutional and other elements of material culture cannot move towards relational ideals without love. Irigaray suggests that if women strive to redistribute power without destabilising and deconstructing existing systems of power, they re-subjugate themselves to 'phallocratic order'.[167] Consequently, for a system to be under transformative process, the unilateral singularity of disembodied male subjectivity must be

---

164 Irigaray, *An Ethics*.
165 Irigaray & Martin, *I Love to You*, 144.
166 Ibid., 82.
167 Irigaray, 1985, 81.

transfigured into an embodied, relational confluence of difference (within her terms, beginning with the mobilisation of the two sexes towards love).

The work of Irigaray has received considerable criticism on the charge of essentialism and heterosexism.[168] While the inflexible centrality of sexual difference within her ontology is problematic in its ethical exclusivity, Irigaray's contribution to the philosophy of love is significant. As Bostic and her other proponents suggest, her work merits genuine engagement in terms of her efforts to destabilise historical male-dominated subjectivity in Western culture, her unique interlinked relational ontology and ethics and her extensive investigation into the philosophy of love, its ethics and practical relationships to culture, politics and institutions.

---

168 See Virpi Lehtinen, *Luce Irigaray's Philosophy of Feminine Being: Body, Desire and Wisdom* (Buffalo: SUNY P, forthcoming 2014); see Judith Butler.

Conclusion: The Relational Imperative of Love

From defining humans as relational beings through love, to conceptualising human togetherness in love as a relational bond, to perceiving the highest form of human relatedness in love or perfect friendship, the classic Greek thoughts have articulated a clear insight into our flourishing life that has already comprised in love's relationality. In fact, this relational dimension of the good life is particularly accentuated in this epoch to be in part our well-being and flourishing. More importantly, love as relationing is also the foundation for us to engage in our communal life and political life, as we shall in the Chapter 7. A relational vision of love as expounded by the classical Greek thoughts points to the good life as a relationally active life of friendships and deep loving connections with others. Through love, others become part of our well-being, and help enlarge our well-being and enrich our good life.

In the theological argument, whether love lies in the innate will of humankind is one of the contentions between St Augustine and St Thomas's theologies. Each of them is also drawn to different metaphors about God. For St Augustine, the distinction between the tripartite human qualities (e.g. memory, intellect and will) that mirror God's trinitarian being is important. By distinguishing these three qualities, love offers a relational grounding to human's path to God and towards transcendence. For St Thomas, God's Trinity defines our relationality and allows the mutual indwelling to feature human's friendship with God, with which to lift humans from a humble position. Both have believed that without God's Grace, human love will not be possible. However, it is Montaigne who asserts the sacred dimension in the self-other relationship to further assumes dignity of being persons in its own right.

Following the Enlightenment and the development of rational, scientific and empirical approach to understanding human nature and our lived realities, in Western thought, there were attempts to liberate humans from the power of pre-ordained authorities (e.g. Christianity and aristocracy). However, neither scientific methods that challenge the predetermined world designed by God nor revolutionary movements that rebel against imposed power had truly provided a satisfying answer to the search for the good life. In particular, amidst the early economic development, humans have been subject to all forms of brutality, physical, psychological, relational and spiritual, in the violent colonisation, enslavement and warring competition. These rational progresses seemed to have created situations where persons could be instrumentalised for the material gains – ironically a totally irrational practice.

During this time, as human living conditions were improved in many ways through the advancement of science and technology, ethical human relationships deteriorated drastically. This phenomenon of putting material wealth ahead of human dignity and well-being has persisted until postmodernity, where sacrificing human's life, or relinquishing living for living's sake to economic gains, is compounded by environmental damage, threatening the integrity of the planet's eco-system as a whole. Given the afore reviewed accounts of love's relationality and its centrality in our flourishing life, the current crises in human and nature's suffering might be considered as a loss of love, or a loss of meaningful relationship with all that is in the cosmos, amongst humans, between man and nature and in connections with the sacred.

In Erich Fromm's analysis of capitalism's domination in Western culture, like other consumer pursuit, love becomes mutual sexual satisfaction and is treated as in part the 'teamwork' to succeed in the world, or to fend off the ever-present aloneness. These are symptoms of 'disintegration of love in modern Western society, the socially patterned pathology of love'.[169] Contemporary individualism that characterises post-modernity tends to lament that love as true bonding and intimacy between people is simply not possible. It talks about how all individuals are islands and what love can contribute is to build bridges linking people who would otherwise be in isolation. However, these bridges tend to be fragile and insecure, which is either a temporary passion that may evade or a calculated decision based on self-interests. A post-modernist conception of love risks being such an alienating consciousness that it is either engulfing the other (by the self) or losing the self to the other,[170] making it impossible to pursue an ethical life in collaboration and communion with others.

Many contemporary theologians and Christian philosophers such as Thomas Merton, Soren Kierkegaard and C. S. Lewis continue to affirm this relational dimension of our being, founded on love as collective human destiny because the meaning of life cannot be understood alone and we cannot flourish without others.

---

169 Fromm, *The Art of Loving*.
170 Cates, "Thomas Aquinas on Intimacy and Emotional Integrity."

CHAPTER 5

LOVE AS CARING

Love loves to love love.

—James Joyce, *Ulysses*

it is both more precise and more fully explanatory to say that there is something we care about […] something we regard as important to ourselves. In certain cases, moreover, what moves us is an especially notable variant of caring: namely, love.

—Harry Frankfurt, *Reasons of Love*

the good social agent should care when people are hungry, when they mourn, when they are persecuted – and should, in her compassion, see the remediation of those bad states of affairs as an urgent task of earthly politics.

—Martha Nussbaum, *Political Emotions: Why Love Matters*

The ways that love speaks of responsibilities and duties of care have been shifting and evolving throughout the Western history of thought. Love as caring expresses an ultimate concern that could be interpreted in two ways: One interpretation is to suggest that to love is to apply the most desirable attitude, such as good will and loving curiosity, to ourselves, people around us, the distant others and other beings in the cosmos, including divine beings such as God. An example of this interpretation is that we take an interest in others. The other is to suggest that to love is to take active responsibility for persons, causes and the goodness in the world.

In the Greek cosmology, the good life is about humans orientating ourselves to the order and harmony of the cosmos according to which humans should act. These acts and ways of being also constitute an ethical life, a flourishing life. For the Greeks, at the core of such an ethical life is love as caring that invites us to be concerned with the good (as manifested in the cosmic harmony) and to be caring (for such harmony and right relationships). In this case, the concern for the cosmic principles should underpin the very structure and practice of human's social, economic and political life. Indeed, the classical Greek thoughts have expressed varyingly how love as caring should be manifested. For instance, according to Plato, an ideal Republic relies on the cultivation of human virtues and for such virtues to characterise the political institutions and structure political processes. These virtues in turn serve as the foundation of a just society. For Aristotle, ethical action is rooted in cultivating a contemplative life which enables us to exercise wisdom and live our ethical principles. For the Stoics, political acts are carried out as a form of self-adjustment, a constant self-observation and self-reflection to ensure that our life is fully aligned with the cosmic vision of the good life.

These ideas are proposed so that they might guide the social order of human life and direct our political processes. In other words, how we live in pursuing the good life must respect and be adjusted to these cosmic principles which are derived from the whole system of nature that fosters justice, beauty and deep loving bond amongst all. Hence the Greek's proposals that the governance of human society must reflect the ways by which the universe is governed and the nature of human society must correspond to the nature of the cosmos (i.e. loving and caring).

From a Christian perspective, the divine order is an expression of God's perfection. Christian theology perceives the cosmos as a structured system that has its origin, order, meaning and destiny. Christian cosmology divides the system into three parts: Heaven, Earth and Hell/the Underworld. In this case, a good life on Earth is a life of seeking salvation, towards Heaven where humans, or the fallen, can be united with the creator, God. Thus, our ultimate concern is directed towards transcendence. Transcendence requires that human actions and our political structures help deliver us from the sins brought by the 'fall' and enable us to be redeemed and liberated by God's love. God is the only organising and animating force of all goodness in the world. This truly directs love as caring uniquely towards God. Where love as caring is directed at fellow humans and other beings, it is ultimately aimed at the essence of God in all beings.

In modernist philosophy, humanist thinkers not only highlighted the individual's natural right and duty to care, but they also conceived persons as beings-in-the-world, whose interests and caring are structured by our primary and necessary involvement in and with the world. Correspondingly, love as caring determines the meaningfulness of our being and our life in and with the world. As we have already seen in Chapter 3 about love as valuing, caring necessarily involves a commitment to what we care, such as the valuable aspects of things in themselves or of persons in themselves, including especially human's well-being. Hence love as caring is regarded as active and proactive and thereby a part of personal, communal, institutional and political process. A particularly compelling modernist perspective on love as caring is as follows: not only do we ordinarily think that love, at its best, should involve sensitivity to the needs, interests, growth and flourishing of the ones we love, but also that this sensitivity should invite, encourage and instigate continued love and caring directed at these. This constitutes an enlargement of the soul as the classical Greeks and Christian theologians have suggested, the extension of our ethical horizons and enrichment of the good life as modernist philosophers have pointed out.

The conception of love as caring is as ancient as it is modern and it is likewise well represented in post-modernist/contemporary philosophical discussions concerning love. Indeed, in light of the growing individualistic tendencies in post-modernist eras, many thinkers, such as C. S. Lewis and Martha Nussbaum, amongst others, have decided to revisit and reinterpret earlier arguments concerning love as caring, especially those in the classical and theological conceptions. By analysing these earlier ideas in the contexts of contemporary challenges, they actively re-imagine how love can be once again instilled in the good life as the guiding principle.

Love as Caring in Classical Greek Thought

> *[…] our purpose in founding our state was not to promote the happiness of a single class, but, so far as possible, of the whole community. Our idea was that we were most likely to justice in such a community and so be able to decide the question we are trying to answer. We are therefore at the moment trying to construct what we think is a happy community by securing the happiness not of a select minority, but of a whole.*
>
> —Plato, *The Republic*

The Greeks were amongst the first people in the Western world to favour rationality and freedom of thought. Therefore, public debates and dialogic reasoning on the goods of democracy were frequent in citizens' assemblies in the polis. The polis was the site where citizen was supposed to have a direct role in political, economic, social and spiritual affairs of the city-state. Love as caring for the common good and appealing to our ultimate concern is therefore at the core of the political life.

For the Greeks, love as caring starts with caring for one's self and one's offspring. It is then extended to caring for others, for the goodness in the world and, ultimately, for the harmony in the universe specified by the cosmic order and justice. As illustrated in the prior two chapters of the book, Platonic, Aristotelian and Stoic philosophies have inherent connections. This chapter will focus on the classical Greek ideas around the social, economic and political implications of love as caring and discuss how acting lovingly and caringly towards oneself, others and the interconnections amongst all beings in the cosmos is a key to the good life in the political communities.

There are a few points worthy of highlighting before we commence the discussion on love as caring. In principle, the ancient Greeks regard the (cosmo)polis to be present prior to the individuals, rather than the other way round as we might conventionally believe. That is to say, it is not that society is made up of individuals, but rather, a political community is established so that humans can pursue a common life together. Thus, the political community is for the sake of the good life and that is its very raison-d'être. Within the polis, humans are teleologically oriented towards the good, which is expressed by our pursuing an active contemplative life with others. Such an active life is in turn nurtured by the systemic design of the polis, such as through its social structure (e.g. the three-tire class model presented by Plato in *The Republic*), law-making and political processes. Furthermore, the flourishing life within the political community requires all persons to live out their virtuous day-to-day qualities in all forms of relationship and in the ways that people collaborate with one another in the myriad socio-economic, political and educative activities in the polis.

The common life in the polis seems, for the ancient Greeks, to be sites where love truly matters. In the contemporary discourse, this active life is also termed citizenship founded on genuine care for each other and for things beautiful and just for their own sake. The Greeks point point out that such caring can only be inspired by genuine love that fosters virtues and human qualities that can enable citizens to live a common ethical life.

***

Plato: Love as a generative caring force

As Plato points out, in the words of Diotima, love is generative (e.g. pregnant in the body and in the soul) and our love for the good, either within us or in others, determines that we are on a path towards self-betterment and humanity, which together are on a path to a better world. Through the 'pregnancy' of the soul, greater wisdom and higher virtues can be aspired and to be given birth. Wisdom and virtues arrive through learning how to lead a life that resembles that of the divine beings (i.e. the gods). In this process, honourable and loving deeds such as caring for our own children, caring for others and caring for all the needy and vulnerable are in part the exercises of our virtues.

Thus, according to Plato, how we love, care and educate our children and each other is entirely a public or political matter. This tendency is connected to the Greeks' concern for transcendence, that is, to overcome mortality and to get as close as humanly possible to possessing the good forever. The creative efforts to reach for something good and valuable involve caring and modelling virtuous conducts or living out values and virtues that constitute the good in our personal and political lives. This is regarded as the highest form of loving pursuit. As a community's common interest is also in the good, people are bound more closely by the shared vision of the good (than being drawn to each other merely by the physical beauty and natural drive for parenthood). Caring bond and co-creation engender the great works, philosophical, political, dramatic or poetical, from which the political community and future generations may in turn learn to love and care for the good, to act nobly in all contexts, to exemplify virtuous characters and to actively contribute to the political lives of the community. The generative force of love as caring further teaches and inspires virtues, wisdom and caring for the good in innumerable future generations – a gift to posterity.[1]

Instilling and cultivating virtues and creativity becomes in part the purpose and activity of the political community and in doing so, people also deepen an appreciation for the beauty of the laws, customs and political processes which promote such cultivation and development. This is, in the words of Diotima, 'inquiring into the ways in which the lives of all citizens might be improved [...] giv[ing] birth to many gloriously beautiful ideas and theories, in unstinting love of wisdom'.[2]

In acting out caring relationships, people can begin to nurture the goodness in each other, as they re-examine laws and other social institutions in the light of the good and the beauty defined by the cosmos. Loving and caring not only cultivates finer children but also engenders stronger and more intense friendships amongst the citizens. Thus, in an article entitled *Plato on Love*, Richard Kraut offers an uplifting summation of Diotima's conception of caring and connects caring with justice.[3]

In *The Republic*, Plato describes a dialogue between Socrates and young people in which they explore what constitutes justice and how a loving and caring political system might nurture just people. In this dialogue, Plato locates justice in love. According to Plato, justice starts with the virtues of the political system – the *polis*. How the polis defines and structures its economic and political processes can have a direct impact on the ways people practise virtues in their personal and political lives. When polis is structured to be loving and caring, the ethical practices can be reflected in the manners that children are nurtured and the ways that people are enabled to participate and contribute to the flourishing of others in the polis. Together these constitute factors of a just world which is characterised by caring people whose loving connection and the affectionate bond engender more refined beings (including ourselves and our offspring) and more dedicated caring in the community.

Put it simply, a political life should be underpinned by love and care. It is an active virtuous life within structural justice which in turn enables and enriches such a life through people's engaging in acts of love and caring. Instead of defining a just person, Plato investigates the characters of just city and suggests that a structure of just governance is composed of three classes

---

1 Plato, *Symposium*, 209b-e.
2 Ibid., 210c-d.
3 Kraut, "Plato on Love," 299.

of people: (1) the rulers, (2) the soldiers or guardians and (3) artisans, farmers and merchants. Justice is what defines the nature of the activities within each class and the nature of relationships amongst the classes and the way they serve the common interest of the polis. This configuration of the polis is analogous to the soul which is comprised of three aspects, that is, reason, appetite and spirit, and each aspect corresponds to a particular class. In locating people in the structure of governance in accordance with the three aspects of the soul, Plato proposes a way to engender political harmony, especially when political life is constantly confronted with internal/psychological conflicts or conflicting physiological urges. For instance, reason can control appetite, or our physiological urges and hence rationality is a key to ensure the goodness of our soul.[4] Whereas spirit is an emotional energy and in a virtuous soul, it is aligned with reason and offers reason the kind of emotional energy to oversee the appetites. Justice in this case consists of cohering these three aspects of the soul in keeping with the principle of the good. As long as the soul allows reason to guide and coordinate our words and thoughts, our deeds and actions will be directed at the good. This is because through reasoning, the needs of the spirit and appetite will be recognised and satisfied and reason can harmonise these three elements within a whole.

When applying this analogy to structural justice of the polis, it indicates that justice is the harmony amongst these three classes of people and these three aspects of governance. This conception of justice also suggests that reason be the gift of the rulers, who, according to Plato, are lovers of wisdom and whose sole purpose is to balance and cohere communal activities, citizens' awareness, political processes and diverse drives and needs within the polis. A wise ruler cares most for what he loves most. Thus, as lovers of wisdom, the rulers will bear no personal interests, and they are only guided by reason. For Plato, enlightened wise rulers are servant leaders, using a modern-day term. Their flourishing lies in their being liberated from the concerns of everyday lives, being respected by their fellow citizens and being a contributor to the peace and harmony of a thriving polis. That is to say, the life of a rule as a lover of wisdom is closest to the divine life of the gods.

In *The Republic*, Plato further highlights that humans are teleologically oriented to pursue reasoned life. Wise rulers who establish structural justice can deter injustice and all forms of tyranny, (e.g. force and aggression). A similar situation can be expected in terms of the relational dynamics between

---

4 Kraut, "Reason and Justice in Plato's Republic."

people in the polis. As already touched upon, just souls, like the just polis, can maintain harmony amongst the drives, needs and forces within oneself through reason. This means that a person will not succumb to strong desires (e.g. lust for sexual gratification), nor give in to greed, anger and other destructive emotional forces. By applying reason, one will not prioritise one's self-interests over those of others, nor take advantage of the weak and the vulnerable. What is implied here is that the good life for one depends on the caring of others in the community and the wider caring culture of the society in which each person is a part.[5] In this sense, Plato's ethical theories, political thoughts and conceptions of love are not separate.

Despite the myriad critiques of Plato's political ideals,[6] the central place of love in his ethics and political philosophy remains significant and positive. Love as caring for wisdom as the highest good determines that the best leaders of the polis are wise persons whose souls are just and harmonised by reason. Love as caring also inspires us to love and care for others for their own sake, in the same way that leaders govern and care for the governed for their own sake. Just world requires love of wisdom and care for non-instrumental values, and these are to be prioritised in laws as part of constructing structural justice.

***

Aristotle: Love as civic and political engagement and action

Following Plato and through the work of Aristotle, especially in his writings, such as *Nicomachean Ethics*, *Politics* and other treatises, there has been a strong tradition that views meaningful yearning and consequent action as being at the heart of love. On such conceptions, the central and most important feature of love is that it involves desiring the well-being of our beloved and acting in pursuit of their well-being for its own sake. Love is thus conceived of as issuing practical imperatives to actions of certain kinds: love as caring commands us to desire and act for the good of our beloved.

Aristotle regards love as caring a vital component of a meaningful and flourishing life and an ideal basis for the cohesion of political communities, the establishment of personal and political justice and the achievement of

---

5 Brown, "Plato's Ethics and Politics in *The Republic*."
6 Notably Strauss, *The City and Man*; Popper, *The Open Society and its Enemies*; Vlastos, "The Individual as an Object of Love in Plato"; Kraut, *The Cambridge Companion to Plato*.

the highest common good. The good, in Aristotle's view, is a matter of fully developing our distinctive and essential natural capacities – the capacities for living well, being well and becoming well. For human beings, this essential and distinctive nature is the possession of reason. The human good, then, involves fully developing our rational nature, through cultivating excellences or virtues of our character, such as intellectual dispositions to think and reason well, moral and practical dispositions to act appropriately and affective dispositions to feel emotions when and to the degree they are appropriate.

For Aristotle, love as caring rooted in the virtues of good character of humans can determine how we live the common life in the community and the society. Indeed, Aristotle famously claims that human beings are both social and political animals and a flourishing life is only unfolded in the polis, or political community. Agreeing with Plato in *Politics*, Aristotle maintains that polis is founded for the sake of our collective life, our living well together. The good life is hence the proper end of the polis.

Aristotle stresses some prerequisites in *Politics* in terms of how we might pursue the good life together. First, a flourishing life in the community requires loving and caring structural features of the polis, such as the protection of law and constitutions that outline how the governance of the city-state can aim to ensure common advantage of all its citizens. This is a basis of social justice – structural fairness and equality.

As political animals, humans naturally engage in complex participatory and collaborative activities directed by the ends of the good and the just. Accordingly, active participation in the political life of the polis constitutes citizenship. Thus, people in the polis should be interested in all citizens' being decent, just-minded and respectable moral persons. These concerns are particularly applicable to those who are in leadership positions, such as lawmakers and politicians. In the case of leaders, according to Aristotle, each should know their fellow citizens personally, be familiar with each other's dispositions, feel connected to them and take responsibility to support their virtuous characters. As we have seen in Chapter 4, this is because friends or fellow citizens are our other selves. The same concerns also apply to the ways that citizens feel for and about each other. In Aristotle's view, love as caring brings forward our shared pursuits which aim to enrich our common life. In other words, living in a political community is as if living in an enlarged family where everyone loves and cares for each other.

The virtues of good character become a matter of fully expressing and acting upon our nature as rational social animals in a political community and living in a proactive way in accordance with our place in the cosmos as a whole. Virtuous character in this sense cannot be static, but rather it marks such a quality of our action that can enable us to pursue an ethical life with others, care for our loved ones and their well-being, and contribute to the good life in the polis. Love as caring in this context becomes civic engagement, working with others towards the common good.

It is important to note that for Aristotle, the common good achieved through collective (and often political) action is not the sum of individual goods attained through cooperation. Instead, the common good is a genuinely collective good belonging to all. The triumphs and fortunes of each person constitute a benefit to or an advantage of every other member of the political community. It is here that Aristotle also devotes a significant amount of attention to civic friendship. Civic friendship or friendship-love is special because although it is a form of advantage-friendship as we have discussed in Chapter 4, it does not have to purely apply to situations where one wants to use friends or friendship for personal advantage, or self-interest. Instead, civic friendship can be formed on the basis of the experience of mutual benefit received through our collective endeavours of participating in the civic life of the political community.

Once again, structural features are important for Aristotle because laws, political processes and governance approaches of the polis can intentionally cultivate civic friendship, allowing people to support and benefit each other. Indeed, Aristotle suggests that good legislators should be more concerned with fostering civic friendship than with putting citizen's relationships on a footing of justice. This is because legislations of justice, when narrowly conceived as legality, can imply a lack of trust, or lack of well-wishing. Whereas when the focus of political structure is directed towards nurturing civic friendship, there is no need for legislations of justice because friends will do what is just for each other and more, out of their love and care for each other.

In *Nicomachean Ethics*, Aristotle highlights the centrality of love as caring:

> those who are merely just in their mutual relations have need also of friendship, whereas those who are friends do not need to become just in addition: they already acknowledge reasons not to harm or work to disadvantage and can be expected to reach an accommodation without having to invoke strict rules of justice. Those who are truly friends will not wrong one another – not, however, out of love of justice and legality, but from love of one another.[7]

---

7 Aristotle, *Nicomachean Ethics*, 1155a26-27.

The last sentence stresses love as caring to serve as an anchor of just society. For Aristotle, the deeper the caring for each other, the more complete the civic friendship and the more just a social system. That is to say, love as the ultimate concern invites caring actions from all citizens. By cultivating civic friendship in a political community, lawmakers can draw on the qualities embodied by virtuous persons in establishing a legal system which in turn will encourage cities to act with affection and care towards all other fellow citizens in the polis.

In recognising that love is at the root of people's moral dispositions, good will towards others and caring actions for the good of the polis, Aristotle affirms that a flourishing life is where love in civic friendship is appreciated non-instrumentally but acted upon with care and justice that can bring advantage and benefit to all. This is a great example of where *non-instrumental* acts can also serve people's shared interests *instrumentally*. By emphasising that human beings are social and political beings, Aristotle points to our natural tendency to live together in political communities and to act in ways that enhance mutual interests and lead to mutual benefits. As Aristotle puts it, love at its best involves acting 'at the right times, about the right things, toward the right people, for the right end and in the right way'.[8]

Love as ultimate concern and caring action is further captured by Aristotle in his articulation of phronesis, which means practical wisdom. Although practical wisdom does not specify what we must care, it does help us understand how we must act in order to pursue the object of our care. In this way, phronesis is a 'reasoned and true state of capacity to act with regard to human goods'.[9] Through reasoning, phronesis, also termed as praxis, engenders acts directed at well-articulated genuine goodness, a key to unifying human virtues in the ways that are both appropriate and balanced (i.e. through the mean, as articulated in *Nicomachean Ethics*). This is pragmatism in our action 'relative to the person, the circumstances and the object'.[10]

Hence love as caring is essential to our taking active responsibilities for our communal and political life – each person must take a positive and active role in promoting the common good. Active life based on love and civic friendship allows space for optimism in cosmopolitanism.

***

---

8 Ibid., 1106b.
9 Ibid., 1140b20-25.
10 Ibid., 1122a25-6.

Epictetus: 'Hope a Little Less, Love a Little More'

Classical Stoic philosophy stresses the importance of living in the here and now, contrary to their counterparts, such as Platonic and Aristotelean philosophies, which tend to have transcendence at their core. For the Stoics, transcendence is important, but it is within immanence that transcendence takes place.[11] This might have explained Epictetus's critique of 'hope'. In his *Discourses*, Epictetus argues that a flourishing life is a life without attachments, devoid of *hopes* and hence fears. It ought to be a life of acceptance and a life lived fully in the present. In doing so, he also maintains that the good life must be fully aligned with the inherent harmony in the divine whole. The question is how one might act from love and care but also from non-attachment.

As we have seen in Chapter 2, feelings and emotions such as 'grief, fear, desire, envy, malice, avarice, effeminacy and in temperance' are regarded by Stoics as the result of inappropriate attachment.[12] These are hindrances to the good life. Rather than being driven by things outside of oneself, we must seek the right attachment, or right relationship. For instance, by looking to God, or nature and attaching oneself to God, or nature, one can turn inwards to the true object of love as the basis for the good life and happiness. This happens when we have 'reached contemplation and understanding and a manner of life harmonious with nature'.[13] For some commentators, this idea of right attachment resembles what is proposed in the classic Eastern philosophical thoughts, such as those found in Buddhism.[14] In the Stoic philosophy, especially in Epictetus's ethics, it is maintained that through love, not attachment, that one cares for, participates in and contributes to a common flourishing life within the cosmopolis.[15]

As a start, Epictetus makes an important distinction between instrumental and non-instrumental ends. He uses the example of going to a festival or fair to illustrate the differences. For some people, the sole purpose of going to a festival or a fair is to trade and make money and therefore their focus is on the animals or things to purchase or to sell, and they have little interest in anything else. This, to Epictetus, is a form of instrumentalisation – instrumentalising

---

11 Ferry, *A Brief History of Thought*.
12 Epictetus, *Discourses*, II, 16, 45.
13 Ibid., I, 6.22.
14 Ferry, *A Brief History of Thought*.
15 This remaining part of the discussion chiefly draws on Magrin, 'Nature and Utopia in Epictetus' Theory of Oikeiōsis.'

one's experiences purely as a means to an end. By contrast, one can go to a festival or a fete and enjoy the scenes, including everything that makes a festival delightful and exciting in and of itself. That is to say, they come to the festival or the fair to experience and take delight in the festival or the fete non-instrumentally. In the latter case, people will participate in the myriad activities and appreciate the scenes for their own sake. These people who take delight in things in themselves and for themselves are called by Epictetus 'lovers of sights' and those who have the capacity to truly appreciate the delightfulness in all the activities and the scenes (or the good in Plato's sense) are called 'lovers of the sight of the truth'.[16] In this case, Epictetus likens the 'lovers of the sight of the truth' to the wise rulers or enlightened lovers of wisdom as in Plato's *Republic*.

Unlike Plato, Epictetus believes that all can be lovers of the sight of the truth. Stoics sees the cultivation of virtuous life as an imperative and such qualities must be pursued by all. How might one become virtuous and therefore live a truly flourishing life depends on how one engages with things worthy of our loving and caring. In other words, it depends on how one directs one's love and care. As the festival analogy illustrates, if one directs one's ultimate concern to things that are mere means to ends, they can be forever chasing ends that are outside of themselves – making money so that we can become wealthier, so that we can feel more secure, so that they can feel more respected, so that ... and so that ... Such pursuit also creates illusions of 'hope' – we are always chasing some ends which hold the promise to fulfil our desires and wants.

As we discussed in Chapters 3 and 4, one of the greatest obstacles to a flourishing life, from the Stoics's perspective, is our emotional attachments which introduce both hopes and fears. Instead of attaching ourselves and our love and care to things that are instrumental, or to ends that are external, people must direct loving and caring inward so as to, in Epictetus's words, 'never to be disappointed in their desires, or fall prey to what they wish to avoid, but to lead personal lives free from sorrow, fear and perturbation'.[17]

Another way of looking at this piece of advice from Epictetus is that we should not only focus on what lies beyond the present moment, in which case, the *beyond* might be equated to the desire for more, for growth and for transcendence. Instead, we are advised to remember that our purpose also lies in appreciating and accepting things of value in themselves for their own sake, such as our life, including all its complexity, in the here and now. By

---

16 Magrin, 'Nature and Utopia in Epictetus' Theory of Oikeiōsis,' 302.
17 Epictetus, *Discourses*, II, 14, 8.

focusing on the present, we can be free from those wants and desires which can disappoint or imprison us, further introducing more wants and potentially more dissatisfaction and likewise more fears and frustrations.

Most importantly, according to the Stoics, in pursuing these instrumental ends that are supposed to take us to the promised future, we are leaving behind the essence of the good life – that is a life *lived* in ways that are aligned with the principles of cosmos. The word *lived* is crucial here as the Stoics's endeavours to be free from attachment, to be liberated from wants, hopes and fears, are precisely by living a good life through partaking in the harmony of nature and by loving and caring for oneself and for others within the cosmopolis. For the Stoics, becoming part of the order of the cosmos and participating in and contributing to the harmony in the cosmopolis is human's true destiny. This means we must accept this life of love and caring as our primary choice, as the fundamental yearning of our soul and as the focus of our being and acting.

Additionally, as we have seen in the earlier chapters, for the Stoics, hope and fear are both undesirable or even dangerous emotions also because they are irrational and can designate the wrong attachment to things. Wrong attachment can further inhibit our active life. For instance, if our life is dominated by fear of loss and fear of death, we can be inhibited from loving those whom we cherish. To escape such a vicious cycle, Epictetus suggests:

> Remind yourself [...] that what you love is mortal, that what you love is not your own. It is granted to you for the present and not irrevocably, not for ever, but like a fig or a bunch of grapes in the appointed season [...][18]

Epictetus is inviting us to actively live out our love for what we truly care, in spite of its impermanence, rather than worrying about the loss of what we love in the future. Luc Ferry's reading of this passage is that Epictetus is advising us 'to content ourselves with the present, to love the present to the point of desiring nothing else and of regretting nothing whatsoever'.[19] Living in the present does not mean to ignore the past nor to neglect the future, but it does mean that each person must live in the moment, in Epictetus' words, 'as if it *were* the last'.[20] It is a matter of conquering our fear of mortality, the cure of the perennial search for redemption, for transcendence.

---

18 Ibid., III, 24 84–8.
19 Ferry, *A Brief History of Thought*, 48.
20 Epictetus, *Meditation*.

Returning to the earlier discussion in this section about the Stoics's focus on the non-instrumental values in their loving and caring, we can see why Epictetus famously proposes that we should all 'hope a little less, love a little more'. The good life consists in loving and caring for the sake of living well and rationality can help clarify the true object of our love and our caring. Equally, rationality can guide us to live in accordance with the harmony of the cosmos.

Christian Perspective on Love as Caring

> *We call to mind, before our God and Father, how your faith has shown itself in action, your love in labour and your hope of our Lord Jesus Christ in fortitude.*
>
> —St. Paul, *Thessalonians, 1:3*

Christian political theology tends to be regarded as rooted primarily in the thoughts of St Augustine and St Thomas who have laid the ethical foundation for Christian principles of politics. In Chapters 3 and 4, we have seen that syntheses on *erôs*, *philia* and *agapē* and relational mutual indwelling are so complete and original that they have simultaneously advanced love as virtue and justice, including the imperative of loving and caring one's self and one another through the love of God. Indeed, God's love sets an example for humans to act with love and care in ways that seek nothing in return. It is God's love that is working in human love. That is to say, we love each other because God loves us all, irrespective of race, background, social status or occupation.

In this sense, unlike their Greek counterparts, Christian political theology is fundamentally concerned with the common good, and less with how to structure the society and how to live together in the political community. Nevertheless, in the light of the wound of the *Fall*, both St Augustine and St Thomas are mindful of the importance of any political regime to be redemptive, reconciliatory and healing. In addition, Augustine and Thomas seem to think that the more the common good is achieved, the more fitted citizens will be for ruling and in turn being ruled democratically. One political structure proposed is a mixed regime with aristocratic and kingly elements.

Amidst Christian thoughts is the emergence of argument for justice as deserving one's due. As we shall see, this argument would have introduced two aspects in the practices of Western democracy: the first is that justice is an individualistic notion, based on what a person deserves and merits; the second is that justice is only made possible through God's love. God's love establishes an authority and a divine order, to which humans must submit ourselves and towards which humans must seek transcendence.

***

St Augustine: Justice as pursuing the right-ordered love

Throughout his extensive corpus, including treatises, sermons and letters, St Augustine intends to teach perennial virtues to humans who are finite and fallible. Because of human limitations and imperfections, no conditions nor institutions would enable us to ever be God-like. In this case, only love as a force can deliver humans closer towards God. In Chapter 3, we point out that, according to Augustine, God is love and love can must be appreciated as love for the sake of love itself and not for the sake of any other ends. In Chapter 4, we explore Augustine's conception of God's Trinity and how the trinitarian qualities are reflected in the human soul and the relational nature of love. In *On Christian Doctrine*, Augustine goes a step further and suggests that one can love and appreciate one's self and one's neighbour in a similar way as loving and appreciating God. This teaching allows Augustine to pave the way for us to understand love as caritas, or caring, which is 'the spirit's motion toward enjoying God for himself and enjoying one's self and one's neighbor for God'. Love as caritas/caring propels us to dwell in union with God and thereby with other fellow beings.

In this chapter, we explore St Augustine's political theology, especially his view on how love as caring might help shape the order of our political and communal life together.

Born and growing up at a time of violent wars, St Augustine's political theology is first reactive towards the lack of peacefulness in the world. For instance, in the *City of God*, he reflects on what the Roman Empire has done, 'in the interests of peaceful collaboration, [that] imposes on nations it has conquered the yoke of both law and language'. He then asks: 'But at what cost! There is one war after another, havoc everywhere, tremendous slaughterings of men. [...] All this for peace?'[21] As we shall see, embedded here is Augustine's vision of peace – positive peace (the presence of peacefulness in one's inner life and in the political community), rather than negative peace (the absence of violence and war). He argues that peace cannot be achieved with violence, and wars are not the solution to end wars. This is a pacifist position, in line with his other writings, for instance in his treatise on freewill, in which he advocates non-violence in that no one shall have the moral right to kill even in defence of life, liberty and honour.

Notwithstanding his insistence on non-violence and positive peace, he goes on and develops his own just war theory. The theory aims to deliberate on the necessary conditions for justifying engagement in war or *jus in bellum* and the necessary conditions for conducting war in a just manner or *jus in bello*. On the former, Augustine presents three conditions as necessary justification to

---

21 Augustine, *The City of God*, 19.7.

engage in war: (1) a just cause, that is, to defend the state from external invasion; and to defend the safety or honour of the state; (2) a rightly intended will, such as the restoration of peace; and (3) a declaration of war by a competent authority. Concerning the latter, Augustine proposes to conduct war only in a manner that (a) represents a proportional response to the wrong to be avenged, with violence being constrained within the limits of military necessity; (b) discriminates between proper objects of violence (i.e. combatants) and non-combatants, such as women, children, the elderly, the clergy and so forth; and (c) observes good faith in its interactions with the enemy, by scrupulously observing treaties and not prosecuting the war in a treacherous manner.

Clearly, there is tension between his position on non-violence and his ideas on what might constitute a just war. The way Augustine deals with the tension is by distinguishing the City of God and the city of man. As justice through love as caring remains the primacy of the Kingdom of God, war is the last resort for the preservation of the worldly kingdom. To maintain peace in the kingdom of man, governments or states will necessarily engage in acts outlined in the just war theory. Indeed, in his political theology, Augustine does not perceive the fundamental role of the government as to inspire peacefulness and engender harmony in the society. Instead, he considers the function of the government to be defending the people against violence, especially external violence, such as invasion or conquest. This does not mean that Augustine encourages governments to use force. For Augustine, governments must create the peaceful conditions where humans can order and harmonise their life in tranquillity. Ultimately, Peace of Babylon cannot be organised by the government but sought by people themselves who actively cultivate love and other virtues and pursue a loving, caring and virtuous (inner) life together. Virtues do require structural conditions to flourish, but Augustine lays emphasis on people cultivating their inner moral compass by aligning themselves to God. Loving God can lead to self-transcendence and hence inner harmony, without which there could not be a peaceful society. In Augustine's words, there is the need for 'right order within man himself'. The right order within man arises from love of God, which, as we shall see, contrasts Thomasian view of structural peace based on love.

For Augustine, an active and well-ordered inner life anchors the society's moral foundation for justice, which comprises what is *right* and thereby what is *just* for the soul, such that each is given what belongs to one, and can claim one's due. This reflects the 'just order of nature', which Augustine describes as the *right order*, applicable to the right relationship between body and soul, as well as between human soul and God. He writes: 'And this holds for the right order within man himself, so that it is just for the soul to be subordinate to God and the body to the soul and thus for the body and soul taken together to be subject to God.'[22] This integrated view sees justice (which is otherwise and conventionally conceived as a social and political dynamic) to be aligned with the right order of a person's inner life, mirroring the right order in nature.

Hence, according to Augustine, justice is integral to his conception of love as valuing, relationing and caring. Augustine argues that love of God is the source of justice, and it is in loving of God that humans experience love of each other, without which a political community will be lacking in the right order and 'devoid of true justice'.[23] Augustinian justice is situated within the two Christian commandments: love of God and love of neighbour. Thus, what people love and how people love would determine the way the society carries out justice. Only by loving God can man live by the right order defined by God, for according to Augustine, God is love and God is truth. In this sense, social justice is determined by love because any common good is always found in love of God which is extended to love of others. Therefore, for Augustine, all governments must be concerned with justice, without which, he asks: 'what are kingdoms but gangs of criminals on a large scale? What are criminal gangs but petty kingdoms?'[24]

A truly just polis must be the City of God, rather than a city of man. The latter is dominated by man's desires and self-interests above love of God and the interests of others. The polis, despite its best intention, will not be able to deliver humans from their fall, nor to impose onto men their teleological end, which is interpreted by Augustine as loving God. Any 'justice' that is self-serving cannot be relational nor restorative.[25] Above all, 'justice' serving self-interest cannot be redemptive nor transcendent. Self-serving justice will remain merely at the level of retributive (*incurvatus in se*). Only in loving God in the fullest sense, man can truly take delight in God's being, which in turn is reflected in his loving actions, including loving and caring for others and loving and caring for the goodness in the world. As what is just mirrors the right order of nature, justice also includes tuning-in towards the natural order that God has bestowed unto the world. Thus, justice is amongst the four cardinal virtues outlined by Augustine (in addition to prudence, fortitude, and temperance),

---

22 Ibid., 19.4.
23 Ibid., 19.26.
24 Ibid., 4.5.
25 Krause, *Augustine on Love, Justice, and Pluralism in Human Nature*.

and justice determines the essence of the Christian life, to be pursued and lived as the good life in accordance with God and nature.[26]

However, for Augustine, although there are four cardinal virtues, there is only one virtue when it comes to conceiving the good life as living by the right order defined by God and exemplified by nature. This is the virtue of love as caring. In the *City of God*, Augustine writes:

> We must, in fact, observe the right order even in our love for the very love with which we love what is deserving of love, so that there may be in us the virtue which is the condition of the good life. Hence, as it seems to me, a brief and true definition of virtue is 'rightly ordered love'.[27]

Clearly Augustine regards justice as the *work* of rightly ordered love and to be just is to reclaim what was lost in the *Fall* of humanity, which can only be healed and restored through the love of God and love of others. To live justly is to re-orient love within one's self in the right order – towards God. In this way, each person is assigned and receives their appropriate due of love. By allowing the fallen to regain their righteous place in the cosmos, Augustine's justice is not only restorative but also generative by fostering an ethic of love that can engender caring for those who have transgressed. More importantly, justice is re-conciliative amongst human beings in the same way that love enables man to reconcile with God.

Therefore, Augustine's account of justice is pro-social, aimed at restoring the relational nature of human's being and returning our polis to its original state (i.e. loving, peaceful and harmonious). Instead of leaving the power of ordering the society to the government, Augustine insists on a spiritual approach to governance by pledging to the loving nature of humanity. A government that is designated to use rules and laws to discipline (and punish) its citizens is only based on man's fear for each other, fear of punishment and desire for domination. Such an approach to governance can only be coercive and imposed from outside of human beings. Whereas in the *City of God*, justice or the right order of love is defined by God's grace and thereby constitutes human dignity and intrinsic worth. Accordingly, in *City of God*, Augustine argues:

---

26 Ibid.
27 Augustine, *The City of God*, 19.

[i]t follows that justice is found where God, the one supreme God, rules an obedient City according to this grace, [...] and where in consequence the soul rules the body in all men who belong to this City and obey God and the reason faithfully rules the vices in a lawful system of subordination; so that just as the individual righteous man lives on the basis of faith which is active in love, so the association, of people, of righteous men lives on the same basis of faith, active in love, the love with which a man loves God as God ought to be loved and loves his neighbour as himself.[28]

This passage highlights a hierarchy of justice in the right-ordered love, in which and through which, we find God's grace at the highest level, followed by the purity of the human soul and then the human body. When integrated and active, the right-ordered love moves from love of one's self to love of others, both of which are expressions of love of God, directed towards love of God. Only when there is such justice based on love, there can be 'association of men united by a common sense of right and by a common interest' and hence the 'commonwealth'.[29] In Augustine's view, such a hierarchy of justice forms the ascending order of human spiritual development elevated by love and through our relationship with Christ, who 'is our peace',[30] each step of transcendence can take us closer to the union with God.

In addition to the ascent through human spiritual development, Augustine also has an ascending vision for the hierarchy of human society. He writes: 'After the city comes the world community. This is the third stage in the hierarchy of human associations. First, we have the home; then the city; finally, the globe.'[31] Clearly, instead of institutions, according to Augustine, governments must be rooted in human associations or our political communities.

What truly distinguishes peace in the City of God and peace in the city of man, for Augustine, is love. The City of God is a just place where God's love permeates all aspects of people's life in the political community. This view of government and governance is progressive, even in our present time.

***

---

28 Ibid., 19.23.
29 Ibid., 19.23.
30 Ephesians 2.14.
31 Augustine, *The City of God*, 19.7.

Thomas Aquinas: Caritas as caring action

Love as caring or *caritas* is a central argument in St Thomas's political theology. Caritas refers to engaging in loving and caring acts with the full appreciation of what these acts are directed at, that is, the good of one's beloved. Acting lovingly and caringly also presupposes that the actor understands God's love and what it means to love and care in ways that are in line with God's definition of love. In other words, caritas is an act based on will and reason. Chapter 4 illustrates how Thomas develops love's relationality through the notion of mutual indwelling which transcends the lover's life experience. According to Thomas, it is love that urges us to respond appropriately to the existence and recognition of goodness, by loving and forming a relationship, paradigmatically and primarily, with God and secondarily, with human beings, who partake in divine goodness. Love yearns for intimacy and relationship which both conditions and is conditioned by benevolent desires. Thomas regards love's yearnings as essential for humans to attain a meaningful and flourishing life. Love seeks the value in union with divine goodness, whether that resides in God, or in the reflected divinity in human beings.

In Part II of *Summa Theologiae*, Thomas explores love as caring in the context of a theological conception of God as love. From a Thomasian perspective, love as caring is instantiating and partaking in God's nature. Following Augustinian idea that God is to be enjoyed for Himself, Thomas proposes that caritas involves that we love God for Himself. This is because God is Himself the end of all things. God does not need any form in order to be good; God's form is His goodness. God's goodness exemplifies all other goods. God is the source of all things good and, therefore, God is to be loved for Himself.

Thomas further maintains that as a virtue, caritas already implies an inclination to a loving and caring act. He suggests that to be loved and cared for is not the true act of caritas but rather, to love and to care is such an act. To love is more proper to caritas because the act of loving and caring is for its own sake, rather than for the sake of something else. Thomas uses two examples to illustrate this point. The first example is found in friendship-love which is for the sake of loving the friend rather than for the sake of being loved by the friend. The second example is found in a mother's love which for Thomas is the greatest act of love and care. Mothers seek to love and to care, not to be loved nor cared for in return.

As a virtuous act, caritas applies to one's friend and neighbour, but it equally applies to one's enemy. Thomas demonstrates the intricate connections between these two acts of love. At first glance, it seems that loving our friend and neighbour surpasses loving our enemy because we are closer to our friend and close to our neighbour, and we are already in union with our friend and to some extent in union with our neighbour. Loving our enemy, by contrast, is not an act based on personal affinity. In fact, we love our enemy for no other reason than for the sake of God. That is to say we love our enemy because we love God. Love for God allows us to extend our affection to those who are most distant and furthest from us (i.e. our enemy). Loving and caring for our friend and neighbour and loving and caring for enemy are directed towards the common good. The common good, for Thomas, is ultimately the goodness of God for which we should all show greater love. Accordingly, other beings, including angels, humankind and all God's creations, have a natural love for God and for the common good.

In *Ethics*, Thomas proposes that an understanding of the common good can serve as the basis for engaging in ethical and political life. For example, the individual good is always secondary in the light of the common good. In this sense, love as caring might be ordered in accordance with the hierarchy of the good. At the base is individual good; next, the good of the community; to follow, the good of the humankind; beyond that, towards the good of the whole that humans are constituted. The truest and greatest common good is always already included in God's goodness. Thus, the 10 Christian commandments are to guard the common good: the first 4 commandments are oriented towards the common good rooted in the goodness of God and the next 6 commandments are oriented towards the common good that is present amongst human beings. The latter are constituted in justice.

In a political community, according to Thomas, love and justice are mutually constituted. The common good of the community can determine how people are treated in the community. For instance, Thomas assumes that anyone who jeopardises the communal common good should be punished. Any punishment, however severe, such as death penalty, must be carried out as an act of love, which both delivers the transgressor from sins and safeguards the political community's common good. For any political community, a punishment is necessary if aimed at preserving the harmony, peace and well-being of the whole community and promoting the common good for all.

With this understanding of the common good as an ethical compass, human society can identify political strategies, such as the exercise of authority, legislation, taxation, exemption, modification, punishment and equally devotion, resistance, sacrifice and so forth, always through the evaluative lens of the common good. For example, in loving and caring for the common good, citizens must be willing to forego their personal goods when required to preserve and enhance the common good. In the same vein, citizens should be prepared to sacrifice their personal goods, such as their well-being, for anyone who is consisted in the common good. This may mean prioritising the well-being of leaders of the community, or defenders of the community, and others. The point here is the act of loving and caring must be directed at the common good which always takes precedence over personal interests.

Take the dispensation of law and justice as an example. In Book V of *Ethics*, Thomas recognises human differences, the inherent limitation and fallibility of human judgement, the contingency of the common good and the historical contexts within which laws apply. In the case when people tend to direct loving act towards one another and towards the common good, Thomas proposes different kinds of justice should pertain to each situation. Justice applicable to loving our neighbour will be different from justice applicable to caring for the common good. For Thomas, the former is prudence and the latter is political prudence. Both are prudent, as if of scale, but in effect, both are prudent because, from Thomas' metaphysical account of the common good, human goods cannot exist independent of the common good and each of these goods is constituted in the good of the whole, which is ultimately God's good.

In political and religious communities, according to Thomas, people should practise obedience to true authority that directs us towards the common good. Likewise, people should practise disobedience and resistance to tyranny that diverts the community from the common good. Both obedience and disobedience are an act of love and justice. The apparent tension between obedience to authority and disobedience to tyranny in the context of both political and religious communities is resolved by regarding love as a moral act of caring and living out our virtues.

***

Martin Luther: Love as acting righteously

For Martin Luther, life's greatest challenge and most important task are for us to decide upon the *right* path to take. In *Two Kinds of Righteousness*, Luther explores the external righteousness and internal righteousness and suggests that we are called to act righteously out of the imperative to love and to care.

External righteousness is termed 'alien righteousness' by Luther because it is the righteousness 'of another, instilled from without'.[32] The source of the external righteousness is through faith in Christ and in God's grace. It is a gift of love from God. Through faith, God's righteousness is bestowed on man.[33] For Luther, the internal righteousness is our personal righteousness, which he calls 'our proper righteousness'. Although personal, the notion does not assume that we work towards it alone, but rather, personal or internal righteousness derives from and is rooted in God's grace, the external righteousness. Internal righteousness consists of loving our neighbour by obeying God, which enables us to live justly and devoutly. Hence, love, joy, peacefulness, goodness and other virtues are the fruit of God's love. Personal righteousness does not seek goodness for our own sake, but for the sake of others and their well-being. This caring, according to Luther, is what living righteously entails and 'it works love'.

Righteousness, as Luther explains, is our soul's commitment to each other's spirit and to God. 'I am yours' is how Luther describes the soul's commitment to another whereby the soul seeks no righteousness in and for itself, but through Christ's righteousness, it seeks only the well-being of others. With this, Luther teaches us not to feel superior nor better than our neighbour. Superiority here is the greatest perversion because it is contrary to love. Instead, we must take it as our own burden when our neighbour is sinful, foolish or weak. Righteousness ensures that we must love more intensely those who are less righteous, less wise and less powerful and serve them more devotedly to restore their well-being. In this way, righteousness means that we are always already bound up with our neighbour and we act in ways that demonstrate we have our neighbour's situations in mind and we care for them deeply.

Shouldn't wickedness and sin be punished? Aren't laws there to ensure punishment? Luther responds that we cannot truly judge and punish the evil and defend the weak and the oppressed. It is only God who can do this. Laws and representatives of laws are only there to serve God's righteousness. For those in the position to serve God's laws, Luther advises that public officials cannot make a case to defend their own interest, but they can invite someone else to be God's representative and make judgement accordingly.

---

32 Martin Luther, *Two Kinds of Righteousness*.
33 Luther recalls in *Two Kinds of Righteousness* the prayer, Psalm 30: 'in thee, O Lord, do I seek refuge; let me never be put to shame; in thy righteousness deliver me!' Therefore, it is God's righteousness.

The same practice of righteousness applies to personal matters. Martin Luther objects to using force on another as vengeance against evil being conducted because violence returns us to evil, even if it appears to be tolerating less evil to avoid greater evil. Luther concludes that passion for one's own advantage must be 'destroyed'. As to those who relinquish revenge and suffer the losses, Luther regards them as the most advanced righteous beings because they forbid and prevent evil. Amongst these, are the poor, the orphaned and the widowed or 'the people of Christ', according to Luther, who grieve for the evil conducted by the offender over their own losses and deprived conditions. Luther quotes Matt. 5:44 that:

> they do this that they may recall those offenders from their sin rather than avenge the wrongs they themselves have suffered. Therefore they put off the form of their own righteousness and put on the form of those others, praying for their persecutors, blessing those who curse, doing good to evil-doers, prepared to pay the penalty and make satisfaction for their very enemies that they may be saved.

This description of the generous act of love and care also characterises love in a spirit of gentleness. From here, humans can seek true justice, where *punishment* is sought as a path towards restoration and betterment in the wrongdoer, rather than seeking to serve one's self-interest and compensate for one's loss. This balance is at the heart of justice and for Luther, true justice is a spiritual act of love as caring.

Indeed, Martin Luther's political theology teaches us how to embrace an ethic of love. Through loving acts of caring for the neighbour and loving response to the wrongdoer, an ethic of love offers a genuine freedom, not the freedom from the burden of a paradise lost, nor a freedom through disobedience and revolution. It is rather a spiritual liberation and transformation in and through love. An ethic of love sets us free, either as a wrongdoer, or as a sufferer of wrongdoing. To such extent, T. S. Tsonchev, in an article entitled "Martin Luther's Political Theology: Freedom is Obedience, Justice is Love", suggests that in Lutheran political theology, Christian freedom is not so much freedom '*from* something, i.e., *against* something, but *for* something'. This kind of freedom is not seeking liberty from bondage, but it is liberty to do what is deemed to be righteous.

Our righteousness arises from the soul, or the spirit, which is nourished by God's righteousness. Humans have access to God's righteousness in Christ as a role model. Any political and ethical acts must start with an inward spiritual foundation without which righteousness will only be served and justified from self-interest rather than from love. Following St Augustine, Luther likewise regards justice as love and discusses how love works in the Kingdom of God and kingdom of the world.

In *Temporal Authority*, Martin Luther suggests that only the worldly kingdom requires governance and laws. This is because without spiritual qualities as ethical pillars, the kingdom of the world will require laws and temporal government to secure external peace, prevent evil and maintain the right order of things. Although worldly kingdom has Christian inhabitants, they are there to serve and support the government. This implies that non-Christians are not virtuous people who are subject to evil deeds and therefore laws and authority are established primarily to constrain, coerce and punish those who do not belong to the Kingdom of God, or the spiritual realm. According to Luther, the unrighteous are what the laws are set up to instruct to do good. Therefore, loving and caring as just act only applies to spiritually enlightened Christians.

That is also to say that Luther is not fully confident that all Christians are righteous people and his only faith is in the power of God who can truly renew humanity and transcend humanity towards the spiritual realm. Hence Luther advocates that both Kingdom of God and the kingdom of world are needed so that the spiritual kingdom will continue to inspire righteousness and the worldly kingdom/government will curtail evil. Church and home are from the Kingdom of Heaven and the city-state is from the worldly kingdom. This points to the co-presence of Church and state. Even the state, for Luther, is governed by people who have been given the authority from God to ensure love, caring and peacefulness.

Modernist Understanding of Love as Caring

There are a thousand prizes for noble discourses, none for noble actions.
—Jean Jacques Rousseau

Modernist understanding of love as caring has initially been heavily influenced by the Enlightenment movement, which underlined individual's natural rights and sought to break free from the stronghold of religious authority over truths and meanings of life. Equally, thinkers of this period were influenced by romanticism as the resistance to a purely rational approach to understanding human experiences.

The development of capitalism further invited corresponding political philosophy such as those claims about man's competitive and hostile 'nature' which must be controlled and regulated. Whilst capitalist economy benefited from unquenchable thirst for capital and materialistic gain; science appeared to provide *evidence* about the natural law of survival of the fittest and the tendency of men's insatiable desire for sexual conquest.

Towards late modernity, the world started to shift dramatically. Erich Fromm, a German social psychologist and philosopher, suggests that at this time, our capacity to love is entirely influenced by the cultural, institutional and political processes and practices. How did these shape human's act to love? To this question, Fromm provides a brief contour of Western capitalistic society, whereby the market serves as a regulator of economic and social relations. Under the market forces, many things become commodities, including acts of love and the hierarchy of values. Humans now not only serve the economic engines in organised fashions, but also become consumers to ensure the continued growth of the market. Such a society moulds people into believing in their *freedom* and *independence* whilst being willing to subject themselves to the authority of market, to be commanded by and to comply with the market in order to get ahead and compete for better positions through social mobility. The result is alienation, from one's self, from other people and from nature.[34]

Therefore, it seems that thinkers, writers and researchers have recognised the risk of the breakdown of an entire cultural tradition founded on loving and caring as the ultimate concern.

***

---

34 Fromm, Erich. *The Art of Loving.*

Tullia D'Aragona (1510–1556): Loving and caring infinitely

Tullia d'Aragona was a writer during the Italian Renaissance. She was also a well-known courtesan of the time. The work by which she was most recognised is *Dialogo della Infinita d'Amore*, translated as *Dialogue on the Infinity of Love*. This dialogue has been regarded as significant in both literary and philosophical senses.

The book captures a dialogue in a Platonic style mainly between Benedetto Varchi, a well-known humanist, historian, and poet at the time, and Aragona. It describes a scenario in her own house where Aragona invites Varchi to explore: 'Is it possible to love within limit?'

The dialogue progresses in three processes.

The first move that Varchi takes is to define the terms. Varchi proposes to start with terms such as 'limits' and 'ends' (which are the same thing) as a way to define love from its essence. He puts forward an idea that 'the things that lack an end will also be without a limit and inversely, those that have no limit will also be lacking an end'.[35] Given the fact that this logical move can promptly lead to a simple conclusion in terms of whether it is possible to love within limit, Aragona sets out to broaden the definition by asking whether love, a noun, and to love, a verb, are the same thing.

Aragona then distinguishes these two terms in the following: Love as a noun connotes meaning without time, whereas love as a verb implies time, or involves a temporal dimension. To this, Varchi introduces the Aristotelean notions of substance and accident and points out that nouns tend to have priority in a sentence over verbs and therefore nouns are assumed greater significance. Despite the grammatical difference, Varchi maintains that regardless of the forms of the words, in their essence, love and to love are, in effect, one and the same thing. Varchi then seeks Tullia's definition of love. In response, she suggests that love as a noun is a desire to enjoy what is beautiful or what seems beautiful to the lover; and love as a verb is to desire to enjoy to be united with what is truly beautiful or what seems beautiful to the lover.

They reflect further that it is the beauty of the beloved that activates and animates love and care in the lover. For lovers to love and to care, there must be a cause that moves them. In this case, Aragona regards beauty as the mother of love, or the beloved, the primary moving force and the lover's 'knowledge' of that beauty, the father of love. She says: 'love is born from the knowledge and desire of beauty, both in the soul and in the intellect of the

---

35 Tullia d'Aragona. *Dialogue on the Infinity of Love*, 73.

person who apprehends and desires it.'[36] However, Varchi thinks that it is the opposite, insisting on love and to love being the same and arguing that love is a cause that results in the lover 'to love'. Hence the act of loving is the effect of 'love'.

In the light of the original question, in this sense, Varchi concludes that lovers do not have an end in sight and when one loves, one does not love within limits. Therefore, love is infinite and to love is to love infinitely. For Aragona, love is finite because she has observed many times in her life that men forsake women after making love. Here is the emergence of another set of opposites: on the one hand love is finite and on the other, love is infinite.

To reconcile these opposites and to explore the question further, Aragona takes the second move by differentiating between two types of love: 'vulgar' or 'dishonest' love and 'honest' or 'virtuous' love. Love that is vulgar is the kind of love that comes to an end after the sensational craving is satisfied and the pleasure of the flesh is no longer the object of desire. It reduces love to a despicable act, and therefore it is instrumental. In fact, sometimes, after the thirst is quenched, the sight of the flesh can be met with disgust. Honest love, on the other hand, is love that characterises noble people who have a refined and virtuous disposition. It is not generated by a desire for bodily pleasure nor for procreation, but inspired by reason. Virtuous love is for the sake of loving and constitutes in itself a continuity to love.

Furthermore, Aragona argues that honest love's main end is becoming the beloved. That is to say, the virtuous lover seeks transformation of one's self into the object of one's love. This is a spiritual fusion, a union of body and soul. It is a richer form of love and the act of loving is noble and dignified. In her argument, Aragona contrasts her holistic and integrated view of body and soul with Varchi's conception of these as separate. Aragona postulates that when body and soul are taken together as one, the fusion is more noble and more perfect than the soul (or body) by itself.

This takes the dialogue to a third move. Here by placing vulgar love and honest love alongside each other, Aragona offers a way to harmonise the two loves – where finite physical consummation is insufficient for the depth of true union, the infinite fusion of souls helps attain it. The act of loving as transformation is a process in which the physical union and spiritual union integrate in order to achieve full mutual identification – the lover with the beloved. The physical and spiritual aspects of love converge in a 'virtuous' process. Hence

---

36 Ibid., 80.

Aragona concludes that the lover 'cannot love with a limit'. Vulgar or corporeal love can thus contain in it the potentiality of the nobility and virtues of honest or spiritual love. When the nobility and virtues are actualised in loving, love as caring can increase even after the physical union.

In the dialogue, the two loves, the physical and the spiritual, shift in their features. Aragona argues that the greatest lovemaking can be experienced as spiritual, and the union of the souls can likewise enrich sensual love. As a feminine voice, Tullia's philosophy of love challenges the Christian conception of morality, which tends to dichotomise the physical and spiritual acts of love. In fact, Christian teaching tends to undermine the sensual nature of love and only regards physical union as purely for the sake of procreation. Sexual pleasure is treated otherwise as sin.

The dialogue also provides a vision of love, as a verb, an act of caring for the beauty and goodness in the thing or the person. Love as a verb, or an act of love, seeks the ultimate spiritual and corporeal union, integrating the transcendence and immanence. The feminine perspective, although continuing to be neglected for a long time, had been present in this engaging dialogue on love. As Rinaldina Russel writes in the 'Introduction' to *Dialogue on the Infinity of Love*, 'What makes Aragona's position unprecedented, however, as well as unsurpassed by subsequent writers, is her linking the discussion of love and sex to gender issues.'

Indeed, Aragona brings to the reader's awareness of the gender bias especially when it comes to the matter of understanding and practising love. Her advocacy for gender equality is consistent throughout the dialogue, especially in the way she presumes the intellectual and sexual equality between men and women in virtuous love.

***

Immanuel Kant: Love as duty to care

As part of Kant's philosophy of love is love as duty to care, associated with Kant's account of different forms of love. For Kant, love of humanity is practical love because of its other-regarding nature that makes it one of our ethical imperatives – the duty to love others. He offers a philosophical-psychological account of how the practice and cultivation of duty to love can have the potential to engender thoroughgoingly rational and moral feelings, relationships and actions.

Kant divides the duty to love and to care into three categories: beneficence, gratitude and sympathy. We will briefly discuss each of these.

In *The Metaphysics of Morals*, Kant argues that beneficence is 'the maxim of making others' happiness one's end'.[37] The Christian command to love one's neighbour has been interpreted by Kant as the command to *act* beneficently. Acting towards other's good will engender appropriate moral feelings of love in one. He explains that:

> The saying 'you ought to *love* your neighbor as yourself' does not mean that you ought immediately (first) to love him and (afterwards) by means of this love do good to him. It means, rather, *do good* to your fellow human beings and your beneficence will produce love of them [*Menschenliebe*] in you (as an aptitude of the inclination to beneficence in general).[38]

Therefore, in Kant's view, love as caring involves a moral duty of beneficence. By making the happiness of others one's own end and acting in pursuit of it, one cultivates the feeling of love of humanity in oneself. This feeling of satisfaction in others' well-being makes one receptive to certain duties one has towards them.

Kant also argues that practical love is *itself* directly subject to a law of duty. This 'is a duty of all human beings toward one another, whether or not one finds them worthy of love'.[39] Kant defines practical love as 'the maxim of *benevolence* (practical love), which results in beneficence'.[40] Practical love is neither mere respect for humanity in general[41] nor the mere adoption of a policy of performing beneficent actions.[42] Instead, Kantian practical love is 'the duty to cultivate a benevolent disposition toward other human beings as well as practical beneficent desires'.[43] We touch upon how Kant seeks to harmonise these two tendencies (i.e. benevolence and beneficence) in Chapter 3 where he suggests that we should be not only *wishing* everyone's well-being as one's own end but also acting with such primacy as our underlying intention. Practical

---

37 Kant, *The Metaphysics of Morals*, 6:452.
38 Ibid., 6:402.
39 Ibid., 6:450.
40 Ibid., 6:449.
41 contra Johnson, "Love in Vain," 46.
42 contra e.g. Wood, *Kant's Ethical Thought*, 270; Guyer, *Kant and the Experience of Freedom*, 384.
43 Fahmy, "Kantian Practical Love," 321.

love is *active* love that irreducibly involves both feeling and caring as moral/rational elements: the feeling of satisfaction in the happiness of others and the rational will to promote their well-being.[44] Because the duty of practical love is a duty to cultivate a benevolent disposition (i.e. love of humanity) and beneficent desires (i.e. acting with such care for the well-being of others as our own), it is a duty that cannot be discharged in a single event of decision or action, but a process of infinitely approaching a moral ideal.[45]

As with any moral duty, in Kant's view, it is impartial and universal, but more importantly mutual – because anyone is merely one self amongst other selves, no different from others in respect of being a rational 'I'. In wanting others to be beneficent towards oneself, one is committed to being beneficent towards others and vice versa:

> In accordance with the ethical law of perfection 'love your neighbor as yourself,' the maxim of benevolence is a duty of all human beings toward one another, whether or not one finds them worthy of love. For, every morally practical relation to human beings is a relation among them represented by pure reason, that is, a relation of free actions in accordance with maxims that qualify for a giving of universal law and so cannot be selfish (*ex solipsism prodeuntes*). I want everyone else to be benevolent toward me (*benevolentiam*); hence I ought also to be benevolent toward everyone else.[46]

As already discussed in Chapter 3 about Kant's notion of categorical imperative where human beings must always be treated as ends in ourselves, the above rational justification suggests that in no way can practical love and our duty to care be instrumentalised. One's rational commitment to practical love is a matter of duty and universal impartiality, *not* of doing good to others in the hope of their doing good to oneself. Hence: 'To be beneficent, that is, to promote according to one's means the happiness of other human beings in need, without hoping for something in return, is everyone's duty.'[47]

This Kantian idea that enacting duty to love and to care is meritorious is of deep significance. He divides the duty to others as human beings into the duty of love and the duty of respect. The duty of love is that 'by the performance of

---

44 cf. Rinne, *Kant on Love*, 111.
45 cf. Fahmy, "Kantian Practical Love," 323–4.
46 Kant, *The Metaphysics of Morals*, 6: 451/215.
47 Ibid., 6:453/217.

which you also put others under obligation', whilst the duty of respect is that 'the observance of which does not result in obligation on the part of others'.[48] Accordingly, fulfilment of the first sort is *meritorious*, whereas fulfilment of the second sort is doing something that is owed. Because one is not owed the treatment one receives through acts of love (even though their enactment is a duty of the lover – not supererogatory), they place corresponding obligations of gratitude and reciprocity on the beloved. This implies that the treatment one receives through acts of respect is merely one's due and so the acts of respect do not carry corresponding obligations of gratitude or reciprocity beyond one's pre-existing duty of respect for other persons.

This leads to the second kind of duty of love, gratitude. Kant regards gratitude as that which is done out of respect for the other and a *'sacred* duty'.[49] This means that ingratitude has the tendency to 'destroy the moral incentive to beneficence in its very principle' and so it is not only *incompatible* with the universal duty to cultivate practical love, but also inexhaustible in that 'the obligation with regard to it cannot be discharged completely by any act in keeping with it'.[50] Therefore, as Kant puts it, 'one cannot, by any repayment of a kindness received, be *rid* oneself of the obligation for it, since the recipient can never win away from the benefactor his *priority* of merit, namely having been the first in benevolence'.[51] Acts of love, therefore, set up a system of mutually reinforcing, mutually enhancing and self-sustaining moral duties within a social and political community that intentionally adopts and cultivates reciprocal benevolent, beneficent and appreciative dispositions.

The third sort, according to Kant, concerns our duty of sympathy. We have a conditional duty of humanity to apply our natural feelings of taking pleasure in another's joy or displeasure at another's pain to promote practical love, or active and rational benevolence. These natural feelings might be regarded as compassion, but Kant argues that compassion is a natural kind of sharing in the joys and sufferings of others which is not a duty. Furthermore, there can be no obligation to share in the feelings of others' good or bad fortunes. Instead, our duty of sympathy is based on our rational reasoning to free will – to sympathise with others.

---

48 Ibid., 6:454.
49 Ibid., 6:455.
50 Ibid., 6:455.
51 Ibid., 6:455.

Kant's identifying beneficence, gratitude and sympathy as duties suggests that love and care are more than attitudes or desires, but that love will move us to act in ways that enable us to live out our loving dispositions. This is the basis of an ideal political community where people relate to each other as friends, respect each other, are benevolent towards each other, take delight in each other's well-being and support each other in cultivating loving dispositions. In such a loving community, all persons would collaborate in achieving the community's highest common good. This would be a true cosmopolitan community of love and respect.[52]

Notwithstanding the aspirational and idealising presentation of love in Kant's conception, practical or active love appears problematic, especially in two respects.

Firstly, despite the strenuous attempt to accommodate and assume an important role to several different feelings of love and even taking the cultivation of these to be an essential part of practical love, their value seems to be ultimately that they encourage selfless beneficence towards others out of duty of care. Bringing these feelings in line with our rational moral duties can facilitate the non-conflicted acts of duties, without any reluctance due to countervailing feelings. This seems at odds with the strong intuition that such feelings towards others are themselves deeply important for meaningful relationships with others and that such relationships are equally important to a flourishing life, an aspect we have elaborated extensively in Chapter 4.

Secondly and relatedly, although acknowledging our duties to cultivate appropriate feelings of love for others, it is, in effect, our beneficent caring action towards others that is primary. Whilst it is an exaggeration to suggest that love is simply a beneficent act towards others, as some have interpreted,[53] it is actually not a drastic exaggeration. However, it does not get to the heart of what Kant thinks as important in the imperative to love. In other words, love in the Kantian conception seems too austere to capture what we take love to be, or why it is important. Unsurprisingly, within a conception of ethics (e.g. Kant's) that emphasises impartiality and universality, strong affective attachment to particular persons and prioritising them and their interest as especially invaluable or important to one, and/or as invaluable in themselves, is almost wholly rejected from an ethical perspective. The latter is what

---

52 Rinne, "From Self-Preservation to Cosmopolitan Friendship," §III.3.
53 e.g. Baier, "Unsafe Loves"; Guyer, *Kant and the Experience of Freedom*; Wood, *Kant's Ethical Thought*.

Kierkegaard terms as preferential love. Therefore, this is not an uncommon orientation in philosophical considerations of love in relation to ethics – the partiality of the perspective of love is often seen as antithetical to the universalism of the perspective of morality and it is particularly strong in Kant and in Kierkegaard, which we shall now turn.

***

Søren Kierkegaard (1813–1855): Love as a caring act

Love has been a central thread in Kierkegaard's philosophical thinking, as well as in his political theology. As a Christian existentialist, Kierkegaard has assumed the task to reconcile the life in pursuit of pleasure (sensual and intellectual) and the life in pursuit of eternal meaning. This attempt to wrestle with the tension between the profane and the religious, or the pleasurable and the ethical, also brings to the fore the acts of love as caring. Love in Kierkegaard's thought is the end of our moral acts, following the divine law of 'Thou shalt love thy neighbor as yourself'.[54]

In his seminal work, *Works of Love*, written in 1847, Kierkegaard reminds the reader in his own Foreword that the reflections captured in his book are not about love, but about the 'works of love'. However, works of love, according to Kierkegaard, cannot be fully described, because the whole wealth of such works is inexhaustible and 'because it is essentially present everywhere in its wholeness', it is impossible to describe it.[55] In many ways, the greatest treasure in the works of love lies in the eternity of our being. This is the starting point of Kierkegaard's reflection:

> How earnest, how terrible existence is, just when it chastisingly permits the self-willed man to act for himself, so that he is allowed to live on, glorying in being deceived, until sometime he has to testify that he everlastingly defrauded himself! What is it which connects the temporal and the eternal, what except love, which just for this reason is before everything and which abides when everything else is past?[56]

In *Works of Love*, Kierkegaard distinguishes two kinds of love: Christian love and preferential love. The former mirrors God's love and is our

---

54 Matthew, 22:39.
55 Kierkegaard, *The Works of Love*.
56 Ibid.

unconditional love and caring for the *neighbour*, whereas the latter is loving and caring act directed to our friends, our beloved and others who are physically closer to us. This is a distinction between inwardly love and worldly love, or spiritual love and human love. In this process, Kierkegaard particularly explores the practice of neighbourly love, an act of love applying unconditionally that draws on the wisdom of God's love. Humans desire to love each other and the imperative for humans to love each other is our response to God's love. This includes our self-love. Hence the law also commands that 'You shall love yourself as you love your neighbor when you love him as yourself'.[57] For Kierkegaard, therefore, 'Thou shalt love' is the divine law that depicts our duty to love and to care. Under this law, there are at least three implications.

The first is about the neighbour who, for Kierkegaard, can be one person, as well as all people. In this instance, the neighbour is anyone other than one's self. Hence, Kierkegaard's humanism is inclusive, based on the equality of all. We love our neighbour not because they are more *distinguished* than us, which suggests partiality and selfishness; nor do we love our neighbour because they are inferior to us, which entails condescension. In all cases, we love each other *as a neighbour*. For Kierkegaard, the neighbour is *every man*, 'for he is not your neighbor through the difference, or through the equality with you as in your difference from other men'.[58] We love each other out of our human equality before God.

Second, Kierkegaard regards one's self and one's neighbour on equal terms and that 'every man unconditionally has this equality and has it unconditionally'.[59] When 'everyone is a neighbour', one's self and others are all placed in the same category of the neighbour. This equality grounds our ethical acts of loving and caring in both individual and universal manners at the same time. The notion of *neighbour* is particularly important for Kierkegaard as he believes that had it not been a duty to love and to care, the notion of neighbour would not have existed. Only with it, we can see that all are loved and cared for equally before the divine law.

Third, love as an ethical act of caring is a universal form of love, which is marked by characterising our life into eternity. Indeed, for Kierkegaard, eternity's mark on everyone determines all to be equal through the spirit's love.

---

57 Ibid.
58 Ibid., 55.
59 Ibid., 61.

However, loving our neighbour does not mean that we are ignoring or undermining our love for our beloved, our friends and others close to us. In fact, Kierkegaard advises that we should let the practice of loving the neighbour to be the ethical compass of our everyday and political life:

> love your beloved faithfully and tenderly, but let the love for your neighbor be the more sacred in the covenant of your union with God! Love your friend sincerely and devotedly, but let your love for your neighbor be what you learn from each other in the confidence of friendship with God! Behold, death levels all differences, but partiality always retains the difference, yet the way to life and to the eternal is through death, and through the leveling of differences: therefore only the love to the neighbor truly leads to life.[60]

At the core of his thoughts, Kierkegaard investigates how loving and caring can help transcend human finitude (e.g. death). With this reflection and question, Kierkegaard identifies the act of loving and caring with something more persistent and more enduring. This conception is in stark contrast with the selfish preferential love which will suffer human finitude. We may not have a beloved or friends and we can lose our beloved and our friends, but we can always love and care for a neighbour of whom death cannot deprive us. The wish for the best for the neighbour must be the focus of loving and caring. It is almost as if a life lived without loving and caring for the neighbour is a selfish life, a life of deception and a life of deception and of loss. Whenever one's life stresses self-interests, it is a form of selfishness, which reduces life's meaningfulness and richness.

What is more, for Kierkegaard, loving our beloved, loving our friends and loving others who are close to us tend to involve an object of love and the act of loving; whereas loving the neighbour doesn't involve the object, it only concerns the act of loving. Preferential or earthly love is qualified by the object of love, whereas loving our neighbour is qualified by love itself. In Kierkegaard's view, loving our neighbour is loving everyone, including loving one's enemy. Such love does not discriminate because all persons bear eternal resemblance before God. In this sense, Kierkegaard is almost saying that one loves the neighbour with eyes closed or by looking away from the difference. Hence Kierkegaard

---

60 Ibid., 79.

concludes that loving the neighbour is the perfect love of eternity, beyond our earthly life, temporality and finitude.

In contrast to Kant's view of love's debt, which places those at the receiving end of love in debt to those who are benevolent and kind, Kierkegaard points out that in loving, one places oneself in debt. The following sentence captures this sentiment:

> One can therefore say that this is the essential characteristic of love: that the lover by giving infinitely comes into – infinite debt. But this is a relationship of infinitude and love is infinite.

With this eternity of love in view, Kierkegaard explains how we must shudder at the caste system, the inhuman separation of man from man, the discrimination of one against another and the rejection of kinship with or caring for another. Anyone is a neighbour, and any unloving and uncaring act violates the dignity of being human. For Kierkegaard, that is exactly what Christianity intends to inspire: the divine in the human through spiritual love.

Hence, being human invites our duty to love and to care. We thus love out of love. True lovers of the neighbour will not seek 'justice', 'equality' or 'fairness' of their own. Instead, as advised by Kierkegaard, 'the true lover understands only one thing: to be fooled, to be deceived, to give everything without receiving the least regard'. Loving and caring for the neighbour without seeking one's own self-interest is when love attains its highest perfection and when humans experience the highest quality of well-being and meaning of life.

***

Max Scheler (1874–1928): The phenomenology of love

As a philosopher and sociologist, Max Scheler explored the place of the affect in the good life and integrated a phenomenology of love with an ethic of caring. Termed as 'sociology of the heart', Scheler's investigations of emotions (e.g. shame, guilt, repentance, resentment, hate, sympathy and, above all, love) provided 'material ethics of values as a systematic alternative to Kantian ethics' based solely on rationality.[61] For Scheler, human's *being* involves our moral agency which does not depend on rationality as argued by Kant. Instead,

---

61 Vandenberghe, "Sociology of the Heart: Max Scheler's Epistemology of Love,", 21.

Scheler proposes that human emotions and feelings are the basis of our ethical ways of being in the world. Fundamentally, Scheler conceives humans as loving beings and that our 'primordial relation to the self, the other, the world and God is emotional and that emotions constitute and disclose the world as a world of values'.[62]

In different books, Scheler develops love as an ethic of caring by first identifying and developing a hierarchy of values, according to which he then explores categories of feelings and emotions. Indeed, at a time when investigations into the world were predominantly located within a positivist framework that tended to ignore value-claims, Scheler's formulation of a values-hierarchy has played an influential role in the recognition that humans are bearers of values and our affective and spiritual experiences are constituted in the good life, alongside the cognitive and the rational.

In *Formalism in Ethics*, Scheler identifies four categories of value and makes distinctions between the higher ones and the lower ones which are founded on five principles. In this case, the higher values: (a) are more enduring; (b) are less divisible; (c) serve as the foundation of the lower ones; (d) introduce greater depth of delight; and (e) are more absolute and independent from how people feel about them. In brief, the higher the values, the less dependent they are on the material, the less divisive, the less they are willed and the less mutable.

Based on these principles, Scheler classifies these values into four categories. From lower to higher, there are the values of pleasure and agreeableness (e.g. embodied emotions and feelings), the values of vitality (e.g. life experiences), then the values of mental perception (e.g. beauty, justice, truth), at the highest level the values of holiness. This scheme has been regarded as coherent between the underlying principles and the categories, from the sensory (e.g. physical and emotional goods), to the vital (e.g. a sense or feeling of life), to the spiritual (e.g. goods that are detached and independent of the embodied and lived environment, such as beauty, justice and truth) and ultimately to the holy (e.g. sacrament, veneration, worship and so forth).[63]

In *The Nature of Sympathy*, Scheler further identifies four corresponding categories of fellow-feelings (*Einfühlung*) based on their capacity to connect oneself with other people through shared feelings and emotions. For Scheler,

---

62 Ibid.
63 Scheler, *Formalism in Ethics and Non-Formal Ethics of Values;* Scheler, *On Feeling, Knowing, and Valuing;* Also see: Cutting, John. "Max Scheler's theory of the hierarchy of values and emotions and its relevance to current psychopathology."

true fellow-feeling is the quality that brings people closer to each other in transformative and transcendent ways.[64] From the lower to the higher, the first is communal feelings, where people can share joy and sorrow, thus creating a bond with each other. At the next level is vicarious feelings, where one can perceive another person's joy or sorrow, but not participate in their feelings (e.g. observing and acknowledging another person's suffering but not feeling it). Seeing people's expressions of their feelings allows us to access their experiences, but we are not feeling their delight on their account or feeling the sadness on their account. At the third level is infectious feelings, as in the example of emotional contagion of mass excitement. However, all three kinds of feelings are not true fellow-feelings.

According to Scheler, true fellow-feelings (Einfühlung) describe the ways that we feel and experience other people's feelings and emotions in the same way as they feel and experience them. Sharing another person's feelings and emotions, vicariously experiencing their feelings and emotions and sympathising with them are not deep attuning. Hence Scheler places mutually identifying and mutually recognising feelings and emtoions at the top level of the hierarchy. So fellow-feelings (Einfühlung), for Scheler, involve emotional identification, whereby we experience others' feelings and emotions as our own, resulting in our bodies and souls to 'go under together in a single passionate surge of collective activity'.[65] In this sense, Einfühlung is an authentic, active fellow-feeling that cherishes the other's joy and respects their suffering they experience it. Fellow-feelings (Einfühlung) require that we participate in other people's experiences as if the feelings and emotions they are going through are our own. Participating in fellow-feelings involves the act of love, 'a true and authentic transcendence of one's self'.[66]

Participating in another's feelings and emotions can only be achieved by integrating within ourselves the act or movement of love as caring. Scheler regards love as the propensity to act in a way that enables (human) beings to transcend ourselves in order to participate in our own and the other's being. Love is the key that can offer us an entry into the mystery of one another.[67]

---

64 Altamirano, "Max Scheler and Adam Smith on Sympathy"
65 Scheler, *The Nature of Sympathy*, 36.
66 Ibid., 46.
67 Vacek, "Scheler's Phenomenology of Love," 156–177.

According to Scheler, 'all of ethics would reach its completion in the discovery of the laws of love [...]'.[68]

Scheler's conception of love is summarised as 'an ascending relation that lightens up things and persons alike so that the highest value that is compatible with their nature is revealed and shines through'.[69] This makes love a primal act, on which all other ethical acts are founded. As a primal act, love as caring is not a mere virtue, disposition, tendency or habit. Love is a concrete act, a spontaneous movement, directed at humans as the bearers of values and not directed at the values themselves. Hence, an act of love is a creative and generative force, propelling us towards our perfection. Love thus:

> promotes the well-being of the beloved, but only where this well-being contributes to the person's overall perfection. The deepest perfections cannot be directly willed into existence; to try to do so would be to usurp the other's freedom.[70]

The other (person or being) is an important notion in Scheler's phenomenology of love. In *The Nature of Sympathy*, Scheler challenges individualism and instrumental mentality and proposes that the other and the common good of the community should have priority over one's self-interest. Scheler maintains that the *I* cannot be/exist without the *we*, and the *we* always already precedes the *I*. It is out of the community that emerges the *I*, whereby any distinction between the *I* and the *other* or an *other* can be made. The primacy of the we or the community affirms the primal act of love as caring and vice versa. The human community is not just a collection of individual persons, it is a vital (embodied living) and spiritual sphere within which we become embodied and en-spirited beings. The primal act of love enables us to move beyond the sensuous vital sphere and reach out to the spiritual sphere from where we 'participate in another being as an end intentionale'.[71] In participating in each other's being as intentional beings who engage in the primal act of love intentionally, we experience transcendence. Thus, the act of love is like a stairway towards ascension:

> In the series of forms of sympathy and sorts of love, the cosmic-vital feeling of oneness and the acosmic love of the person, grounded in the love of God,

---

68 Scheler, *Formalism*, 261, quoted in Vacek, "Scheler's Phenomenology of Love," 163.
69 Vandenberghe, "Sociology of the Heart," 30.
70 Vacek, "Scheler's Phenomenology of Love," 158.
71 Scheler, *Selected Philosophical Essays*, 110.

stand thus at opposite poles. All the other forms of the series lie between them like the stairs of a case.[72]

The ascension is also a form of freedom. Indeed, for Scheler, spiritual love can liberate us from isolation and alienation and help break the chains of social conditioning, such as class, histories, cultural constraints and traditions and from biases and prejudices thus fostered. An act of love transcends these limitations and restrictions. Hence, without spiritual love, humans are no different from other animals.

Scheler's phenomenology of love transcends the separation between reason and emotion and between life as embodied, lived and life as spiritual and as holy. The meaning of life is lived through a full immersion and participation in the world and through loving and caring for the world. In this case, love is an uplifting and constructive action in and over the world. Hence, love, 'in this account, was always a dynamic becoming, a growing, a welling up of things in the direction of their archetype, which resides in God'.[73]

Although in his earlier texts, Scheler's phenomenology of love appealed to God, he ended this work with pantheism, which pointed to the spiritual dimension of human's being and thereby the spiritual notion of love as deep caring.

---

72 Scheler, *The Nature of Sympathy*, 137.
73 Scheler, *Selected Philosophical Essays*, 109.

Post-Modernist Ideas on Love as Caring

> *Politically speaking, it is that under conditions of terror most people will comply but some people will not, just as the lesson of the countries to which the Final Solution was proposed is that 'it could happen' in most places but it did not happen everywhere. Humanly speaking, no more is required and no more can reasonably be asked, for this planet to remain a place fit for human habitation.*
>
> —Hannah Arendt, *The Origin of Totalitarianism*

> *For millennia, man remained what he was for Aristotle: a living animal with the additional capacity for political existence; modern man is an animal whose politics places his existence as a living being in question.*
>
> —Michel Foucault, *The History of Sexuality*

> *We cannot have a duty to feel love for particular persons, but we can have a duty to be loving and an obligation to cultivate love in our lives.*
>
> —La Caze, *Love, That Indispensable Supplement*

Post-modern concerns are characterised by questioning power dynamics and the continued and evolving human problems that have been defined by power. These are reflected in our social positionalities, identities, narrative and discourse. We see philosophers interrogating the origin of totalitarianism, the control of institutions, such as hospital, prison and schools and likewise, people's lived experiences through sociological lenses such as sexuality, class, ethnicity, skin colour, gender, physical ability and so forth.

As Michel Foucault pointed out in his oeuvres, politics, since the eighteenth century, have gradually become both a means and process to dominate the human life. The conceptions and representations of power have been instituted in the consumptions of goods, economically, socially, romantically and personally. To a certain extent, the human existence becomes highly prescribed, highly controlled and highly fragmented. The technology of life is the pre-occupation of politics. This is, for Foucault, biopolitics, aimed at disciplining bodies and regulating people's embodied experiences of the population. Politics under the culture of consumption have given rise to the economic structure which itself also shapes a hierarchy of values, at the top of which sits the value of capital.

Politics of resistance and people's refusal to partake in subjectivities deliberated and inculcated by representations of consumption further mark the post-modern thoughts. Whilst the technology of life reduces human's being to commercialised existence, the decolonial approaches reinstate human dignity with practices and acts of loving and caring.

***

Hannah Arendt (1906–1975): The politics of love as caring for the world

Hannah Arendt was a political philosopher and one of the most influential thinkers of the twentieth century.[74] In Chapter 3 of this book, I touched upon Arendt's interpretations of love in St Augustine's theology, such as 'cupiditas' and 'caritas'. Here in this chapter, our focus is on Arendt's political ethics, especially her conception of love, 'amor mundi', or love of/for the world that articulates how love must be an active force for public bond as the basis for our common life of well-being.

In her highly influential book *The Human Condition*, Arendt writes that 'love, for reason of its passion, destroys the in-between which relates us to and separates us from others'.[75] This quote appears to suggest that Arendt separates love from passion. The quote also reads as if Arendt sees that love is private and apolitical. However, for many interpreters of Arendt, her political philosophy has *amor mundi* at its core.

How does Arendt understand amor mundi?

In *Love and St. Augustine*, Arendt already identifies that our active life (what she terms as vita active in *The Human Condition*) hinges on neighbourly love, an appreciation and care of our common bond as humanity. So, it would appear that Arendt's notion of amor mundi not only sits in-between philia, or friendship amongst citizens, and agapē, or love of humanity, but more importantly, it concerns how people can pursue a good life together in the world. So amor mundi is love and kinship between people and amongst people, which takes place in the world, that is, the political or public sphere, and it is also our bond with the world.

---

74 Hannah Arendt, although her books were published from 1930s until 1970s, her political thoughts have been regarded as broadly post-modernist by many interpreters, not least Bonnie Honig, Dana Villa and Tuija Pulkkinen. That is why I have placed Arendt as a contemporary thinker.
75 Arendt, *The Human Condition*, 242.

For Arendt, the political/public sphere can be constituted in the spaces between our private and political interests, our capacities to experience freedom and equality and institutional or worldly conditions within which our social or common lives and related activities arise and flourish. For citizens to live out an active political or public life together, it requires love to characterise these spaces so that people can experience oneself and each other as humans and can extend friendship and caring towards solidarity.

Why does love matter in the active political/public life? According to Arendt, our political activities are located in spaces where people meet one another, share perspectives, discuss differences, seek consensus on aspirations and identify shared solutions to our common challenges. Political life, for Arendt, does not only concern power but also involves people living an active life within public spaces in a common world. Hence in agreement with other Western philosophers already mentioned in this book, Arendt also recognises that community or society cannot be a mere collection of individuals, each doing their own things separately from others, pursuing their private interests and perceiving the world from their own lenses. Instead, the political community and public common space already precede the individuals.

Without the act of love, citizens will only be a lot of private 'I's. With the act of love as caring, the public sphere can help enlarge our collective sense of ourselves to become 'we' through political friendship of mutual caring. When acting as 'we', our differences, diverse interests and myriad ways of going about things will not serve as the basis for separation and hence violence. Instead, multiplicity and plurality are just forms of mutual participation in the public life. The 'we' also permits our participation in shared power through collective deliberation, political agency and common action. Amor mundi, as an underlying principle for constituting a community,[76] enables people to direct their socio-political processes at caring for the common world.

Arendt further qualifies that the 'we' is indeed political friendship. Challenging Aristotelean notion of philia as rooted in sameness and homogeneity, Arendt argues, in her collection of essays entitled *Men in Dark Times*, that political friendship recognises and respects human diversity, plurality and heterogeneity amongst people. Acknowledging our difference is an important departure from the Greek philosophy of love, whereby friendship-love implies homogeneity. In an extended quote from an article

---

76 Chiba, "Hannah Arendt on Love and the Political: Love, Friendship, and Citizenship," 505–35.

entitled 'Among Lovers' of the Journal *Arendt Studies*, Liesbeth Schoonheim quoted a passage from Arendt's diary that really illustrates this point:

> We are born into this world of plurality where father and mother stand ready for us, ready to receive us and welcome and guide us and prove that we are not strangers. We grow up to become like everybody else, but the more we grow, the more we became equal in the way of absolute, unbearable uniqueness. Then we love, and this world between us, the world of plurality and homeliness, goes up in flames, until we ourselves are ready to receive the new arrivals, newcomers to whom we prove what we no longer quite believe, that they are not strangers.[77]

What Arendt is saying here is that love applies to all persons as equals regardless of our differences. Indeed, for Arendt, it is such loving and caring regard for the other that can sustain political friendship in spite of our difference. Thus, love embraces the other in their multitudes of particularity. This means that friends can engage in discussions of things that they do not necessarily agree with, but without falling out or resulting in breaking the bond of the group or community. According to Arendt, political friendship can only be enriched in and through the political processes, or in and through political discourse, conversation and dialogue. In conversing about the world and ourselves in it, we can 'humanize what is going on in the world and in ourselves only by speaking of it and in the course of speaking of it we learn to be human'.[78] People meet and encounter each other in public spheres to act together and address things that are of equal concern to each person, be it our work, education, other social activities and so forth. In this sense, our active political life is not mere means to an end, it is the end itself – in living out our active life together, we build a flourishing world and achieve collective well-being.

What is emergent in such dialogic world-making political process, according to Arendt, is a strong shared political identity, an enduring political 'we'. Amor mundi can inspire not just politics of common action but also politics of resistance.[79] Politics of resistance can further be inferred to mean our collective resistance to violence, divisiveness and alienation. In *The Human Condition*, Arendt proposes that love through forgiveness, especially political forgiveness,

---

77 Schoonheim, "Among Lovers," 117.
78 Arendt, *Men in Dark Times*, 25.
79 Chiba, "Hannah Arendt on Love and the Political."

can support the community's resistance to vengeance and violence. Forgiveness enables the political community to reconstitute itself following aggression or transgression, liberating human beings from the imperfection of wrongdoings. Hence true freedom is the freedom from revenge and from the dichotomy of victim and perpetrator. This suggests that Arendt's amor mundi goes beyond philia and contains within it the strength of agapē, whereby persons who have committed wrongdoings or who have transgressed can be returned to and re-integrated in the political community. Amor mundi expresses justice in the collective act of loving and caring.

Can this understanding of amor mundi as a form of caring political action relieve. Arendt from her greatest concern about the tyranny of power? In *The Origin of Totalitarianism*, Arendt suggests that it is precisely by limiting the public spheres and by pressing people against each other, the spaces for political discourse, dialogue and action are destroyed. Hence Arendt states.

> Totalitarian government does not just curtail liberties or abolish essential freedoms; nor does it, at least to our limited knowledge, succeed in eradicating the love for freedom from the hearts of man. It destroys the one essential prerequisite of all freedom which is simply the capacity of motion which cannot exist without space.[80]

Accordingly, the fervour and revolt of the masses are the result of the individual's atomised state and the loss of communal relationships and political friendships. For Arendt, this spaceless human existence created by the totalitarian system is founded upon the utilitarian principle whereby everyone and everything can be disposable as means to ends when found superfluous to the system. Hence there is the evil of extermination through what Arendt terms as 'factories of annihilation'. Within such a system, there is little love or caring for the individual, let alone for the world.

Amor mundi might provide the answer to political resistance whereby we celebrate human diversity in our equal particularities. Multitudes of public space are created for political dialogue and civic engagement. These are not just political processes to achieve some ends, but rather these are the emplaced sites for relational flourishing. Arendt insists that no persons should be reduced to their identity labels in these public spheres, and all persons can participate in political processes and explore mutual concerns.

---

80 Arendt, *The Origin of Totalitarianism*, 612.

Here, in the communal spaces, the social and the political converge in our care for the flourishing of our common world.

***

Harry Frankfurt (1929–): Loving and caring actively

Harry Frankfurt has written two important books on love. One entitled *Necessity, Volition and Love* and the other *The Reasons of Love*. His most influential account of love starts from the observation that there are certain kinds of action that a person simply *must* take, not because one is compelled or compulsive, but because one has no choice but to act in these ways. Frankfurt calls these 'volitional necessities', some of which are necessities of prudence, 'indispensable to the attainment of our settled goals'; others are necessities of duty, which peremptorily require us to act in accordance with our moral duty; a third class refers to the 'necessities of love', actions that are required of us by virtue of loving someone or something.[81]

What is central to Frankfurt's conception of love is that it involves caring deeply and actively about what is loved and that it shapes the ways in which a person is motivated or inclined to act, affecting their preferences and choices. Although the objects of a person's love will most commonly and obviously be a specific other person, Frankfurt suggests that this be not essential to love and that someone might just as well love something more abstract: a moral ideal such as social justice, scientific truth, or a family tradition. What one loves is entirely contingent to, for instance, personal circumstances, character and history. Therefore, it might seem to be entirely a matter of chance in terms of whom or what one ends up loving.

However, argues Frankfurt, love is in effect not so impartial nor so random because we would (if suitably placed) all end up loving similar things. In this respect, according to Frankfurt, the actions that love requires of us are just as contingent as the necessities of prudence. This contrasts starkly with the supposed universalism and impartiality of moral imperatives. At the same time for Frankfurt:

[t]he claims that are made upon us by our love of our children, or of our countries, or of our ideals may be just as unequivocally categorical as those

---

81 Frankfurt, *Necessity, Volition, and Love*, 129.

that are made upon us by the moral law. In cases of both kinds, there is no room for negotiation: we simply *must not* violate our moral obligations and we simply *must not* betray what we love.[82]

That the necessities of love leave us no other options but to act by loving and caring, for Frankfurt, offers a source of freedom. Following Kant, Frankfurt argues that such freedom of choice and action, or freedom of the will, constitutes 'the most genuine freedom'.[83] The highest degree of freedom is that in willing something, one follows what there is decisive reason to want and to do something that one cares about and cares for. To love something, in Frankfurt's conception, is to adopt a particular kind of care for what one loves and in doing this, a person actively shapes their volitional nature. They become bound by practical necessities to act in ways that focus on the good of their beloved. By loving someone or something, one is committed to caring for them.

Frankfurt makes an important distinction between passive and active love. Love of either variety, in Frankfurt's conception, 'implies conduct that is designed to be beneficial to the beloved'; whereas an act of love is passive, however, when such actions are motivated by the further goal of 'obtaining or continuing to possess the object of his love [who] will be beneficial to him'.[84] Whether a lover has such ulterior motives, however, may not be something they are guaranteed to know about themselves. This kind motivation, which is characteristic of passive love, is essentially self-regarding and has its source in a lover's preoccupation with their own good. This self-regarding is central to what makes love passive. Here, Frankfurt explains, 'love is conditional upon attribution to beloved of a capacity to improve the condition of life'.[85] When an act of love is conditional in this way, it is easy to abandon its practical requirements for how one's acts lack the stringency (which can make one free). It is a matter of chance whether someone has the capacity to improve the condition of one's own life and if one's love and its practical requirements depend on such winds of fortune, this makes one's love passive in the face of its shifting gusts.

According to Frankfurt, possessiveness in one's attitudes and actions, so familiar a phenomenon in our daily encounters with reputedly loving

---

82 Ibid., 130.
83 Ibid., 131.
84 Ibid., 133.
85 Ibid.

relationships, is detrimental to love. At its worst, possessiveness implies a lack of care for the beloved, perhaps by seeing them as an object to be acquired. An object to be possessed has no independent good, interests, or agency of their own. Even if they do have these, possessiveness means seeing them as undeserving of care and respect and subjugating their good to one's self-interests. Without such malign extremity, when one feels that possessing and controlling another who does deserve care and respect for their intrinsic worth somehow reflects upon oneself, this is still a narcissistic and egoistic attitude. As long as one loves and cares for others for the sake of one's self-interest, such acts of passive love are mere means, instrumentalising both love and the beloved.

In contrast, active love involves non-instrumental motivation – an interest in caring for and serving the goods and ends of the beloved. Active love is loving for the sake of loving and caring for the sake of caring for beloved and their well-being and for the end of preserving and respect for what one loves. Taking the example of parental love for their children, Frankfurt observes that although a parent has personal interest to love and care for their child, such interest is utterly selfless. For Frankfurt, in such active love, we are captivated by what we love. We are not free to choose what to love about our beloved, nor can we cease loving or caring about their flourishing. In this sense, active love is compelling (but not compulsive), and we are not free in the face of it. Intense passions of jealousy or addiction are compulsive whereby one is overwhelmed by their force, whether or not it moves us in a direction we can identify with and endorse. Compulsion has no authority and makes no claims on what we ought to do. The demands of compelling love, in contrast, have an inescapable authority (even if we might sometimes flout it). Accordingly, Frankfurt explains:

> The fact that a person loves something does imply ... that he cannot help caring about its interests and that their importance to him is among the considerations by which he cannot help wanting his choices and his conduct to be guided. His readiness to serve the interests of his beloved is not just a primitive feeling or an impulse toward which his attitude may be as yet totally indeterminate. It is an element of his established volitional nature, and hence of his identity as a person.[86]

Active love is also subtly reflexive. Frankfurt explains that a lover cares, in the distinctive way involved in love, about how they themselves act and what kind

---

86 Ibid., 137.

of people they themselves are. Active love means that one simply cannot help but care about how what one does affects the beloved and so cannot help but care about one's self and the ideal kind of person one might become:

> In being devoted to the well-being of his beloved as an ideal goal, the lover is thereby devoted to an effort to realize a corresponding ideal in himself – namely, the ideal of living a life that is devoted to the interests and ends of his beloved. Someone who loves justice, for instance, necessarily wants to be a person who serves the interests of justice. He necessarily regards serving its interests not only as contributing to the realization of a desirable social condition, but also as integral to the realization of his ideal for himself.[87]

Active love also involves this kind of concern for oneself and the kind of person one is. Because of this, by betraying the requirements of love, for example, the demands to act in service to the good of what one loves, one simultaneously betrays oneself, which 'ruptures inner cohesion or unity' and brings about a division within one's own will. Such betrayal, therefore, involves inflicting damage to oneself and injuring one's psychic unity and manifests a lack of self-respect as well as respect and care for what one loves. This, for Frankfurt, is the ultimate source of love's necessities, which is the very inviolability of the demands that love makes upon oneself. To transgress these demands entails violating, betraying and 'rupturing' oneself.

Frankfurt's active love constitutes the basis of ethics of care. To truly care about someone or something involves one's will and an attitude directed simultaneously at the beloved, the world and at oneself. The caring not only shapes one's identity as a person, but it also points to the actions that one must take.

---

87 Ibid., 139.

Conclusion: Love as Caring for a Flourishing Common Life

Politics or *Politiká* in Greek concern the affairs of the polis, the political community. It involves the process of making decisions that apply to and affect all members of a community. As demonstrated by classical Greek thoughts, politics is a space and process to sustain congenial relations, achieve positions of governance and exercise meaningful power within a human community. The end of politics, as we have seen, is not power, or control. The end of power is the good life of people in the polis, or in the political community.

How we achieve a flourishing common life with one another and with other beings in the cosmos is truly the focus of the ethic of love and caring in politics. From loving and caring for children and educating virtuous youths, to designing structural justice in the cities, to identifying socio-economic system aimed at harmony amongst all; from cultivating personal virtues for civic engagement, such as friendship-love, to caring for communal well-being and to ensuring the integrity of the political community. In the Platonist and Aristotelean thoughts, love remains to be an animating force that serves to inspire caring and to transcend human life towards higher level of flourishing. Platonic erôs itself is an energising force or animating power that enables humans to aspire for the perfect goodness. It illustrates the true integration of love and power by justice that defines how love and power manifest in people's personal and social lives. Similarly, Aristotle doesn't consider the world (in the highest and most perfect form) not as the cause but the object of love, enabling the goodness in people and in the world from the potential to be the actual, from *dynamis* to *energeia*, two notions that are constituted in power.

Meanwhile, Aristotelean eudaimonia, or living for living's sake, also consists of the proposition that the meaningfulness of the good life lies precisely in the living of it. In other words, where there is too much focus on the transcendence (i.e. the redemptive future), we can miss out the opportunity to partake in the valuable nature of all our activities and processes in the present, such as loving and caring for our children, enjoying the scenes in the festival, or concerning ourselves with all that is happening within our personal, communal and political lives.

This Aristotelean proposition has an echo in the Stoic advice on living in the present. Indeed, for the Stoics, love is actively caring for what we are experiencing in the here and now. In other words, love concerns enriching our being in the present which is simultaneously about our becoming. In living in the present through loving and caring for what is truly valuable, uninhibited by the worries of our finitude and mortality, unattached to the hopes and fears of tomorrow and untethered by the regrets and shames of the past, human beings can achieve transcendence within immanence.[88] Stoic wisdom in this respect distinguishes itself from the classical Greek philosophy of love which tends to seek transcendence.

However, the Stoic vision for the mutuality of transcendence and immanence was quickly succeeded by Christianity's political for redemption because in the Stoic vision, the persons who participate in the harmonious flow of the cosmos are anonymous because they are part of nature. This Stoic anonymity, according to Luc Ferry, does not seem to advance personal redemption and self-transcendence as the Christian promise can offer.[89] Christian thinkers offered visions of justice by establishing the individual's right, a moral claim to what would be their due. This could be the premise for the emergence of individualism in the West.

A typical analysis of the West's rise to modernity tends to view it as the consequence of the capitalist expansion in the sixteenth and seventeenth centuries, including the brutal exploitation of enslaved labour, empirical and colonial invasion and oppression. In addition to geographical and natural conditions, the cultural, philosophical, religious and institutional legacies from the Greeks, Romans, mono-theistic Christian conceptions of nature, human nature, citizenship, governance processes, as well as scientific and technological development, all converged to give rise to the Western modernity's domination in the world. It also extends to the philosophical discussions of, for instance, Schopenhauer, Kierkegaard and Nietzsche, whereby will/power has primacy in love, despite in different ways. In these philosophical landscapes, there is an underlying assumption that love defines being in an ontological sense which enables people to live a particular kind of ethical life with others and with the world, including the cosmos and the divine.

In this process, the earlier hierarchy of power that placed the cosmos or God at the top gave way to individualism. In the capitalist mode of production and obsession with wealth-accumulation, philosophical and political thoughts struggled to fill in the gap between the aspirations for the good life based on love and caring for what is truly valuable and the practices that instigate the pursuit of materialistic wealth which is effectively the means to the good life and well-being.

---

88 Ferry, *A Brief History of Thought*.
89 Ibid.

Paul Tillich has a famous sentence in his book *Love, Power and Justice*: 'Life is being in actuality and love is the moving power of life.'[90] Did the West lose life's beingness in actuality in the modern and post-modern capitalist fixation? At minimum, modernist conceptions of love as caring constituted the continuous attempts to determine the ways that we may act justly, lovingly and caringly. Metaphysics of meaning in life is in part the epistemological questioning about the value scheme and how we might live accordingly. The most striking evolution is the shift from love as disinterested interest and a rational act supported by objective reasoning to love as embracing feelings and emotions which tend to ground our motivation or propensity to act. In contrast to classical and Christian views of salvation, modernist view the route towards human becoming not by being lifted towards ascension by a transcendent being. Instead, some modernist thinkers have proposed a pathway through cultivating our outward relational ethics in social and political lives by nourishing our ethical being from within, with love.

Politics became processes to organise public conversations, safeguard the sovereignty of nations and ensure material and technological resources for human comfort and well-being. Ethical values, such as the primacy of human life and well-being, justice, benevolence, beneficence, equality and spirituality have become increasingly more recognised. These are beyond personal virtues that are actively sought in the classical and theological accounts of love as caring.

The post-modernist realities have frustrated many Western thinkers. They analysed the structural changes in Western societies, in terms of our relationship to capital, labour, other people, especially those who are different and the world, including nature. The concentration of wealth and centralisation of capital, the growing privatisation of enterprises and the bureaucracy of power further cause alienation in contemporary societies. What capitalism also does is to champion individual deserve and merit as justice, which tends to turn a blind eye to the relational nature of social and political processes and further discourages mutual caring and structural caring. This results in a general impersonal culture in many Western societies, with little sense of sharing and solidarity. Notions such as the common life and nature as in part our global commons are being buried by privatisation and individual ownerships. The uneven, unequal and unjust economic development has engendered fragile states and marginalised communities, politically vulnerable, poverty-stricken,

---

90 Tillich, *Love, Power and Justice*, 1954.

tormented by historical dehumansiation and continued legacies of structural violence. Accompanying economic injustice is identity politics, competing victimhood and political antagonism. Love as an ethic of caring is thus truly needed to create convivial spaces for relational politics that can transcend antagonistic identities and for caring co-actions that draw on our myriad differences.

Twentieth- and twenty-first-century thinkers have built on this particular critique of capitalism and supported politics of love and an ethic of caring. For instance, Tillich has urged us to consider the ontological question of being itself and suggests that love, power and justice must be considered together as a reflection of the nature of our being. From a metaphysics perspective, being itself is the working of eternal laws that bind all in a perpetual system of harmony. It is in such a harmony that love, separation, reunion and restoration mark the movement of the different constitutive elements within the whole.

CHAPTER 6

LOVE IN PRACTICE

Society must be organized in such a way that man's social, loving nature is not separated from his social existence, but becomes one with it. If it is true [...] that love is the only sane and satisfactory answer to the problem of human existence, then any society which excludes, relatively, the development of love, must in the long run perish of its own contradiction with the basic necessities of human nature.

—Erich Fromm, *The Art of Loving*

A real democracy must take as its basis, today, a just relationship between man and woman. A distorted relationship between them gives rise to many forms of antidemocratic power. Unless we can transform this, the most everyday element of our lives, we will never bring about change across the world.

—Iragaray, *Democracy Begins between Two*

Without an ethic of love shaping the direction of our political vision and our radical aspirations, we are often seduced, in one way or the other, into continued allegiance to systems of domination—imperialism, sexism, racism, classism. It has always puzzled me that women and men who spend a lifetime working to resist and oppose one form of domination can be systematically supporting another.

—bell hooks, *Love as Practice of Freedom*

In this book, I have proposed to apply a triadic conceptual framework for capturing the understanding of love already present in Western thought. This threefold agenda involves love as valuing, love as relationing and love as caring. Here love is conceived as a verb, not as a noun. This triadic conception of love allows us to offer a unitary lens to further explore how an ethic of love has been essential for living the good life

Under the first prong of the triad, love as valuing, this book has discussed love as the animating force that can enrich the valuable qualities and aspects in humans and other beings. In seeking and appreciating these enduring qualities, love has been understood to be able to transcend human finitude and limitation. At the same time, love is also conceived as an energising process that recognises, invites and cherishes the valuable aspects in persons and in things in their own right.

Through the lens of the second prong of the triad, this book has investigated love as relationing, including sustaining the in-between spaces where opposites are transcended and conflicts harmonised, towards mutual indwelling with the divine and intimately connecting with all beings in the cosmos or in the world. Love's relationality also insists on our commitment to other's people's well-being for their own sake.

Within the last prong, this book has examined love as acting on our ultimate concern with care, such as living together in political communities and expressing and acting on our caring for each other, for other beings in nature and for the flourishing of our common world.

This triadic framework suggests that these three dimensions of love are not independent, but rather, to love means to integrate the intrinsic values, relational processes and caring actions in our pursuing the good life together.

The triadic framework can also help us to understand how love is lived and practised in our everyday life. In particular, the conceptions of love discussed in this book demonstrate that life can only be lived as an active life (even the contemplative life is not inactive), and it is in living out our ethical values, relationality and caring acts that life becomes meaningful. Hence love affirms the recognition of living for living's sake. It also suggests that living involves practising the art of loving. As Erich Fromm points out in his book, *The Art of Loving*, that mastering such an art must be a matter of ultimate concern. Yet, after two millennia's deep-seated yearning for love and continued articulation of love's meanings and longings throughout Western thought, for some reason, love remains to be less important in comparison, for instance, to money, power, status or prestige. Hence the collection of postulations on love captured in this book can serve to remind us and truly highlight that there cannot be anything else in the world that is more important than learning and practising the art of loving.

Indeed, through this three-fold agenda, we can begin to evaluate whether social policies, political processes and institutional cultures and practices reflect our collective aspirations for love, as valuing, as relationing and as caring. For instance, values-based imperatives, such as the UN Charter of Human Rights, can only have genuine positive impact on diverse people's experiences when global institutions begin to actively nurture and practise the art of loving. In this case, love's triadic framework can help examine whether institutions cherish and treat human beings as intrinsically valuable, create spaces for respectful dialogue and non-instrumental relationships and design governance processes that cultivate people's dispositions and actions to care for each other, care for the work we do and care for the world we live in. Without institutions' embracing an ethic of love and without their practising the art of loving through structures and processes, aspirations for equal human rights will remain abstract and irrelevant.

Similarly, an organisation may want to stress the importance of relationships and provide spaces and time for staff to develop self-love and other-love and a sense of mutual belonging and fellowship. However, unless the organisation's loving endeavours are also aligned with the valuable nature of the good causes in the world that it aims to serve, its therapy-like processes for relational enrichment might be seen as mere self-indulgent.

A further example concerns the pursuit of human development, progress and growth. An over-emphasis on transcendence can treat all else as a dispensable cost, including the dignity of work, our well-being in the here and now and the integrity of the ecological system. Globally, we are experiencing climate and humanitarian crises brought on by a growth-focused economy. In front of the escalating catastrophes, we must return to the questions that the notion of love invites us to ponder: What constitutes the good life? How might we live well together?

Love's interconnected tri-domains can help us to gauge society's orientations and urge us to direct our attention to the good life of all. They remind us that valuing, relating and caring must be mutually reinforcing. Neither is to be treated as a separated singular focus of our personal and public life. So, in this chapter, we will examine how love in practice might look in fields such as politics, economy, community, education and ecology. I will do this by reflecting on specific cases and discussing the ways that they might illustrate the work of love.

It is worth noting here that love as conceived in this book remains to be an aspiration. This means although some organisations have intended to embody all three domains of love in their process and culture, in practice, human endeavours still have a long way to go to fully align our valuing, relationing and caring with an ethic of love. Nevertheless, practical examples can be precious to illustrate how love can be integrated into our common life on Earth.

Politics of Love

Politics in contemporary Western societies seem to be riddled with flaws. Typical criticisms include (1) short-termism which does not encourage governments to focus on long-term commitments to policies nor support coherent policy continuity; (2) distrust in leaders from the general public who believe that politicians can be corrupt and do not have the common good as their mission; (3) domination by the elite whereby political processes and policies become captured by the interests of the wealthy class; (4) antagonism and animosity during election which can exacerbate societal divisiveness and undermine solidarity and coherence; (5) voters ignorance and irrationality which tend to result in unsuitable national leaders being elected, such as the Presidency of Donald Trump. Furthermore, contemporary Western liberal politics also wrestle with people's negative psychological factors that can inhibit collective aspirations for justice and solidarity.

In her book *Political Emotions: Why Love Matters for Justice*, Martha Nussbaum discusses some of the negative emotions, such as selfishness, fear, disgust and envy which, according to her, are endemic even in societies that are considered to be good. Indeed, whilst globalisation has brought people closer through mobility, internet, social media and international politics, globalisation has not yet united people and, instead, has stirred these negative emotions in personal, public and political spheres. Nussbaum is joined by many other global thinkers and religious leaders to call for an ethic of love in politics. Let's examine four of these proposals and related practices, all reflecting the ideas put forward by Western thinkers already captured in this book.

First, it concerns instilling an ethic of love as the underlying principle for engaging in politics. Many people seek positions in politics, and what motivate them to serve can determine how they serve as leaders. It is here that an ethic of love matters. Let's explore a set of questions provided by *Fratelli Tutti: On Fraternity and Social Friendship*, the third Encyclical of Pope Francis signed in October 2020. The letter starts with an emphasis on an ethic of love as a transcending force inspired by St Francis of Assis's theology. What is of particular relevance to our discussion here is that in Article 197, Pope Francis invites leaders to reflect on the following:

> At times, in thinking of the future, we do well to ask ourselves, 'Why I am doing this?', 'What is my real aim?' For as time goes on, reflecting on the past, the questions will not be: 'How many people endorsed me?', 'How many voted for me?', 'How many had a positive image of me?' The real,

and potentially painful, questions will be, 'How much love did I put into my work?' 'What did I do for the progress of our people?' 'What mark did I leave on the life of society?' 'What real bonds did I create?' 'What positive forces did I unleash?' 'How much social peace did I sow?' 'What good did I achieve in the position that was entrusted to me?'

What if political leaders at all levels continue to reflect on these questions throughout their public service? What answers might they come up with or want to come up with? What answers might they live with and want to live with? What if these leaders reflect publicly on these questions, for example, in front of the people and with the people?

In this book, in examining how love must be an ultimate concern underlying political processes, we have seen suggestions for creating public spaces for listening and dialogue and for reflection on the common good. Pope Francis's questions offer a sharper focus for these political engagements. When love is at the core of public inquiries and mutual exploration, Pope Francis's questions and the ways that these questions are phrased can ensure that politics serve as a site for deepening our civic friendships, enriching human bonds and affirming mutual belongingness. More importantly, if leaders can take time to discuss these questions together, they can have an evaluative framework to consider how political processes and political institutions are themselves loving and caring.

Second, it is about ensuring the direction of the political project to be aligned with an ethic of love and the good life of all. Let's reflect briefly on the UK-based movement *Compassion in Politics*, which has introduced a compassion threshold into UK policy making. The threshold signifies qualities of life below which no new piece of legislation would be allowed to fall. This threshold would enable both legislators and the public to review policies from the perspective of human well-being. This is particularly relevant in the present context whereby some government policies seem to push people into further vulnerability (e.g. unemployment, homelessness, poverty and depression). In addition, *Compassion in Politics* advocates respect, decency and honesty in political campaigns and encourages respectful, inclusive and collaborative approaches to day-to-day parliamentarian practices. Compassion not only characterises political processes, thereby sustaining political friendships amongst politicians and leaders; compassion also denotes human experiences as the effects of politics.

In other words, compassionate politics can introduce social policies and governance practices in such ways that people can feel valued non-instrumentally and recognise their well-being respected and even cherished in the society. *Compassion in Politics* invite intentional opportunities and spaces for leaders and citizens to engage in and contribute to decision-making that benefits the common life of all.

Third, it involves orienting the justice system within the paradigm of love. Let's review the example of restorative justice, a practice that is in total contrast to the Western legal systems' primary focus on a retributive paradigm whereby prosecutors and victims are encouraged to punish the offending party for the wrongdoing. Instead, restorative justice exemplifies the ideas advanced in the book in that it equates justice to love. It seeks to offer an opportunity for offenders to self-transform and self-transcend by mediating reconciliation between those who have transgressed and those who have been harmed by the transgression. The communities from which both parties are part will too be involved in the reconciliatory process. Restorative justice works by creating a safe space for the wrongdoer and the injured party to meet, along with members of the community. During the meeting, all parties will discuss the offence that was committed, examine the resulting harm and damage, as well as determine a path to move forward in ways that address the needs of both sides.

These restorative meetings and their eventual outcomes are supported by the justice system in the community. This means that the offender is not incarcerated, but instead is charged with fixing the wrongdoing and repairing the damage. Although having transgressed, the offender is still treated as a human being who is worthy of love and respect and deserves an opportunity to put the wrong right and to be returned to the community as a valued member.

Furthermore, such a justice system avoids putting young offenders in prison. Instead, restorative justice approach connects the the young offenders with other members of the community who can mentor and guide them so that the chance of future re-offending will be reduced.

The practice of restorative justice is rooted in an ethic of love. It recognises human fragility and vulnerability and focuses on the needs for healing and well-being of both parties tied in the act of wrongdoing and the healing and well-being needs of the communities bound together in an act of transgression.

A fourth example is political forgiveness, such as Truth and Reconciliation Commission, aimed at healing the trauma of intercommunal violence and building positive peace. Key practices involve (a) giving the harmed party a voice for truth-telling and expressing their pain and recounting the harms done to them; (b) allowing the perpetrators (e.g. political leaders) to offer apologies and accept responsibility for the wrongdoing; (c) institutionalising a process of restorative justice to acknowledge the wrongdoing and restore the well-being of the harmed; (d) embracing forgiveness that re-affirms shared human dignity and provides opportunity for people to renew their narratives of transformation; and (e) paving the paths towards collective healing through psychosocial processes and transforming socioeconomic systems for human empowerment and flourishing.

Forgiveness can be seen as a necessary part of political process and strategies to build sustainable, enduring and just peace. National politicians' publicly offering apologies, asking for forgiveness and making commitments to right the wrongs can be powerful moral acts that recognise human dignity and our intrinsic values as persons. Forgiveness stresses the importance of our relational reconciliation and create socio-political conditions for caring and well-being. When followed by an understanding of the causes of individual and large-scale moral wrongdoings, developing structural justice, addressing the roots of violence, it can be received and experienced as a profound act of love.

These four examples, echoing conceptions of love highlighted in this book, recognise that human emotions can help bring to the fore what we value, why situations in the world affect us and how we respond to other people's lived realities and experiences with care. Whilst negative political emotions might serve to alienate people from one another, increase aggression and exacerbate distrust, positive emotions such as compassion, empathy and forgiveness can pave the path to values-based, relationally congenial and caring political processes.

***

Economy of Love

In most Western societies, a capitalist economy is the predominant system, which tends to have four main features. First, the raison-d'etre of capitalist economy is maximising the increase of capital for its own sake. This feature determines that when people perform their roles within a capitalist structure, their actions will necessarily have profit-maximising aims and instrumentalising consequences. Thus, capitalism has exploitation built into the very structure of the mode of production. Second, with maximising profit as the sole purpose, within a capitalist economic system, everything else is instrumentalised, including our work, human consumption, the natural environment, social relations and even the markets themselves. All are fundamentally and ineluctably mere resources for that single purpose. Third, a capitalist system is competitive and expansionist. Competition can sometimes result in hostility and corruption and expansion can lead to colonial occupation, cultural appropriation, or political domination, or imperialism when it involves state power. Lastly, capitalist economy tends to breed inequality and alienates an underclass who are robbed of their livelihood, power and voice.[1]

This brief sketch of the capitalist economic system and its effects demonstrates that human beings, our well-being, environment, other beings in nature and even life itself can risk becoming means to the end of economic growth. Putting instrumental end (e.g. materialistic pursuit) in front of human well-being, at the cost of the integrity of ecosystem, is dehumanising. Such an economic system is devoid of non-instrumental values, congenial relations and caring acts.

So, what might an economy of love look like? We will explore three examples.

We can begin with the global movement of well-being economy. In light of growing dissatisfaction with dehumanising effects of capitalist economic system and the increased awareness of its damages, not least climate change, inequality, deliberately created vulnerability in non-European communities, a global movement has been underway to explore alternative to capitalist economy. One such attempt is *well-being economy* that regards the primary aim of economy to be holistic human well-being and the good life of all. Under different names, such as well-being economy, economy of happiness and *buen vivir* or good living, well-being economy seeks to reimagine an economic system that does not instrumentalise human life, our work, consumption, or our relationships with each other and with other beings in nature.

As articulated in this book, the good life in well-being is conceived as being well, living well and becoming well. This is rooted in an ethic of love, as discussed in Chapter 2. When we come to realise that economy is an activity, a process and a system that has our collective well-being and the flourishing of other beings on the planet at its core, we can move away from the instrumental mentality and eliminate the damaging effects of profit-maximising economy. This means certain love-based principles can serve as underpinning pillars that facilitate the construction of well-being-centred economic system, including a shared vision for a common human future, an understanding of what constitutes holistic well-being, the nature of our work and purpose of our consumption and how to create spaces for enriching relationships and identify ways to relate to other beings in the natural environment.

---

1 Gill and Thomson, *Understanding Peace Holistically*.

An emphasis on economy as the process to enable our collective well-being and co-flourishing can help decolonise the prevalent system of production that is by nature purely instrumental. This emphasis can overcome the perennial defects (such as inequality and injustice) inherent in the capitalist system. Put simply, well-being economy aims to serve human beings rather than the other way around. Economic factors only matter insofar as they contribute to a common good life on Earth.

In Chapter 2, I used the dignity of our work as an example to illustrate an ethic of love in human life as living for living's sake. Let's now take our work as an example to demonstrate the integration of instrumental and non-instrumental values in the good life in the context of well-being economy. In well-being economy, in sharp contrast to an instrumentalised view of labour whereby our work is a mere means to earning a salary, work becomes a highly significant aspect of our being well, living well and becoming well, or flourishing. Although it is a means to our livelihood which is instrumental, work does have intrinsic value, or is valuable for itself. The intrinsic value of work lies in the following aspects which already reviewed in Chapter 2: work is (a) an integral part of our life; (b) an expression of our talents; (c) a process through which we develop and become more fully human; (d) a space to be with others in synergetic relationships; and (e) an opportunity to do things for others and to serve the common good. These facets of work combine in a well-being economy, the being, the expression, the learning, the relationships and the service to others. All these reflect the triadic conception of love.

Furthermore, we can also apply an ethic of love as a lens to understand our consumption within a well-being economy. Instead seeing consumption as making a purchase, thus increasing the movements of goods and money and the revenue of businesses and corporations, meaningful consumption requires relation to life activities and experiences of non-instrumental value. In this sense, meaningful consumption as an economic activity is more than spending money; it pertains to our well-being.

Ultimately, through the lens of an ethic of love, we can see that well-being economy (including its values, conceptions of work, consumption, and our relationships with other beings on the planet and nature itself) is a system that values humans and other sentient beings in nature intrinsically. It supports the congenial and harmonious relationships amongst all, and cares for the well-being and flourishing of all.

The second example is the growing development and application of local currencies (as an aspect of well-being economy). These currencies are part of a system of exchange that is established in a physical location or around a demarcation of community. The community chooses a currency (including the printing of special notes, debit cards, etc.) that can only be used within the community. These currencies form physical representations of the way that money moves through a community. To a certain extent, local currencies can highlight the values embedded in our economic transactions through meaningful consumption.

Meaningful consumption means that when we make a purchase using local currencies, we are committed to the valuable nature of being-in-community, to the close relationships we can initiate and nurture within the community and to our caring for our collective flourishing. For instance, it encourages us to shop face-to-face rather than online. In facilitating this exchange, we also come to know the work and care of our local farmers, bakers, florists, artists and entrepreneurs. It promotes dialogue about how local business contributes to the vibrancy of the community and keeps small businesses alive and supports healthy competitiveness (against multinational corporations).

In a community that uses a local currency, our consumption becomes a way of valuing each other and valuing our relationships. It makes our consumption more personal rather than impersonal, and hence more meaningful. Any transactions carried out with the local currency can become an investment in the community's vibrancy and solidify an intention to support local businesses even if the operating costs of these businesses mean their products are more expensive than products that are mass produced (often using exploited labour). Understanding the processes of product development and thereby paying for the appropriate costs for the goods and services also ensure that as consumers, we are not exploiting people's work, but rather we are respecting the dignity of work.

The businesses that accept these local currencies are taking part in a relationship with the community in which their work and the fruit of their work (e.g. product and produce) are seen as more than commodities. Instead of trying to drive costs down as much as possible, business owners have greater latitude to remunerate their employees with fair wages for their work, source better ingredients for the products, and align the products and services to the well-being of the community. In sourcing better ingredients, businesses may also use the local currency to get these resources locally. This builds a network of values that create higher quality products and better work conditions. Finally, for the employees, the local currency might be used to supplement wages. This reflects the value of the worker in the community system because their work is turned into meaningful consumption within the community.

The third example is *Economy of Communion*. Initiated by the founder of the global Focolare movement, Chiara Lubich, in 1991, *Economy of Communion* proposes a new economic paradigm to underpin global enterprises and businesses. Briefly, the paradigm can be captured in the following three core features:

The first is its affirming communion or relationing as a mission of life. Hence it considers love as a fundamental value for the economy. This is translated into caring for the qualities of relationships amongst all stakeholders in the economic system. It also means moving away from a purely hierarchical structure of economic institutions and placing human beings at the centre of these institutions' processes.

The second feature is based on the original teaching of the Focolare movement, which is caring for the *poor* and the vulnerable. This means paying attention to any difficulties and hardships in the workplace and making these occasions precious opportunities for expressing love and caring and for everyone's growth and maturity.

The third feature is co-creating shared values amongst all stakeholders. This implies time and space for listening, for dialogue and for sharing experiences.

In doing so, *Economy of Communion* can contribute to the global economy in a number of ways. For instance, it coheres to businesses' economic profit and community's well-being benefit. This avoids pursuing economic profit for its own sake and makes an economic profit for the sake of community's collective well-being. At the same time, *Economy of Communion* enables everyone to partake in the process of creating values and sharing the valuable aspects of the co-creation. It allows companies and economic institutions to empower everyone to contribute to value-generation and to collective well-being and the good life for one and all.

In doing so, businesses can in turn be motivated to improve the quality of goods and services, to encourage creativity and inspire more work opportunities and activities. This is a proactive approach to inclusion by ensuring the participation in economic activities of all people. Such care for people(s) and communities is naturally extended to all beings on the planet. In this process, the paradigm of love and communing further extends a culture and ethic of love and communing.

Additionally, for those participating in the *Economy of Communion*, there is a recognition that the presence and support of what the Focolare community calls the 'Invisible Associate' allows people from all faiths and beliefs to feel included. This *invisible partner* is love itself.

***

Community of Love

Politics of love and economy of love can create conditions for people to live in beloved communities. 'Beloved Community' has been one of the most inspirational contemporary notions. Against the backdrop of racial segregation, white supremacy and other dehumanising legacies of slavery and colonialism, Dr Martin Luther King Jr (1929–1968) outlined a non-violent vision for living harmoniously in pursuit of the good life together. Informed by Christian philosophy and influenced by other peaceful practices, Beloved Community is rooted in an ethic of love. In particular, it values human dignity which, for Dr King, is contained in an all-inclusive friendship-love. An important aspect of Beloved Community is the commitment to relationing which defines the practices of conflict transformation and reconciliation amongst adversaries. Positive emotions such as love, compassion and empathy can overcome fear, hatred and vengefulness and help break the cycles of violence. Thus, the spirit of goodwill and friendship should prevail in social movements and activism and underpin our collective pursuit of the good life and well-being. Dr King in a speech once said:

> It is this type of spirit and this type of love that can transform opponents into friends. It is this type of understanding goodwill that will transform the deep gloom of the old age into the exuberant gladness of the new age. It is this love which will bring about miracles in the hearts of men.[2]

In our common life within communities, an ethic of love has been translated by Dr King as a relational practice where interpersonal and intercommunal reconciliation and friendship can serve as the basis for creating the Beloved Community. In the acts of forgiveness and redemption, people in the community can re-establish passionate love for the good life, friendship-love and love for the sake of loving and extending goodwill to all, including goodwill to our enemies. Within the Beloved Community, love is experienced as a total generative relatedness, an integration of the collective objective for living well together through mutually valuing each other's dignity, absolute commitment to congenial relationing and actively caring for each other's well-being.

---

[2] Martin Luther King Jr made a speech at a victory rally following the announcement of a favourable U.S. Supreme Court Decision desegregating the seats on Montgomery's buses.

Beloved Community, for Dr King, is just community and that injustice anywhere is a threat to justice everywhere. This means homeless, poverty, hunger, discrimination and abuse cannot be tolerated as they violate human dignity. It is equally in the dignity of all persons to act upon an ethic of love and support the deliberation from such indignity. Justice is mutual liberation and mutual emancipation. Any injustice can damage the fabric of the community, fragmentise the bonds amongst people and result in antagonism. Hence Dr King advanced an important principle that justice seeks to overcome injustice, but not through punishing people because, for Dr King, those who have perpetrated and transgressed are also suffering from harm – the harm to their spirit in the act of dehumanisation.

Dr King's vision for Beloved Community is confronted with a contemporary challenge of individualism and the pursuit of atomic independence. Both individualism and self-centred independence have significantly weakened the bonds amongst people, and sabotaged the fabric of the community. For example, we might find that we seldom have genuine interaction with people in our neighbourhood. In structuring our living spaces around individual privacy, a great deal of intrinsic value in communing and relationing goes unnoticed and unappreciated.

Against such a backdrop, however, there is the global emergence of intentional communities, such as ecovillages.[3] These are effectively beloved communities in which members of the community make a conscious decision to see each other and in many cases the environment as well, as beings of intrinsic and non-instrumental value rather than simply a means. These communities are characterised by the practices of mutual valuing, loving kindness, caring and extending good will to all, including to beings in nature. Here are a few examples of intentional communities:

Hertha Living Community near Aarhus, Denmark is a community that places special attention and care on the needs of differently abled people. These individuals are loved in the sense that their humanity is equally appreciated, and the community builds its amenities and facilities around the diverse needs of its residents. Furthermore, this model demonstrates the bestowal characteristics of love by considering the residents' needs and seeking to gift or provide value

---

3 https://www.mutualaidhub.org/resources; https://www.resilience.org/stories/2013-08-26/how-lending-circles-mutual-aid-groups-create-community-resilience/; http://www.deanspade.net/wp-content/uploads/2020/03/Mutual-Aid-Article-Social-Text-Final.pdf

without the expectation of indebtedness. The Hertha Living Community stands in stark contrast to many capitalist societies where developmentally challenged individuals are often not valued or are even explicitly regarded as burdensome.

Los Angeles Ecovillage is another compelling example of intentional community. The Ecovillage began in 1993 and has expanded to include collective ownership of land and buildings and a support network of ecological initiatives and businesses. Here love is practiced in the development and the enrichment of the community. From valuing the environment and the skills that each of the diverse neighbours can bring to the community, to the creation of value in collaboratively retrofitting houses to be zero emissions capable, or hosting community-building events, love is practiced through intention. Decisions are made through dialogue and listening, leading to collective consensus on the projects that they intend to carry out. Each member of the community pledges to uphold the values decided upon as a group. Love is expressed and experienced in the collective caring for the well-being of each other.

Focolare movement, already mentioned, takes the practice of love to another level. It recognises that physical separation is not the only challenge that confronts humanity today and that spiritual isolation is also widespread. Spiritual isolation can be felt in the mainstreaming of individualistic principles and ideas. Pop culture, the news and the media tend to highlight narratives of separation, violence and hatred. In this media environment, it can be difficult for spiritually minded people to find one another. The Focolare movement is rooted in the Catholic Church's practice of actively reaching out to people of all religions, faiths and beliefs and bringing together people who are committed to building a united world. Focolare's members are dedicated to loving God and loving all people without exclusion, renounce material wealth and devote their lives to the communing with oneness. To achieve such radical love, daily practice of the art of loving is the foundation to acquire loving qualities. In the words of the founder of Focolare, Chiara Lubich, such practices of love help 'penetrate to the highest contemplation while mingling with everyone […]'.

Mutual Aid has an extensive history of empowering the disenfranchised and enabling resources to be shared amongst members of a community. In essence, the project aims to combine the strengths of each individual and address the needs of the community at large. In recent times, Mutual Aid projects have been established to remedy the failure of the state to adequately protect citizens from catastrophes and pandemics.

Mutual Aid typically begins with a small group of neighbours who band together to address a challenge in the community. These neighbours describe their talents as well as their weaknesses. Since mutual respect is tantamount, each member searches for ways that their talents might resolve the challenges that others face. This can take the form of direct economic aid, manual labour, construction of art, childcare and so on. In each case, the aid is 'gifted' with no expectation of remuneration. The gift is thought of as a contribution to the community rather than to any one individual. Mutual Aid projects are inherently loving because they encourage compassion and connection. They demonstrate an 'appreciation' definition of love by recognising that each individual is invaluable and has their own gifts. This is also extended into the 'bestowal' characteristics of love because these unique gifts that each person has are shared rather than kept in isolation.

The combination of both 'appreciation' and 'bestowal' present in Mutual Aid projects set it apart from a traditional conception of charity. In contemporary Western societies, charities typically involve a bestowal form of love in which the loving relationship goes from those possessing more resources to those with little. It is a benevolent act. Gauging from the triadic notion of love advanced in this book, charity as such can increase isolation because it reinforces the power dynamics separating the gift-giver from the receiver. Mutual Aid transcends the limitations of charity through normalising giving and enabling all neighbours to recognise their value and potential. It acts upon beneficence whereby the person who gifts takes the other's well-being needs seriously.

Mutual Aid returns power and co-belonging to communities through bonds of love. Mutual Aid networks can be a model for loving neighbourhoods, businesses and even larger enterprises. Mutual Aid does not replace the function of government or business, but it shows that unless these institutions are structured in ways akin to loving communities, people can and will find their own ways to express equal consideration amongst their neighbours.

***

Education of Love

In this book, we have observed that many thinkers and philosophers have postulated that an ethic of love must first and foremost be cultivated in and through education and formation. As Rousseau proposed in *Emile*, when education focuses on love, it can enable children and young people to become loving, caring and compassionate persons. Carefully set within an ideal environment of relational depths and intellectual richness, Emile's education, in the absence of societal influences and pressures, has enabled him to experience *love* in their idealised forms. Education thus provides a moral compass and ethical sensitivity for fostering civic identity grounded in virtues and hence right relationships with oneself, with other people and with goodness in the world.

From the classical Greeks to contemporary thinking, education has been consistently recognised as a most important site to advance the art of loving, through nurturing values, enriching generative relationships and fostering inquiring spirit. When embracing an ethic of love, education cannot be merely the transmission of skills and information, but instead, it involves a broader mission – enabling us to become more fully human.

In this book, proposals for education of love include those activities and pedagogies that intentionally cultivate human virtues, friendship-love and mutual caring. Some schools in contemporary Western societies deliberately teach students how to be loving and caring by providing ethical education, citizenship education and service learning. Other educators would join many of the thinkers in the book and suggest that ethical education be more than building good moral characters and personal virtues, but rather education should be about learning to be loving.

Key ideas emerging from this book in the context of education, or learning to be loving, entail these five aspects, including the arts of valuing, cultivating persons, listening and dialogue, relating and caring.

The first is valuing humans non-instrumentally. For a long time, critics have pointed out that our current educational system is infused with instrumentality and is driven by testing performance, resulting in the loss of mean-ing, and, above all, at the cost of students' well-being. Meaningful relationships in schools are increasingly trivialised and where there are attempts, they can be superficial and devoid of human touch. To counter such a culture, an ethic of love must be rooted in schools as humanising places permeated with an ethos of valuing everyone non-instrumentally. Valuing in this way is constituted by our self-respect and respect for others. Likewise, when valued as such, students, teachers and parents are more open to actively participating in each other's realities, being present and availing themselves to each other, thus restoring the community.

The second is the intention for education to cultivate persons. Educational systems in many Western countries dictate a national curriculum that prescribes to the teachers the contents to be learned by the students. What underlies such a national curriculum is often a fixed idea of what kind of end-product education should aim to deliver, treating persons as objects, who are reducible to functions, roles and categories. To liberate schooling from such a factory model, an ethic of love proposes that the aims of education must be the formation of human beings. An ethic of love highlights that in learning to become more fully human, education can contribute to our self-transcendence, relational enrichment and greater engagement with others and with the world in order to transform human conditions. This means that curriculum contents cannot be limited to information and knowledge mastery and should include important activities and experiences such as those in arts, music, theatre, literature, dance, movements, sports, scientific inquiry, exploration of nature and community engagement.

The third is focusing on the arts of listening and dialogue. Pedagogically, an ethic of love prioritises the persistent presence of teachers and a central feature of teaching as listening and dialogue which constitute a 'pedagogy of encounter'. Listening and dialogue in classrooms can be experienced as a form of love, a spiritual presence to each other and deep listening can enable students and teachers to hear each other out – into presence and into relationships. The challenge is for the teacher's presence and listening to be a constancy and ethical education will provide opportunities for teachers to reflect on their practices and learn how to better facilitate listening and dialogue.

The fourth is co-creating spaces for meaningful and generative relating. From an organisational perspective, schools must create safe spaces for children and young people to come together and share feelings, emotions and experiences of life. Equally, teaching and learning should intentionally offer students time and spaces to attend to and participate in an array of relationships and discuss ways to enrich friendships and relationships. Sharing can transcend the solitary self and egoism and deepen our experiences of 'we'.

The last one is constructing schools as caring communities. An ethic of love stresses that the 'I' is always already part of the 'we', which can be experienced more vividly when schools are constructed as caring communities. A caring community can enable relationships and interactions beyond the roles or functions that people occupy (under the titles such as principal, teacher, counsellor, teaching assistant, student and cleaner). It can help members of the learning community to surpass the designated categories for self-identification (e.g. colour, ethnicity, gender, sexuality, age, social class, ability and other identity labels). Such transcending does not imply that one abandons one's responsibility, sense of one's self and one's place in the world. Instead, in a community, people care for each other and care about each other because the other is part of one's self and our friendship, and caring relationship is already constituted in our well-being. In this way, learning through being a part of community helps expand students' horizons and qualities – the real promise of becoming.

Through learning the art of loving, children, young people and all persons can perceive one another through the lens of goodness and beauty. Studies in social, political, economic and natural sciences and technology are better placed to involve wider and direct experiences in the natural world and in the community. Equally, schools can engage in spiritual explorations through practices such as prayer, contemplation, meditation, silent walk, storying, meal-sharing, inner listening and deep dialogue. Above all, learning to love requires educators and caregivers (parents, teachers and community members) to create loving spaces in educational settings, to avail themselves to students and to enable students to partake in their human-being-ness. In many ways, nurturing loving consciousness is a process of practising love. These orientations can equally apply to informal and non formal education, such as educative activities that take place in families, communities, universities, workplaces, societies and beyond. That is to say, the *world* in which a child grows up, a person matures, a being becomes and flourishes and to which all human belong must be understood as in part the 'school' of love.

***

Ecology of Love

This book outlines some of the Western thinkers' arguments on why beings in nature and non-human life on Earth must be valued and appreciated alongside human well-being and flourishing. These are intrinsic values and, therefore, nature cannot be treated as pure means for human purpose. The ideas, such as those of Spinoza's, go further by suggesting that there be no separation between the human world and our environment, or the natural world. In fact, nature is already constituted in the life of humans, and nature is comprised in our well-being. Therefore the 'we' already includes both human and non-human beings on our planet.

This means that our well-being involves a self-aware consciousness that humans are part of this more inclusive 'we', allowing us to extend valuing, relationing and caring to all beings because they are part of us. This integral view does not recognise any separation between human beings and other beings in nature. Non-dualism may prevent and protect us from acting upon the separation. Loving nature is synonymous with loving ourselves. Likewise, the act of loving nature is to become as concerned with the well-being of the natural world. Love engenders an ethic of caring for the environment.

Globally, there are many programmes that aim at reconnecting us to nature and inviting us to take part in the stewardship of the world that is needed.

Million Pollinator Gardens Challenge by the National Pollinator Gardens Network in the United States is one such project. The project hopes to protect bees and other pollinators from extinction by reversing the trend of keeping manicured lawns over gardens with wildflowers and natural diversity. A Pollinator Garden involves the planting of local flowers, elimination of pesticides and safe nesting places for common pollinators such as bees, bats and birds. Homeowners and Business owners signed up for the project and pledged to transform their gardens to reconnect to nature. They shared their efforts and successes with pictures and stories on social media. The project has already exceeded its goal of building a movement of over a million pollinator gardens, and they are continuing to provide resources for others to follow suit. They encourage schools to plant pollinator gardens in order to teach young children about the immense beauty and intrinsic value of the natural world. Philanthropic sponsors of the movement donate seeds in addition to monetary resources, demonstrating a commitment to the paradigm shift that the project requires.

The Million Pollinator Gardens mission exemplifies love in practice because the process of turning a lawn into a garden is both intentional and about caring deeply for another. First, the decision to change from the status quo is motivated by the recognition that nature is part of our well-being, and when natural environment is in danger, we must act to heal and nurture it. Second, the planning for such a garden cannot be motivated by selfish reasons. The garden must be planned using plants found naturally in the environment where one lives rather than being chosen for purely aesthetic or convenience purposes. Again, this step shows reverence for the needs of another and demonstrates an ethic of love in service to nature. Third, with the garden planned the next step involves continuous care and attention. Unlike a lawn that can be passively tended, a garden that is committed to not using pesticides requires continuous attention and maintenance. And finally, when the garden is in full bloom it should be clear that a loving relationship is shared between the garden and all its beings, and the gardener(s). The garden values the gardener for the nurturing attention, watering and tending and in turn gifts back to the gardener(s) natural beauty, tranquil experiences with wildlife and perhaps even food. The gardener, having exhibited love as an beneficent act in the tending and nurturing, also loves the garden for its natural splendour and appearance. This symbiotic relationship in love is a microcosm of the actions that need to take place to restore our connection with nature, but it is an accessible one.

Conclusion

Through practice of love in these intersectional domains, this chapter illustrates that recognising love's values in a holistic way is a starting point towards shifting our collective consciousness and transforming our cultures, systems and practices. An ethic of love affirms the understanding that the good life resides precisely in our being truly part of nature, the sacred, the divine and the greater harmony in which all participate and to which all contribute.[4] This is the essence of the paradigm of love that involves a deep appreciation of the good life, as well as of the kinds of situations and conditions that propagate goodness for humanity. The question is how to pursue love, the good life, by aspiring to the greater values and acting with love and care in the here and now, aimed at continued human growth. As already outlined, this understanding thus has profound implications for different fields of human action, not least those explored, for example, politics/governance, economy, family/community, education and ecology. These fields are not isolated and cannot be viewed as such, instead, they are part of an intertwining, interconnected whole. In other words, the paradigm of love inspires systems thinking that acknowledges the dynamic, complex and interdependent nature of our life and our world.

---

4 Such a view is prefigured in Spinoza; see Chapter 2.

CHAPTER 7

TOWARDS A PARADIGM OF LOVE

The Now is what measures time backwards and forwards, because the Now, strictly speaking, is not time but outside time. In the Now, past and future meet. For a fleeting moment they are simultaneous so that they can be stored up by memory, which remembers things past and holds the expectation of things to come. For a fleeting moment (the temporal Now) it is as though time stands still, and it is this Now that becomes [...] eternity.
—Hanah Arendt, *Love and Saint Augustine*

Our starting point for this book's inquiry was that the world urgently needs a new narrative concerning who we are, what we ought to value and what sort of lives we should live together on Earth. Conceptions of what constitutes human flourishing are thus revisited with the hope that they might inspire the systemic transformation that our time requires. This is especially pertinent when the prevailing narrative of growth and development is incapable of informing and guiding us in our pursuit of being well, living well and becoming well together. On the contrary, decline has been observed in many dimensions of our personal and political lives, such as in our mutual relatedness, in how we conduct and organise our societies, institutions and political associations and in how we confront the challenges of the twenty-first century.

It was this inadequacy that prompted the inquiry (and its findings) reported in this book. The intuition was that any narrative to serve as an inspiration for a new way of being, living and becoming human together must concern love. The fundamental question in the pursuit of meaningfulness in life is: 'What is valuable and important in human life?' This is the question that has been central to virtually all conceptions of and narratives about the good life since Socrates' invitation for us to live an examined life. For such a narrative to be capable of transcending current impasses and transforming us in all aspects of human life, it must involve an understanding of the nature of love and the qualities and manifestations of love in our collective life on Earth. As a consistent thread across major accounts of the good life, love has offered an opportunity for humanity to learn from, develop and go beyond those conceptions in the course of arriving at a new future-making and world-making narrative.

This question has helped the book to present our inquiry into the good life by following the evolution of love's accounts throughout the ages. This approach has allowed us to observe that love is not a contemporary invention, nor is it a long forgotten past vision, nor a pure romantic idea. Instead, love has a profound root in human thoughts since antiquity and conceptions of love, although varied at different times, have remained central to human's quest for a common flourishing life. In particular, we have chosen to explore three aspects of the notion of love, that is, love as valuing, love as relationing and love as caring or acting with caring. As a part of a triadic framework, these have served as the interlocking perspectives that give rise to the imperative of love in the twenty first century.

There is much we have learned in this inquiry which is particularly meaningful in highlighting what should constitute the good life in the present time. Let's recall the major accounts in this book:

Platonic, Aristotelean and Stoic thoughts have all provided conceptions of love that has transcendence at its core. Love's ladder and love's justice are both avenues that aim to help humans to come closer to a cosmic order and a place beyond the human. Together, these articulations and postulations on love seem to marry metaphysics with ethics, pointing towards a practical wisdom or praxis to guide the ways for us to live the common life together in congenial relations, through different structural designs that facilitate relational processes at multiple levels, as well as by engaging in different domains of transformative actions.

In Christian mysticism, love is a transcendent vision in that humans can strive to rise above ourselves and to attain the highest goodness, beauty and truth or supreme value through spiritual ascension. Christian philosophers have even identified steps of enlightenment as a pathway to reach God, as in Diotima's ladder, taking all that is in the universe (God's creations) closer to the divine.[1] However, such ascension is only possible by God reaching human through God's bestowal of love, as if a reverse ascension – human self-transcendence is achieved when God reach down to humans and help liberate humanity's burden of seeking salvation on our own. Thus, faith has become a

---

1 For instance, St Bonaventure (1217–1274).

critical element in Christian agapē where humans can depend on God's gift in order to be delivered from our limitedness, imperfection and sins.

Accordingly, Christian love is gift, Grace and true bestowal. Human love, including self-love, friendship-love or neighbourly love, is the fruit of and for the sake of God's love. On this account, C. S. Lewis claims: 'human loves deserved to be called loves at all just in so far as they resembled that Love which is God'.[2] It might also be argued in this case that God's love is realised by human love.

The modern world has seen an unprecedented increase in human interest in understanding love and exploring love's values and expressions in our individual and collective lives. Love becomes the end of our ethical pursuit, and love is pursued as a valuable good in that it contributes to what is non-instrumentally valuable, including our well-being, dignity and integrity.[3] Instead of being regarded as a mere pathway to transcendence, modern conception of love recognises and appreciates the intrinsic non-instrumental value in being human and our being part of the greater cosmos (i.e. nature). Thus love's immanence is placed alongside love's transcendence.

By locating love within our understanding of the good life and well-being, this book highlights that to qualify love as valuing, we must focus on the beings who are bearers of values whose intrinsically valuable nature must be acknowledged and embraced. For instance, love's valuing points to that what we want is the goodness and well-being of our beloved for their own sake and not instrumentally for the sake of furthering other aims. This is a recognition that what we desire as the goods for our beloved must be constituted in their well-being and flourishing. This approach should be supported by many contemporary thinkers. In the case of focusing on the bearers of values, Robert Nozick claims that life has meaning when one relates to things of value beyond oneself and when life contains a positive insight of great importance that we do not want to lose. Life is more valuable and meaningful when one is connected to things of value outside oneself. This places humans in an important place in engaging in, facilitating and ensuring values in our self-recognition, in our activities that constitute our life, such as enjoying beauty, in our relational processes and in our action towards the common good in the world. In this book, we regard these as dimensions of well-being.

That is to say, as bearers of values, humans are respected for the intrinsic worthwhile nature of our being and equally humans must assume greater

---

2 Lewis, *The Four Loves*, 1.
3 Friedman, 1993.

responsibility for caring for each other, for other beings in nature and for striving for good causes towards the well-being of all, for engaging in the pursuit of meaning beyond the limits of our own life. By appreciating the value of things beyond one's own life, as bearers of values, we can enrich our own and each other's well-being.

Our analysis of love's profound meaningfulness must be extended to identifying ethical anchors and practical ideas for transforming the conditions of our life. As Erich Fromm advises:

> To analyze the nature of love is to discover its general absence today and to criticize the social conditions which are responsible for this absence. To have faith in the possibility of love as a social and not only exceptional-individual phenomenon, is a rational faith based on the insight into the very nature of man.[4]

This includes the ways that love can inspire new understandings in terms of how institutions, political processes and economic systems necessarily facilitate human well-being and flourishing of all.

Nygren identifies ambiguities in the meaning of love, power and justice and suggests the confusion has resulted in misconceptions of the relationships between these three notions. Clearly, it is erroneous to consider that love and power are opposite. For Nygren, it is a mistake to identify love with 'a resignation of power' (or powerless love) as it renders love a mere emotion and power 'a denial of love'. However, the opposite, or loveless power, is likewise a flawed idea, as it connects power with force. It seems that without tracing love's ontological significance, we will continue to separate personal realities from public practices; spiritual life from social, economic and political engagements. Thus ethics must assume a meaningful interconnection between 'the element of love in structures of power and the element of power without which love becomes chaotic surrender'.[5] The same might also apply to our understanding of justice which cannot be conceptualised as demanding a fair and proportional resource distribution, or as insisting on each person deserving their due. Love can too transcend justice, allowing us to escape the domination of abstract laws and locate justice as right relationships in the lived human realities, through forgiveness, atonement and good will.

---

4 Fromm, *The Art of Loving*.
5 Nygren, *Agape and Eros*, 129.

The question is: have our efforts to revisit the accounts of love served to resolve the ambiguities identified by Ngyren? In many ways, this book, in outlining key relevant discussions in selected Western philosophies across the time span of human history, has indeed helped illuminate and clarify relationships between love, power and justice in the common life of humanity.

For instance, the Greek and Christian cosmology tends to suppose that humans must seek transcendence as our collective growth, to attain qualities that are greater which are only found in the sacred realm. We then showed that where humans aspired for transformation, we could also find ourselves enslaved by the 'higher' powers in their ideology and beliefs about meaningfulness of human life. Thus humanistic philosophers began to apply rationality rather than pure theistic doctrines in deconstructing religious authority and introduced scientific ways of knowing as a counter-narrative to discern meaning and explain the world. This shift of narrative from cosmology and monotheistic theology to rationality and empiricism might seem to be liberating, but it nevertheless offers yet another grand narrative only to be deconstructed by post-modern thinkers.

In each historical period, there has been construction and critique of ideas, but the perennial quest has never been withdrawn and deconstruction is unending, aiming at understanding better what constitutes the good life. For instance, one of the central tenets of the critique has been on our present system of production, which has never found a satisfactory alternative. This is a system of instrumentalisation that has now been embedded in the Western economy and societal fabric since the late 1500s when humans were captured and traded as commodities and enslaved brutally. Mass enslavement for the sake of financial gain marked the beginning of structural dehumanisation that has continued until today. Europeans in Europe and people of European descent in North America have built their so-called civilisations and materialistic wealth partly by instrumentalising people and exploiting the lands in other continents including Asia, Africa and North and South Americas. For nearly five centuries, the system of instrumentalisation and dehumanisation is increasingly becoming so deeply seated that it seems to be the only language through which we can talk about economics, politics, public welfare, common good and education. This is the language of measurement based on materalistic gains; it is also the language of growth for the sake of growth, once again in the realm of material wealth. Many have indeed attempted to explain how, when instrumentalisation is carried out at a structural level, it not only frames our institutional ethos and practices as instrumental, it may also re-configure human thoughts, our relations, the practices of our institutions and the cultures of our societies as such.

Love's evolution and revolution suggest that it be a concept that is full of contentions and contradictions. Here I highlight three:

Ascension. Cosmocentric and theocentric conceptions articulate that love embodies an ascension, from Diotima's ladder to the Christian salvation. In the Greek conception, the ascension is connected to the extent and the kinds of value that are appreciated, including, the value of beauty in the body, the value of beauty in the soul, beauty as an ethical and aesthetic value itself, at which level, we can 'know just what it is to be beautiful [...] pure, unmixed, divine, uniform and devoid of the great silliness that mars the beauty of human beings'.[6] In Christian salvation, this ascension entails steps that can take humans from Earth to God, each level of which finds us more perfect, more pure and more enlightened than the previous level.[7] Salvation promises mankind the possibility to infuse with the divine and even become one with God through love's elevation. Christian erôs helps ordinary persons to rise above the transient, imperfect world through stages of spiritual development to reach God's perfection. Such ascension also exists in the realm of human love, with sexual love being regarded as close to animal instinct, thereby at the lowest level, followed by passionate or romantic love, then friendship-love and the highest being caritas, love for all things of value. In each case, the ascension aims at going-beyond, seeking becoming more than ourselves. Thus, in each ascending process, there is an implication that love's gifts are being treated as means, in Diotima's words, 'using these beautiful things ... as steps',[8] suggesting that true ends are beyond the human.

Clearly, this rising-above, or going-beyond, does not always fare well in all contexts. It has resulted in the critique of this ascension view, which has been recognised by feminist philosophers as within the domain of the masculine. By contrast, the lived everyday experiences are located in the immanent and are placed in the domain of the feminine. Transcendence instrumentalises immanence, perpetuating not just a value hierarchy but also a potential system of exploitation. For this project, we can see that simply placing the tension within the realm of the clash between the masculine and the feminine does not

---

6 Kraut, "Plato on Love," 296.
7 May, *Love: A History*.
8 Plato, *Symposium*, 211c.

cover the complexity of the issue at hand, and our concluding remarks on de Beauvoir's view of an integrative approach may also be too abrupt.

Furthermore, there is a structural question about who has the authority to bestow love and how such authority ought to be perceived. In the context of love's value, power can either be perceived as strength and energising force or as control and domination. Several contemporary philosophers reviewed here have argued that religious doctrines and Christian churches have become a part of the greater system of control and domination, threatening human's liberty and freedom. Control can be perceived as a form of dehumanisation, reducing persons to objects, rather than co-subject. Likewise, love's value may also be misplaced to treat other people as means to one's own passion, pleasure and desire. Marriage, motherhood and even human body can be emplacement of instrumentality. Sexual liberation, gender equality and debate on abortion have come to the fore not just due to the incompatibility of sex and love, basic human needs and morality, and also because of the tension between instrumental and non-instrumental values.

On this note, Martin Luther King Jr developed love levels based on the different forms of values and what to be valued. At the bottom level, he suggests, lies the utilitarian love, where we love each other for mutual usefulness, out of needs. This is to apply the instrumental value of love. At the next level is *erôs* or romantic love, which, according to King, although egoistic also has a sense of altruism. For example, one can love another person for the sake of loving. Hence erôs is above utilitarian love. King suggests that mother's love be placed at a higher level as it is non-instrumental and purely giving. However, even mother's love can be limited as it tends to be oriented towards her own children. Therefore, King proposes that friendship-love or perfect philia be at the next level up. It is regarded at a higher level because friendship-love can embrace more people. It is broader than mother's love and more generous. Better still, for King, is humanitarian love, which is greater than friendship-love because it comprises the humanity as a whole. What is even higher, as King highlights, is agapē, 'unmotivated [...] spontaneous [...] overflowing [...] seek[ing] nothing in return'.[9] This, as King puts it, is gift-love and available to all, encompassing all, including one's enemy. At a highest level, we find non-instrumental love – the value of love as of itself.

Clearly, by focusing on love as valuing and by discerning the different kinds of value that love embodies, King is able to present love's levels without

---

9 King, "Levels of Love."

resolving it beyond the human. Although it does not resolve the tension between going-beyond the human and appreciating the human in the here and now, it does help cohere the idea of transcendence and the notion of immanence. In this model, King offers love as a continuum, an integration of instrumental and non-instrumental values where needs are met, cares are provided, love is given and love is appreciated in its own right. Despite its pointing to seemingly a hierarchy, King's vision is in effect a vision of harmony of love's values where instrumental values and non-instrumental values complement each other in a coherent way. We hence included King's proposal of living in the beloved *community* held together with love as the thread, which intends to illustrate that such a conception of love can wave a beautiful tapestry of harmony through sharing, caring, collaborating and co-acting synergetically in the pursuit of a good life for one and all.

Love of persons. There are two sides to the love of persons, each presenting some ambiguity in the literature. On the one hand is the love of one's self or self-love. Self-love has been both celebrated and criticised in our review so far. To love at all requires one to value oneself. As we have seen, this is the first condition for the highest form of Aristotelian love – one must love oneself. Without such a self-directed basis, one cannot extend sympathy and affection to others. This may lean on a Kantian notion of self-respect too. To love oneself, it relies on self-knowledge, or our soul's awareness, in the words of Thomas Aquinas and our rational capacity to appreciate ourselves and our qualities. This applies in particular when examining our nature and our value or worthiness to merit divine or God's love. Alternatively, self-love is regarded as a self-delight, allowing ourselves to pursue our interest. According to Velleman, love is a distinctive response to appreciating something and someone's value as a 'self-existent end'.[10] It is a distinctive way of valuing someone's humanity or personhood, especially that of one's own.

At the same time, self-love as satisfying one's own desire and meeting one's own needs can imply a more ego-driven conception. It poses an irreconcilable tension with self-love as valuing our own dignity. This tension pertains to the ongoing explorations of love in more recent literature throughout late twentieth and early twenty-first centuries. Self-love has evolved into contemporary notions such as self-concept, self-esteem and self-respect. These tend to be concerned with one's sense of value in relation to others and within a given society.[11] The latter development on self-concept would bear no resemblance

---

10 Velleman, 1999, 65.
11 Rosenberg, *Society and the Adolescent Self-Image*.

to the kind of self-love that the classic philosophers and Christian philosophers have conceptualised.

The other side is love of other persons. Once again, there are ambiguities, especially where other people are valuable in relation to one's needs, desires and interests. That is to say, on the one hand, love of other people can be instrumental, where we are drawn to others by our own desire for their qualities as a way to respond to and satisfy our own need; on the other hand, we can love other people non-instrumentally whereby because they embody the non-derivative value in their own right. There is more to the latter which is yet to be explicitly treated in philosophy. Let's take a brief look here.

No doubt the valuable aspect of love is the other person, the loved one. By this, we do not mean just that the beloved feels important to the person who loves, although that is, of course, true. Rather the point is that, in loving someone, we can become connected to the valuable nature of the other person. One aspect of that connection is that the other person feels important to us in their own right, not because of. In other words, one recognises that there is a being, the other person, of value distinct from one's self and one becomes deeply connected and involved with that other life. We can see these in particular in friendship-love discussed in this book.

Part of the beauty and wonder in the love of other people is that we can realise and feel this self-regarding value of others as part of nature and thereby participate in it as Spinoza suggests. We can do so simply by connecting to another as a person, which, according to Kant, implies a feeling of respect and care for the other person. Moreover, one aspect of loving another person is learning how to see things from their perspective, participating in their life and entering their phenomenological world. It involves appreciating their subjectivity. More specifically and more intimately, we can connect to their valuable qualities or virtues, if using a Christian notion.

This point shows that love as 'feeling towards'[12] and other forms of commitment are, in a sense, under-determined. There are good reasons for loving those we care for. For instance, they are our friends, or families, or they have special and loveable qualities. However, our friends and our families are almost certainly not unique in having such qualities. Part of love is appreciating the loveable qualities of the person one adores, but one can also recognise that many other people have similar qualities. This makes love's value under-determined. This realisation can enrich our view of the world. By recognising

---

12 Hamlyn, "The Phenomena of Love and Hate."

that other people have equally loveable qualities, one can perceive strangers as potential friends and families. The strangers might also include one's enemies.

This beautiful and ethical aspect of loving and appreciating the values of persons, including oneself and other people, can help us confront systemic othering: people from different backgrounds can find themselves defined by socio-economic and political institutions as the Other and thus be made to feel vulnerable and dehumanised. These 'others' tend to be women, people of ethnic minorities and those who are considered different as defined by the Western norms. To challenge structural discrimination and oppression, it requires such a conception of love for other people to embrace the ethics of love's under-determined value, which makes love of the Other possible.

Emotions. Due to the limited scope of the review and owing to their deeply ambiguous nature, we have avoided getting entangled in romantic love and sexual love, although these have been implied. In so doing, I have omitted to review important discussions on the value of emotions and emotional experiences as part of human life. Love of other people must involve the values of emotions in their rich arrays and complexities.

Martha Nussbaum has regarded love as the emotional foundation of human life. For Nussbaum, love 'lies at the root of all the other emotions'.[13] She argues that erotic love is constituted by judgements or appraisals that something is of great value and importance, in itself and to one's own flourishing. Although valuable, erotic love can also be beyond one's control and make one vulnerable to the contingencies of the world. Hence love is at the root of our emotions and human life also consists in the emotional dimension. One of Nussbaum's primary concerns is with how emotions are constituted in an ethical life, and how they can be legitimate inputs to ethical deliberation in politics, for instance, and warrant encouragement and support by society and its institutions. From this ethical perspective, Nussbaum is able to defend that erotic love and emotions are essential in a flourishing life. Not only is such a defence needed, but it is also urgent, for emotions in general have often been viewed with suspicion as antithetical to living well in the Western philosophical traditions. For example, in the Helenistic philosophies, particularly Epicureanism, or Stoicism, in which *ataraxia*, or the state of the soul (that is free of emotional upheaval), is viewed as a central component of happiness. In contrast, strong sexual desire is viewed as antithetical to human happiness, owing to the attendant tumultuous emotions

---

13 Nussbaum, *Upheavals of Thought*, 459.

that it inevitably invites.[14] Other philosophers, such as St Augustine and David Hume, have joined the Stoics to suggest that emotions be an irrational force, consuming, imprisoning our mind and preoccupying our thoughts, making us become obsessed with the object of our emotions.

Rather than such brute forces, emotions, according to Nussbaum, are states of mind which are *about* some more or less specific things that 'involve often complex beliefs' and 'are concerned with *value*'.[15] If the judgements that constitute emotions concern value, how are we to understand the nature of the value they ascribe to things? Here, Nussbaum's view is subtle and complex. It is common for ethicists to distinguish between conceptions of values which take them to be objective, existing intrinsically in things independently of us or what we think or feel about them and those which take them to be subjective, dependent on what we feel or how think about things; or even as a 'projection' of our attitudes onto things which, in themselves, are evaluatively neutral. Nussbaum insists that the value which is attributed to things in judgements of emotion is of a particular sort, the kind that enables one 'to make reference to the person's own flourishing'.[16] Whilst things and persons may be highly valuable and important for one's flourishing, this needn't mean that they are merely instrumentally valuable, to be treated merely as means to our pursuit of happiness and the good life. Similar to the above argument about love of other people, other people are valuable because they constitute in part our own good life, in this case, 'emotions appear to be *eudaimonistic*, that is, concerned with the person's flourishing'.[17]

Essentially acknowledging them being comprised in our natural and spiritual vulnerability and recognising their being intrinsically constituted in human well-being, emotions thus conceived can be regarded as an ethical foundation of human life. This ethical aspect is at odds with individualism and self-sufficiency both of which seem to be venerated by neoliberal ethics, politics and economics. In its structural connection to narcissistic and possessive paternalism, fear, anger, jealousy, hatred and vengeance, erôs risks being incompatible with the compassionate conception of ethics and the good life. To this, we might add Kant's objection that:

---

14 Cf. Nussbaum, "Compassion: The Basic Social Emotion," Ch. 4–5, 10, 12; Chadwick, 1998, in Augustine, 1998, xvii.
15 Nussbaum, *Upheavals of Thought*, 30.
16 Ibid., 31.
17 Ibid., 31.

> [sexual love] makes of the loved person an Object of appetite [...] Taken by itself it is a degradation of human nature; for as soon as a person becomes an Object of appetite for another, all motives of moral relationship cease to function because [...] a person becomes a thing and can be treated and used as such by every one.[18]

In order to reconcile emotion with ethics and make a claim for emotions to have a place in the meaningful life well lived, Nussbaum argues that loving emotions must incorporate three key criteria: individuality, compassion and reciprocity. It can thus rule out instrumentalising and objectifying the human.

Responses to Objections

I am fully aware of criticisms and objections to this book's proposition.

As a start, one may point out that by following a progression in the conceptions of love, there is a risk of giving the impression that the development of these has proceeded in a clear and linear fashion. This would suggest a naive and superficial understanding of the complexity.

To respond: In writing this book, I have been particularly mindful of the shifting landscapes and dialectics in our understanding of love. In particular, I was constantly reminded of Ervin Singer's caution that 'we still have to recognise that history – the history of ideas in this case' that:

> doesn't march in a linear fashion. Ideational changes are like changes in the stock market. They go in one direction and then there is a reaction against them [...].[19]

As well as recognising the non-linear nature of the Western history of ideas, I am also aware that the development of the narrative of love is confronted with the already identified tensions between the different ends of life's meaningfulness. For some, '[t]he history of love is intellectual warfare between bestiality on the one side and divinity on the other'.[20] For others, the debate is between the 'theological' and the 'naturalist' principles: philosophers of the former

---

18 Kant, *Lectures on Ethics*, 163–4; also See Baier, "Unsafe Loves," (esp 433–8, 446–8) for a fuller consideration of the risks undertaken in opening oneself to love – to society, to oneself and to one's lover.
19 Singer, *Philosophy of Love: A Partial Summing-Up*, 13.
20 Solomon, *In Defence of Sentimentality*, 166.

tradition tend to 'conceive of us primarily as souls in relation to other sinful souls or to a sovereign God', whilst the latter 'take umbilical cords, navels and other basic anatomical reminders of our mammalian condition more seriously than they take our immortal and sinful souls'.[21] Such complexity is investigated in the book rather than simplified. Similarly, the iterative processes of putting forward accounts of love over time are also accentuated.

Another challenge is the argument that a love-based narrative speaks to the obvious. It is good that few would object to the thesis, but then it has little added value. Indeed, as illustrated in Chapter 2, the word *love* has been used in such a way that it risks losing its meaning.

To respond: This book is meaningful because despite this cultural ubiquity, within the sphere of scholarship, love has received a seemingly disproportionate lack of systematic investigation. Notwithstanding philosophers and theologians, throughout the ages, have argued for the paramount significance of love in our ethical life, a few books that do explicitly explore the philosophy of love (e.g. those by E. Singer, S. May, L. Ferry and L. Secomb) only serve to illustrate this lack.

A further question about the validity of such a book might be raised. For instance, one might argue that the goodness of love, being loving and feeling loved has always been accepted in our contemporary world. In psychology, for instance, the benefits of love include increased mental health, an elevated sense of self-worth and better character.[22] Likewise, feeling loving or being loved has been credited with lowering stress and increasing good family relationship and longevity,[23] and loving connections between people produce greater self-knowledge.[24] The list of known benefits or gains from love goes on. (Of course, there is also a wealth of literature that poses unrequited or misplaced love as the ultimate torment.) These claims also tend to boast their empirical basis, proving their verity and adding a sense of rigour. Why do we need close reading and thorough investigation and analysis of rich accounts of love?

To answer, I would say that recognising these instrumental values of love does not necessarily bring us closer to a deeper understanding of love as the core of the good life or human meaningfulness, nor can it inspire us to fully integrate love or live lovingly in our everyday personal and political lives. To

---

21 Baier, "Unsafe Loves," 438–9.
22 LaFollette, 1996.
23 Helm, 2017.
24 Badhwar, 2003.

prove the significance of love in human life through scientific measures only reinforces the causal link between love and the good life. It doesn't, however, offer any insights into the nature of love and how love gives rise to meanings. On the contrary, instrumental rationality can actually reduce the spiritual significance of love to mere utility, causing us to lose sight of the wonder of how love makes sacred the human.

Others may challenge by suggesting that accounts of love, although interesting to know and even helpful for people to recognise their value, e.g. the importance of mutual respect, can do little to confront the present perplexity as humanity reaches another crossroads. How does love matter when we must make choices that either determine a safe passage forward or lead to the peril of humanity altogether?

To respond, as the book illustrates, the power of love goes beyond a solely rational argument for the imperative of respect or appreciation.[25] It is also about our care for the other, including the greater Other, that is constituted in what is made sacred by love. Indeed, as Ferry suggests, the sacred really refers to that which is so valuable that it is worthy of *sacrificing* one's life for. The revered and sacrosanct is precisely what gives meaning to life and what makes life good and worthwhile. Thereby an ethic of love would help us become more fully conscious of the valuable nature of being human, our common life together, in communion with all that is and our collective well-being and flourishing. An ethic of love urges us not only to understand love but, more significantly, it motivates us to engage in acts of valuing, relationing and caring and to take an active responsibility for safeguarding all that is sacrosanct.

---

25 As in Kant, *Grounding for the Metaphysics of Morals*.

BIBLIOGRAPHY

Altamirano, A.. "Max Scheler and Adam Smith on Sympathy,". *The Review of Politics* 79 (2019): 365–387.
Aquinas, Thomas. *Summa Theologica*, translated by the Fathers of the English Dominican Province. Westminster: Christian Classics, 1981.
Arendt, H. *The Human Condition*. Chicago: University of Chicago Press, 1958.
———. *Love and Saint Augustine*, edited and translated by J. V. Scott and J. C. Stark. Chicago and London: University of Chicago Press, 1996.
———. *Men in Dark Times*. Boston, MA: Mariner Books, 1970.
———. *The Origins of Totalitarianism*. New York: A Harvest Book, 1968/1951.
———."Kant on the Emotion of Love." *European Journal of Philosophy* 24, no. 3 (2015): 580–606.
Aristotle. *Nicomachean Ethics* (2nd ed.), translated by Terence Irwin. Indianapolis, IN: Hackett, 1999.
Asmis, E. "Choice in Epictetus' Philosophy," in *Antiquity and Humanity: Essays on Ancient Religion and Philosophy*, edited by A. Collins and M. Mitchell, 385–412. Tübingen: Mohr Siebeck, 2001.
Atkinson, T.-G. "The Descent from Radical Feminism to Postmodernism", Presentation on the Panel 'How to Defang a Movement: Replacing the Political with the Personal' at the conference A Revolutionary Movement: Women's Liberation in the Late 1960s and the Early 1970s, Boston University, March 27–29, 2014.
Augustine. *The Confessions of St. Augustine*, translated by R. Warner. New York: Mentor, 1963.
———. "The Trinity." In *The Fathers of the Church: A New Translation, vol. 45*, translated by S. McKenna. Washington, DC: The Catholic University of America Press, 1963.
———. *The Works of Saint Augustine*. New York: New City Press, 1993.
———. *On Christian Doctrine*, translated and edited by R.P.H. Green. Oxford: Clarendon Press, 1995.
———. *The City of God Against the Pagans*, edited and translated by R.W. Dyson. Cambridge: Cambridge University Press, 1998.
Avnon, D. *Martin Buber. The Hidden Dialogue*. Lanham, MD: Rowman and Littlefield Publishers, 1998.
Baggini, J. *What's It All About? Philosophy & the Meaning of Life*. Oxford: Oxford University Press, 2004.

Baier, A. "Unsafe Loves." In *The Philosophy of (Erotic) Love*, edited by K. Higgins and R. Solomon. University of Kansas Press, 1991.

Barnes, J., ed. *Complete Works of Aristotle*, Princeton, NJ: Princeton University Press, 1984.

Beauvoir, S. de. *The Ethics of Ambiguity*, translated by B. Frechtman. New York: Citadel Press, 1947.

———. *The Second Sex*, translated by S. Borde and S. Malovany-Chevallier. New York: Random House, 1949.

Bertram, C. "Jean Jacques Rousseau." In *The Stanford Encyclopedia of Philosophy*, plato.stanford.edu, 2020

Bicknell, J. "An Overlooked Aspect of Love in Spinoza's "Ethics"." *The Jerusalem Philosophical Quarterly* 47 (1998): 41–45.

Biss, M. "Aristotle on Friendship and Self-Knowledge: The Friend Beyond the Mirror." *History of Philosophy Quarterly* 28, no. 2 (2011): 125–140.

Bjerke, A. R. "Hegel and the Love of the Concept." *The Heythrop Journal* LII (2011): 76–89.

Black, R. "What Did Adam Smith Say About Self-Love?" *Journal of Markets & Morality* 9, no. 1 (2006): 7–34.

Bostic, H. "Introduction: The Recent Work of Luce Irigaray." *L'Esprit Créateur* 52, no. 3 (2012): 1–10.

Brentino, F. *Psychology from an Empirical Standpoint*. London: Routledge and Kegan Paul, 1973.

Brown, E. "Plato's Ethics and Politics in *The Republic*." In *The Stanford Encyclopedia of Philosophy*, edited by E. Zalta, 2017. https://plato.stanford.edu/archives/fall2017/entries/plato-ethics-politics/.

Buber, M. *Between Man and Man*, translated by R. G. Smith. London: Kegan Paul, 1947.

———. *I and Thou*, translated by R. G. Smith. Edinburgh: T. & T. Clark, 1958.

Burch, K. "Rousseau on Love, Education, and Selfhood in "Emile"." *Counterpoints, Erōs as the Educational Principle of Democracy* 114 (2000): 115–141.

Burns, B. St. *Thomas Aquinas's Philosophy of Love: A Commentary on Mutua Inhaesio (Mutual Indwelling) as the Most Proper Effect of Love in IA IIAE, QQ26-28 of the Summa Theologiae*. Dallas, TX: University of Dallas, 2013.

Cates, D. "Thomas Aquinas on Intimacy and Emotional Integrity." *Studies in Spirituality* 16 (2006): 119.

Chiba, Shin. "Hannah Arendt on Love and the Political: Love, Friendship, and Citizenship." *The Review of Politics* 57, no. 3 (1995): 505–535.

Cooper, J. *Plato: Complete Works*. Indianapolis, IN: Hackett, 1997.

———. *Reason and Emotion: Essays on Ancient Moral Psychology and Ethical Theory*. Princeton, NJ: Princeton University Press, 1999.

Cory, T. *Aquinas on Human Self-Knowledge*. Cambridge: Cambridge University Press, 2013.

Cottingham, J. *On the Meaning of Life*. London: Routledge, 2003.

Cutting, John. "Max Scheler's Theory of the Hierarchy of Values and Emotions and Its Relevance to Current Psychopathology." *History of Psychiatry* 27, no. 2 (2016): 220–228.

Delaney, N. "Romantic Love and Loving Commitment: Articulating a Modern Ideal." *American Philosophical Quarterly* 33 (1996): 375–405.

Deleuze, G. and Guattari, F. *A Thousand Plateaus: Capitalism and Schizophrenia*, translated by Brian Massumi. Minneapolis, MN: University of Minnesota Press, 1987.

De Rougemont, D. *Love in the Western World*, translated by Montgomery Belgion. Princeton: Princeton University Press, 1983.

Dent, N. and O'Hagan, T. "Rousseau on Amour-Propre." *Proceedings of the Aristotelian Society* 99 (1999): 91–107.

Dolson, G. "The Influence of Schopenhauer upon Friedrich Nietzsche." *The Philosophical Review* 10, no. 3 (1901): 241–250.

Ebbersmeyer, S. "The Philosopher as Lover: Renaissance Debates on Platonic Eros." In *Emotion and Cognitive Life in Medieval and Early Modern Philosophy*, edited by M. Pickavé and L. Shapiro. Oxford: Oxford University Press, 2012.

Epictetus. *Discourses and Selected Writings*, translated by Robert Dobbin. London: Penguin Classics, 2008.

———. *Enchiridion*. Mineola, NY: Dover Publications Inc. 2004.

Fahmy, M. "Kantian Practical Love." *Pacific Philosophical Quarterly* 91 (2010): 313–331.

Ferry, L. *A Brief History of Thought*, translated by T. Cuffe. Edinburgh: Canongate Books, 2010.

———. *On Love*, translated by A. Brown. Cambridge: Polity, 2013.

Foucault, M. *About the Beginning of the Hermeneutics of the Self. Lectures at Dartmouth College, 1980*, edited by H.-P. Fruchaud and D. Lorenzi and translated by G. Burchell. Chicago, IL: University of Chicago Press, 2016.

Freire, P. *Pedagogy of the Oppressed*. London: Continuum, 1970.

Frankfurt, H. "Autonomy, Necessity, and Love." In *Necessity, Volition, and Love*, 129–141. Cambridge: Cambridge University Press, 1999.

———. *The Reasons of Love*. Princeton, NJ: Princeton University Press, 2004.

Friedman, M. "Romantic Love and Personal Autonomy." *Midwest Studies in Philosophy* 22 (1998): 162–181.

Fromm, E. *The Art of Loving*. New York: Harper and Row, 1956.

Gallagher, D. "Thomas Aquinas on self-love as the basis for love of others." *Acta Philosophica* 8, no. 1 (1999): 23–44.

Gill, S. and Thomson, G. *Understanding Peace Holistically*. New York: Peter Lang, 2014.

Gingrich-Philbrook, C. "Love's Excluded Subjects: Staging Irigaray's Heteronormative Essentialism." *Cultural Studies* 15, no. 2 (2001): 222–228.

Gracia, J. J., Reichberg, G. M. and Schumacher, B. N. (eds.) *The Classics of Western Philosophy: A Reader's Guide*. Oxford: Blackwell Publishing

Goldman, E. *Anarchism and Other Essays*. New York and London: Mother Earth Publishing Association, 1910.

Guild, E. "Montaigne on Love." In *The Oxford Handbook of Montaigne*, edited by P. Desan. New York: Oxford University Press, 2015.

Guyer, P. *Kant and the Experience of Freedom: Essays on Aesthetics and Morality*. Cambridge: Cambridge University Press, 1993.

Hagglund, B. "Melanchthon versus Luther: The Contemporary Struggle." *Concordia Theological Quarterly* 44, no 2-3 (1980): 123–133.

Halperin D. "Why is Diotima a Woman?" In *One Hundred years of Homosexuality*, 113–151. New York: Routledge, 1990.

Hamlyn, D.W. "The Phenomena of Love and Hate." *Philosophy* 53, no. 203 (1978): 5–20.

Harari, Y. N. *21 Lessons for the 21st Century*. London: Jonathan Cape, 2018.

Heaton, J. and Roige Mas, A. *The Metaphysis of Love: An Annotated Bibliography*. First Edition, 2014, Available at http://www.themetaphysicsoflove.com/publications/.

Hegel, G. W. F. *Early Theological Writings*, translated by T. M. Knox. Philadelphia, PA: University of Pennsylvania Press, 1971.

———. *The Phenomenology of Spirit.*, translated by Terry Pinkard. Cambridge: Cambridge University Press, 2018/1807.

———. *Introduction to the Lectures on the History of Philosophy*, translated by A.V. Miller. Oxford: Clarendon Press, 1985.

———. *Lectures on Natural Right and Political Science: The First Philosophy of Right, Heidelberg 1817–1818*, translated by J. Stewart and P. Hodgson. Berkeley, CA: University of California Press, 1917–8/1995.

Henry, P. "Saint Augustine on Personality." In *The Saint Augustine Lecture Series: Saint Augustine and the Augustinian Tradition*, edited by R. Russell. New York: The Macmillan Company, 1960.

Hobbes, T. *Leviathan*. London: Penguin Classics, 2017.

von Hildebrand, D. *The Arts of Living*. Steubenville, OH: Hildebrand Project, 2017.

———. *Nature of Love*. South Bend, IN.: St. Augustine's Press, 2009.

Irigaray, L. *Between East and West: From Singularity to Community*, translated by S Pluhácek. New York: Columbia University Press, 2003.

———. *Democracy Begins between Two*, translated by K. Anderson. London: Athlone Press, 2001.

———. *An Ethics of Sexual Difference*, translated by C. Burke and G. Gill. Ithaca, NY: Cornell University Press, 1993.

———. "Introducing: Love between Us." *Women: A Cultural Review* 6, no. 2 (1995): 180–190.

———. *Sharing the World*, New York: Continuum, 2008.

———. "Sorcerer Love: A Reading of Plato's Symposium, Diotima's Speech." *Hypatia, French Feminist Philosophy* 3, no. 3 (1989): 32–44.

———. *The Way of Love*. New York: Continuum, 2002.

Irigaray, L. and Martin, A. *I Love to You: Sketch for a Felicity within History*. New York and London: Routledge, 1996.

Jenkins, C. "What is Love? An Incomplete Map of the Metaphysics." *Journal of the American Philosophical Association* 1, no. 2 (2015): 349–364.

Johnson, R. "Love in Vain," *The Southern Journal of Philosophy* 36 (1997): 45–50.

Johnson, R. and Cureton, A. (2019). "Kant's Moral Philosophy." In *The Stanford Encyclopedia of Philosophy*, edited by E. Zalta. 2019. https://plato.stanford.edu/archives/spr2019/entries/kant-moral/ (accessed in April 2020)

Jones, E. "The Future of Sexuate Difference: Irigaray, Heidegger, Ontology, and Ethics." *L'Esprit Créateur* 52, no. 3 (2012): 26–39.

Kant, I. *Grounding for the Metaphysics of Morals* (3rd ed.), translated by J. Ellington. Indianapolis, IN: Hackett, 1993/1785.

———. *Lectures on Ethics*, translated by L Infield. Indianapolis, IN: Hackett, 1980.
———. *The Metaphysics of Morals*, edited by L. Denis and translated by M. Gregor. Cambridge: Cambridge University Press, 2017.
———. *Practical philosophy*, translated and edited by M. Gregor. Cambridge: Cambridge University Press, 1996.
Kaufman, D. *Love, Compassion and Other Vices: A History of the Stoic Theory of the Emotions.* Ann Arbor, MI: UMI Dissertation Publishing, 2013.
Kerr, F. *Thomas Aquinas: A Very Short Introduction.* Oxford: Oxford University Press, 2009.
Kierkegaard, S. *The Works of Love*, translated by D Swenson & L Swenson. Princeton, NJ: Princeton University Press, 1946.
King, M. "Levels of Love." In *Sermon Delivered at Ebenezer Baptist Church.* Stanford, CA: The Martin Luther King Jr. Research and Education Institute, 1962.
Klein, J. "The Stoic Argument from Oikeiōsis." *Oxford Studies in Ancient Philosophy* 50 (2016): 143–200.
Kolodny, N. "The Explanation of Amour-Propre." *Philosophical Review* 119, no. 2 (2010): 165–200.
Korsgaard, C. *Creating the Kingdom of Ends.* Cambridge: Cambridge University Press, 1996.
Krause, P. *Augustine on Love, Justice, and Pluralism in Human Nature*, 2018. https://voegelinview.com/augustine-on-love-justice-and-pluralism-in-human-nature, accessed June 2020
Kraut, R., ed. *The Cambridge Companion to Plato.* Cambridge: Cambridge University Press, 1992.
———. "Plato on Love." In *The Oxford Handbook of Plato*, edited by G. Fine. Oxford: Oxford University Press, 2008.
———. "Reason and Justice in Plato's Republic." In *Exegesis and Argument*, edited by E.N. Lee et al. Assen: Van Gorcum, 1973.
La Caze, Marguerite. "Love, That Indispensable Supplement: Irigaray and Kant on Love and Respect." *Hypatia* 20, no. 3 (2005): 92–114.
Levinas, Emmanuel, *Totality and Infinity: An Essay on Exteriority*, Alphonso Lingis (trans.), Pittsburgh, PA: Duquesne University Press, 1969.
Levine, Philippa. "So Few Prizes and So Many Blanks': Marriage and Feminism in Later Nineteenth-Century." *Journal of British Studies* 28, no. 2 (1989): 150–174.
Levy, D. "The Definition of Love in Plato's Symposium." *Journal of the History of Ideas* 40, no. 2 (1979): 285–291.
Lewis, C. S. *The Four Loves.* London: HarperCollins Publishers, 1960.
Liao, S. M. "The Idea of a Duty to Love." *The Journal of Value Inquiry* 40 (2006): 1–22.
Locke, J. *An Essay Concerning Human Understanding*, four books, edited by P. Nidditch. Oxford: Clarendon Press, 1975.
———. *Two Treatises of Government*, edited by P. Laslett, Cambridge: Cambridge University Press, 1689/1988.
Long, A. *Epictetus: A Stoic and Socratic Guide to Life.* Oxford: Clarendon, 2002.
Luther, Martin. "An Introduction to St. Paul's Letter to the Romans." In *Martin Luther*, translated by R. Smith. Erlangen: Heyder and Zimmer, 1854.
———. "The Smalcald Articles in Concordia." In *The Lutheran Confessions.* Saint Louis: Concordia Publishing House, 2005.

Magrin, S. "Nature and Utopia in Epictetus' Theory of Oikeiōsis." *Phronesis* 63 (2018): 293–350.
Malherbe, A., Ferguson, E., and Meyendorff, J. *Gregory of Nyssa: The Life of Moses*. Mahwah, NJ: Paulist Press, 1998.
Mannermaa, T. *Two Kinds of Love: Martin Luther's Religious World*. Minneapolis, MN: First Fortress Press, 2010.
Marcel, G. *Being and Having*, translated by Katharine Farrer. Westminster, UK: Dacre Press, 1949.
———. *Le Monde Cassé Suivi de Position Et Approches Concrètes du Mystère Ontologique*. Paris: Desclée de Brouwer & Cie, 1933.
———. *Metaphysical Journal*, translated by B. Weil. Chicago, IL: Henry Regnery, 1952.
———. *The Mystery of Being, Vol. I: Reflection and Mystery*, translated by G. S. Fraser. London: The Harvill Press, 1951.
———. *The Philosophy of Existence*, translated by Manya Harari. New York: Citadel Press, 1949.
Marshall, P. *Demanding the Impossible: A History of Anarchism*. London: HarperCollins, 1992.
May, S. *Love: A History*. London: Yale University Press, 2011.
McDermott, T. St *Thomas Aquinas, Summa Theologiae: A Concise Translation*. London: Eyre and Spottiswoode, 1989.
McEvoy, J. "The Other as Oneself: Friendship and Love in the Thought of Thomas Aquinas." In *Thomas Aquinas: Approaches to Truth*, edited by J. McEvoy and M. Dunne. Dublin: Four Courts Press, 2002.
McGowan, T. (2017) "Hegel in Love." In *Can Philosophy Love? Reflections and Encounters*, edited by C. Zeiher & T. McGowan. London: Rowman Littlefield International, 4–24.
McShea, R. J. "Spinoza on Power", *Inquiry* 12, no. 1–4 (1969): 133–143.
Meconi, D. *The One Christ: St. Augustine's Theology of Deification*. Washington DC.: Catholic University of America Press, 2013.
Metz, T. "The Meaning of Life." In *The Stanford Encyclopaedia of Philosophy*, edited by Edward N. Zalta (Winter 2021 Edition), 2021. https://plato.stanford.edu/archives/win2021/entries/life-meaning.
Montaigne, M. *The Complete Essays*. London: Penguin Classics, 1993.
———. *The Complete Works of Montaigne*, translated by Donald Frame. New York: Everyman's Library, 2003.
———. *On Friendship*, translated by M. A. Screech. London: Penguin, 2004.
Morris, M. "Akrasia in the *Protagoras* and the *Republic*." *Phronesis* 51 (2006): 195–229.
Moseley, A. (n.d.). "Philosophy of Love." *Internet Encyclopaedia of Philosophy*. Accessed December 20, 2019, https://www.iep.utm.edu/love/
Nietzsche, F. *Beyond Good and Evil*, translated by R. Hollingdale. London: Penguin Books, 2003.
———. *The Birth of Tragedy*, translated by S. Whiteside and edited by M. Tanner. London: Penguin, 1992.
———. *Human, All Too Human*, translated by M. Faber and S. Lehmann. Harmondsworth: Penguin, 1984.

———. *Thus Spoke Zarathustra*, translated by R. Hollingdale. London: Penguin Books, 2003.

———. *The Will to Power*, translated by W. Kaufmann and R. Hollingdale. New York: Vintage, 1968.

Norton, D. and Kille, M. *Philosophies of Love*. Totowa, NJ: Rowman & Littlefield Publishers, 1971.

Nozick, R. *Anarchy, State and Utopia*. London: Blackwell Publishing, 1974.

———. "Love's Bond." In *The Examined Life: Philosophical Meditations*, 68–86. New York: Simon & Schuster, 1989.

Nussbaum, M. "The Ascent of Love: Plato, Spinoza, Proust." *New Literary History* 25, no. 4 (1994): 925–949.

———. "Compassion: The Basic Social Emotion." *Social Philosophy and Policy* 13, no. 1 (1996): 27–58.

———. "Human Functioning and Social Justice: In Defense of Aristotelian Essentialism." *Political Theory* 20, no. 2 (1992): 202–246.

——— *Upheavals of Thought*. Cambridge: Cambridge University Press, 2003.

Nygren, A. *Agape and Eros*, translated by Philip S. Watson. Chicago: University of Chicago Press, 1982.

O'Dwyer, K. "Nietzsche's Reflections on Love." *Minerva – An Internet Journal of Philosophy* 12 (2008): 37–77.

Pakaluk, M. *Other Selves: Philosophers on Friendship*. Indianapolis, IN: Hackett Publishing, 1991.

Pangle, L. "Friends as Other Selves." In *Aristotle and the Philosophy of Friendship*, 142–154. Cambridge: Cambridge University Press, 2002.

Phillips, J. "Loving love or ethics as natural philosophy jacques derrida's politiques de l'amitié." *Angelaki: Journal of Theoretical Humanities* 12, no. 3 (2007): 155–170.

Plato. *Meno*, translated by G. M. A. Grube, in Cooper, *Plato: Complete Works*.

———. *Protagoras*, translated by S. Lombardo and K. Bell in Cooper, *Plato: Complete Works*.

———. *Republic*, translated by H.D.P. Lee and Desmond Lee, London: Penguin Classics.

———. *Symposium*, translated by A. Nehamas in Cooper, Plato: Complete Works.

Popper, K. *The Open Society and its Enemies, Volume I: The Spell of Plato*. 5th ed. Princeton, NJ: Princeton University Press, 1945/1971.

Ricoeur, P. *Oneself as Another*, translated by Kathleen Blamey. Chicago: University of Chicago Press, 1992.

Rinne, P. "From Self-Preservation to Cosmopolitan Friendship: Kant and the Ascent of Love." *Kant-Online*. 2018. Accessed at: www.kant-online.ru/en/?p=933

———. *Kant on Love*. Berlin: Walter De Gruyter, 2018.

Rist, J. *Augustine: Ancient Thought Baptized*. Cambridge: Cambridge University Press, 1994.

Roberts, R. *How Adam Smith Can Change Your Life: An Unexpected Guide to Human Nature and Happiness*. New York: Penguin, 2014.

Robinson, D. "How Stoicism Influenced Christianity." In *The Lecture Series: The Great Ideas of Philosophy*. Chantilly, VA: The Great Courses, 2016.

Rorty, A. "The Politics of Spinoza's Vanishing Dichotomies." *Political Theory* 38, no.1 (2010): 131–141.

———. "Spinoza on the Pathos of Idolatrous Love and the Hilarity of True Love." In *The Philosophy of (Erotic) Love*, edited by R. Solomon and K. Higgins. Lawrence, KS: University Press of Kansas, 1991.

———. "The Two Faces of Spinoza." *The Review of Metaphysics* 41, no. 2 (1987): 299–316.

Rosenberg, M. *Society and the Adolescent Self-Image*, revised edition. Middletown, CT: Wesleyan University Press, 1989.

Ross, W. *The Student's Oxford Aristotle: Volume V - Ethics Ethica Nicomachea*. Oxford: Oxford University Press, 1942.

Rousseau, J.-J. *The Social Contract and Discourses*, translated by G. Cole. London and Toronto: J.M. Dent and Sons, 1923.

Russell, B. *A History of Western Philosophy and Its Connection with Political and Social Circumstances from the Earliest Times to the Present Day*. New York: Simon and Schuster, 1945.

Scheler, Max, *On Feeling, Knowing, and Valuing*, edited by Harold J. Bershady. Chicago. The Chicago Press, 1992,

———. *Formalism in Ethics and Non-Formal Ethics of Values*, translated by Roger L. Funk and edited by John Wild. Evanston, IL: Northwestern University Press. 1973.

———. *The Nature of Sympathy*, translated by Peter Heath. Hamden, CT: Archon Books, 1970.

———. *Selected Philosophical Essays*, translated by David R. Lachterman. Evanston, IL: Northwestern University Press, 1973.

Schoonheim, L. "Among Lovers." *Arendt Studies* 2 (2018): 99–124.

Schopenhauer, A. *On the Basis of Morality*, translated by E.F. Payne. Indianapolis, IN: Bobbs-Merrill, 1965.

———. *The World as Will and Representation*. Abingdon and New York: Routledge, 2016.

———. *The World as Will and Representation*, translated by E. F. Payne. New York: Dover Publications, 1966/1819.

Schott, N. "Bergson's Philosophy of Religion." In *Interpreting Bergson: Critical Essays*, edited by A. Lefebvre and N. Schott (pp. 193–210). Cambridge: Cambridge University Press, 2019.

Secomb, L. "Amorous Politics: Between Derrida and Nancy," *Social Semiotics* 16, no. 3 (2006): 449–460

Sherwin, M. *By Knowledge and by Love: Charity and Knowledge in the Moral Theology of St. Thomas Aquinas*. Washington, DC: Catholic University of America Press, 2005.

Schoonheim, L. "Among Lovers: Love and Personhood in Hannah Arendt." *Arendt Studies* 2 (2018): 99–124.

Singer, I. *Meaning in Life: The Pursuit of Love*. Cambridge, MA: MIT Press, 2010.

———. *The Nature of Love: Plato to Luther*. Chicago: University of Chicago Press, 1984.

———. *Philosophy of Love: A Partial Summing-Up*. Cambridge, MA: MIT Press, 2009.

Smith, A. *The Theory of Moral Sentiments*, edited by D. Raphael and A. Macfie. Oxford: Oxford University Press, 1759/1976.

———. *The Wealth of Nations*, edited by R. Campbell and A. Skinner. Oxford: Oxford University Press, 1776/1976.

Solomon, R. *In Defence of Sentimentality*. Oxford: Oxford University Press, 2004.
Spinoza, B. *Ethics*, edited and translated by E. Curley. Princeton, NJ: Princeton University Press, 1985/1677.
———. *Short Treatise on God, Man, and His Well-Being*, edited and translated by A. Wolf. Edinburgh: Black Publishing, 1910.
Stiglitz, J., Fitoussi, J.-P., and Duran, M. *Measuring What Counts: The Global Movement for Well-Being*. New York: The New Press, 2019.
Strauss, L. *The City and Man*. Chicago: University of Chicago Press, 1964.
von Strassburg, G. *Tristan*, translated by A. Hatto. London: Penguin Classics.
Streiker, L. "The Christian Understanding of Platonic Love A Critique of Anders Nygren's "Agape and Eros"." *The Christian Scholar* 47, no. 4 (1964): 331–340.
Stump, E. "Love, by All Accounts." *Proceedings and Addresses of the American Philosophical Association* 80, no. 2 (2006): 25–43.
Taylor, C. *Hegel*. New York: Cambridge University Press, 1975.
———. *Sources of the Self: The Making of the Modern Identity*. Cambridge: Cambridge University Press, 1989.
Taylor, G. "Love." *Proceedings of the Aristotelian Society* 76 (1976): 147–164.
Thomson, G. *Ancient Philosophy*. Long Grove, IL: Waveland Press, 2016.
———. *An Introduction to Modern Philosophy*. Belmont, CA: Wadsworth, 1993.
———. *On the Meaning of Life*. Belmont, CA: Wadsworth, 2003.
Thomson, G. & Gill, S. *Happiness, Flourishing and the Good Life: A Transformative Framework for Human Well-Being*. London: Routledge, 2020.
Tillich, P. *Love, Power and Justice: Ontological Analyses and Ethical Applications*. New York: Oxford University Press, 1954.
Toner, J. *The Experience of Love*. Washington, DC: Corpus Instrument, 1968.
Torchia, J. *Exploring Personhood: An Introduction to the Philosophy of Human Nature*. Lanham, MD: Rowman & Littlefield Publishers, 2008.
Vacek, E. *Love, Human and Divine: The Heart of Christian Ethics*. Washington, DC: Georgetown University Press, 1994.
———. "Scheler's Phenomenology of Love." *The Journal of Religion* 62, no. 2 (1982): 156–177.
Vandenberghe, F. "Sociology of the Heart: Max Scheler's Epistemology of Love," *Theory, Culture & Society*, 25, no. 3 (2008): 17–51.
Vlastos, G. "The individual as an object of love in Plato", in G. Vlastos, *Platonic Studies* (pp. 3–34). Princeton: Princeton University Press, 1973.
Walter, G. "Promise in Martin Luther's Thought and Theology", *Religion* (2017). https://oxfordre.com/religion/display/10.1093/acrefore/9780199340378.001.0001/acrefore-9780199340378-e-342
Wehus, G. "Freedom, Slavery, and Self in Epictetus." *Teologisk tidsskrift* 8, no 4 (2019): 227–242.
Wicks, R. "Arthur Schopenhauer." In *The Stanford Encyclopedia of Philosophy*, edited by E. N. Zalta. 2019. https://plato.stanford.edu/archives/spr2019/entries/schopenhauer/
Wilde, L. "Embracing Imperfection: Plato vs. Nussbaum on Love." *Philosophy Now* 122 (2017): 12–14.
Williams, B. *The Sense of the Past*. Princeton, NJ: Princeton University Press, 2006.

Wolf, S. *Meaning in Life and Why It Matters*. Princeton, NJ: Princeton University Press, 2010.
———. *The Variety of Values: Essays on Morality, Meaning, and Love*. New York: Oxford University Press, 2015.
Wood, A. *Kant's Ethical Thought*. Cambridge: Cambridge University Press, 1999.
Zeiher, C. & McGowan, T., eds. *Can Philosophy Love? Reflections and Encounters*. London: Rowman Littlefield International, 2017.

INDEX

Abrahamic religions 15
absolute unity 133–34
acting righteously 180–83
acting-*for* 20
acting-*with* others 21
active desire 63
active emotions 63
active love 205–8
advantage/utility friendship 97–98
affection 16, 33, 46, 100–101, 104, 112–13, 129–31, 162, 167, 179
agapē 56–59, 93
Agathon 38
amarer 16
amor 16–17
amor amicitiae 53–54
amor concupiscentia 53–54
amor fati 73–75, 137
amor mundi 201–5
amour-de-soi 124–26
amour-propre 124–26
Anarchy, State and Utopia (Nozick) 116
antiquity 2–3, 30–31, 60
Apollo 137–42
appetitive power 110
appraise/appreciation 16, 44; God's goodness 50–53; of human qualities 128–29; of human spirit/soul 49; love and 22–24, 44
apprehensive power 110
Aquinas, Thomas (1225–1274) 53–56, 172; in *Ethics* 179; on friendship-love 54, 110; on knowledge in love 55, 108–10; on love as desiring good 53–56, 110; on love as mutual indwelling 108–11; one's self and another, likeness between 54; philosophy of love as caring 178–80; political theology 178–80; *Summa Theologiae* 53, 108–9, 178–79; theory of love as relationing 111
Arendt, Hannah (1906–1975) 31, 201; *amor mundi* 201–5; *Human Condition, The* 201, 203–4; interpretations of love in St Augustine's theology 201; *Love and St. Augustine* 201; *Men in Dark Times* 202–3; *Origin of Totalitarianism, The* 204; passion *vs.* love 201; on political friendship 202–4; on political/public sphere 202; on politics of love as caring for world 201–5
Aristophanes (c. 450–388 BC) 94; allegory 94–95; contribution to *Symposium* 95; human oneness/wholeness, myth of 94–95; on humans as spherical 94; on love as perpetual yearning for union with beloved 94–95
Aristotle (384–322 BC) 13, 35, 93, 209–10; ethical action for 158; eudaimonia 39–40, 209; on friendship-love in flourishing life 97–100; on human qualities 42–44; on love as caring 164–67; on love as civic and political engagement and action 164–67; love for humanity 93; *Nicomachean Ethics* 99, 164–67; philia 37, 42–44, 93, 99–100; phronesis 167; *Politics* 164–65;

self-love for 43–44; on virtues 42–44; vision of love 37, 42–44
Art of Loving, The (Fromm) 214
ascension 238–40
Athens 35
attraction 112
Augustine of Hippo (354–430) 50, 172; *On Christian Doctrine* 50, 173; *City of God* 173, 176–77; *Confessions* 50; on cupiditas *vs.* caritas 104–5; God's Trinity 106–7, 173; on justice 172–77; on love as appreciating God's goodness 50–53; on love as caring 172–77; on love as fellowship with God 104–8; political theology 173–77; position on non-violence 173–74; vision of peace 173
Austin, Jane 14, 78
authentic love 85

beauty/beautiful (καλόν) 38–42, 71, 110, 112
becoming well 19
being-for-itself 135–36
being-in-itself 136
being-*with* others 21
beloved communities 224–27
beneficence: *vs.* benevolence 68, 188–91; practical love as 188–89
benevolence 130–31, 188–90; *vs.* beneficence 68
Bennett, Elizabeth 14
Bergson, Henri 17
bestowing 24
Birth of Tragedy, The (Nietzsche) 137–42
Black Lives Matter movement 7
broken world 144
Brontë sisters 78
Buber, Martin 145
Buddhism 168

capacity to love 184
capitalism 79, 184, 219
care/caring 16; doing work for relationships with others 21; love as 28–30, 157–212 (*see also* love as caring)
caritas: see love as caring

Cartesian meditation 115
Castiglione, Baldassare 31
categorical imperative 66–67
character friendship 97–98
Christian agapē 49, 56–59, 93
Christian conceptions of love's relationality 103–14; Aquinas, Thomas on 108–11; Augustine of Hippo on 104–8; de Montaigne, Michel on 111–14; in Judaeo-Christian theology 103
Christian perspective on love as caring 158, 172–83; Aquinas's philosophy of 178–80; Luther's theology 180–83; St Augustine 172–77
Christian political theology 172–73
Christian theology on love as supreme virtue 48–59; Aquinas, Thomas on 53–56; Augustine of Hippo on 50–53; Luther's theology 56–59
City of God (Augustine) 173, 176–77
civic friendship 30, 166–67
climate crisis 1
colonialism 219–20
coming-together (communion) 110
commercialisation of love 15
commodification of love 15
common good 179–80
communal feelings 197
community of love 224–27; Focolare movement 226; Hertha Living Community 225–26; King's vision for 224–25; Los Angeles Ecovillage 226; Mutual Aid 226–27
compassion 123, 190, 217–18
Compassion in Politics 217–18
compassionate politics 217–18
complacency 110
Comte-Sponville, André 112
conatus 63
concupiscence, love of 54
Confessions (Augustine) 50
cosmic harmony 4
cosmic order 3–4
cosmos 5–6, 33–36, 160; harmony of 3; love's rootedness in 8–9; nature in 26; other beings in 8, 18, 28–29; *see also* God

Index

COVID-19 pandemic 1, 7
cultural mythos 1–2
cupiditas *vs.* caritas 104–5, 201
currencies 221–22

daemon 95–97
d'Aragona, Tullia (1510–1556) 31, 185; *Dialogue on the Infinity of Love* 185–87; gender equality, advocacy for 187; on love as caring 185–87; Varchi, Benedetto and 185–87
de Beauvoir, Simone (1908–1986) 13, 31; on ethical love 85; *Ethics of Ambiguity* 82; on freedom 83; on love as integrating transcendence and immanence 82–87; perspective on women 83–87; *Second Sex, The* 13, 83
de la Boétie, Etienne 111, 113
de Montaigne, Michel (1533–1592) 31, 111; *On Friendship* 111–12; on friendship-love 111–13; on love as fusion of souls 111–14; philosophy of love 111–14
dehumanisation 7, 34, 79, 145–46
Deleuze, Gilles 19
delight 119
Descartes, René (1596–1650) 115
desires 16, 62–63, 175; active 63; for good 53–56, 128; passive 63; sexual 93; for union/closeness 91
Dialogue on the Infinity of Love (d'Aragona) 185–87
dignity 19, 65–70, 101, 131–32
Dionysian affirmation 137–39
Dionysus 137–42
Diotima of Mantinea (c. 440 BC) 38–41, 92–93, 95, 161–62, 234, 238; on love as relationing as daemon/in-between-ness 95–97; love as valuing, conception of 96
Discourse (Epictetus) 45–46, 168–69
Discourse on Inequality (Rousseau) 122
disenchantment 115
dishonest love: *see* vulgar love
disobedience 180
divine 60
divine beings 92, 96, 104, 157, 161

doing work: for being well 20–21; to betterment of world 21; for each other 21; for human becoming 21; life and 20–21; for live out (caring) relationships with others 21; for living well 20–21; for ourselves 21; for partake in relational processes 21; to serve others 20–21
doing-*for* 20
doing-*with* others 21
Doll's House, A (Ibsen) 78
duty: of beneficence 188; of gratitude 190–91; of human beings 188; law of 188; of love 188–90; of sympathy 190–91

ecology of love 230–31
economic injustice 212
Economy of Communion 222–23
economy of love 219–23; competitive 219–20; currencies 221–22; ethic of love 221; expansionist 219–20; human well-being 220–21; increase of capital 219; maximising profit 219; meaningful consumption 222
education of love 227–30; arts of listening and dialogue 229; co-creating spaces for meaningful/generative relating 229; intention for education 228–29; pedagogies 228; schools as caring communities 229–30; valuing humans non-instrumentally 228
Einfühlung: *see* fellow-feelings
élan vital 17
elation 119
emancipation 79
Emile (Rousseau) 124, 227
emotional affinity 115
emotional attachments 169
emotions 46, 63–64, 74, 109, 118, 168, 195–96, 216
empathy 127
empiricism 116
Enchiridion (Epictetus) 46
Enlightenment movement 116, 184
Epictetus (c. 50–130) 100–101; contribution to Stoicism 45; on

cosmopolis 102; critique of hope 168–71; *Discourse* 45–46, 168–69; *Enchridion* 46; ethics 168; idea of choice 45; on instrumental *vs.* non-instrumental ends 168–70; love as caring, philosophy of 168–71; on love as self-belonging and/other-belonging 100–102; love as valuing nature of things, philosophy of 45–47; 'lovers of sights' 169; on lust *vs.* love 46–47; on notion of control 45; virtues for 45
erôs 37, 61, 96
ethic of love 216–17, 221
Ethics (Spinoza) 61–62, 118
Ethics of Ambiguity (de Beauvoir) 82
ethics of love 5–6, 85, 150–51
Ethics of Sexual Difference, An (Irigaray) 150–51
eudaimonia 39–40, 209
existing-in-and-for-itself 136
external righteousness 180–81

factories of annihilation 204
faith 53, 58, 181
false opposites 74, 74n144
fears 168–69; *vs.* love 134–35
feelings 74, 168
fellow-feelings 127–28, 196–97
Ferry, Luc 2–4, 170, 210
Ficino, Marsilio 31
flourishing life 20, 22, 30, 37, 44, 157–58, 168–69; friendship-love in 97–100; love as pathway to 114, 118–21; within political community 160–61; *see also* well-being
Focolare movement 222–23, 226
forgiveness 57, 203–4, 218–19
Formalism in Ethics (Scheler) 196
Foucault, Michel 19, 200
Fragment on Love, The (Hegel) 132–33, 135
Frankfurt, Harry (1929–) 18–22, 24–25, 205; conception of love 205–8; on freedom 206; on love as caring 205–8; *Necessity, Volition and Love* 205; on passive *vs.* active love 206; *Reasons of Love, The* 205

Fratelli Tutti: On Fraternity and Social Friendship 216
free love 80
freedom 4, 76–80, 83; of action 206; of choice 206; of will 206
freewill 122, 173
Freire, Paulo 32
friendliness 16
friendship 37, 42–44, 110; advantage in association 42; advantage/utility 97–98; Aquinas on 54; Aristotle on 97–100; character 97–98; civic 30; forms of 42; goodness 37, 42–44; love as 42–44, 97–100; on moral goodness/virtues 42–43; perfect 42–44; in philia 42–44; pleasure 42, 97–98; political 202–3
friendship-love 97–100, 110–13, 166–67, 178–79, 202–3, 224
Fromm, Erich 22, 91, 184, 214, 236
fusion of souls, love as 111–14

Geist 135–36
gender equality 187
gendered performance of love 14
general feelings of love 16
generative force of love as caring 161–64
gentleness 182
gift 81
globalisation 7, 216
glory *vs.* cross, theology of 59
God 3–4, 26, 33, 61–65, 82–83; agapē 56–57, 93; in Christ 59; definition of 62; as eternal 64; existence 109; forgiveness 57; goodness 50–53; hidden *vs.* revealed 59; image of 55; as inherent in humans 50–53; Kingdom of Heaven 6; and love 5, 48, 50–53, 61–65, 104–8, 172–77, 192–93; with nature 62–63; as relational being 104–8; responsive *vs.* creative love 56–57; righteousness 181; self-knowledge 109; as supreme form of love 54–55
God's Trinity 106–8, 173
going-inwardly (mutual indwelling) 110

Index

Goldman, Emma (1869–1940) 31; capitalism, criticism of 79; on 'free love' 80; on human liberty/freedom 76–80; on love as valuing love in its own right 77–80; on marriage 77–79; *Marriage and Love* 77–78; *Tragedy of Women's Emancipation, The* 79–80
good *vs.* evil 45–46, 74, 74n144
goodness 3–4, 36, 38–42, 112; friendship 37, 42–44; God 50–53; in others 110
grace 112
gratitude 190–91
greater whole 7–8
Greek conceptions of love as relationing 93–102; Aristophanes thoughts 94–95; Aristotle's thought on 97–100; Diotima of Mantinea on 95–97; Epictetus's thought on 100–102
Greek philosophy of love as caring 158, 160–71; Aristotle's 164–67; Epictetus's 168–71; Plato's 161–64
Greek thought on love as valuing 35–47; Aristotle's thoughts 13, 42–44; Epictetus's philosophy 45–47; Plato's thought 37–42
Groundwork of the Metaphysics of Morals (Kant) 66–67, 188
Guild, Elizabeth 113–14

happiness 22, 50–53, 60, 91, 119–20, 127–28; *see also* flourishing life; well-being
Harari, Yuval Noel 1–2
harmony 3–4, 36, 174
Heaven 158
Hegel, G. W. Friedrich (1770–1831) 116–17, 132; on fear *vs.* love 134–35; *Fragment on Love, The* 132–33, 135; on Geist 135–36; on love as mutual participation in generative relations 132–37; for mutual-constitutedness 133–34; *Phenomenology of the Spirit, The* 135–36; philosophical development 132; *Spirit of Christianity, The* 132–33; vision of love 132–37
Heidegger, Martin 143
Hertha Living Community 225–26
high-mindedness 118
Hobbes, Thomas (1588–1679) 116–17; *Leviathan* 116–17; on self-serving people 116–17
holiness, values of 196
Holy Spirit 108–9
honest love: *see* virtuous love
hooks, bell 32
hope 53, 168–71
human becoming 17
human beings 3–4, 7–8, 60, 165; as political animals 165–66; as social animals 165–66; virtues of good character of 165–66
Human Condition, The (Arendt) 201, 203–4
human dignity 19, 65–70
human emotionality 65–70
human experiences 70–72; intuition 70–72; perception 70–72
human flourishing 44
human good 54–55, 165
human individuality 76–80
human intuition 70–72
human liberty/freedom 76–80
human life: *see* life
human nature 4, 72–74, 82, 116–17, 123, 127, 143, 154, 210, 244
human oneness 94–95
human qualities 42–44
human well-being 220–21; *see also* well-being
human wholeness 94–95
humanism 60
humanity 1–4, 7–8, 83, 127–32
humans as relational beings 94
humans as spherical 94
human's state of nature 116–17

Ibsen, Henrik 78
idolatrous love 121
'I–It' relation 145
imago Dei 55
immanence 82–87, 210

immanent Trinity 108–9
immortality 41
in-between-ness 26–27, 95–97
independence 134
individual good 179
individual/individualism 120–21, 138; Irigaray on 149–53; love as relationing 143–53; Marcel on 144–49
inequality 123
infectious feelings 197
inherent dignity of persons 65–70
inquiry 9–10
Inquiry into the Nature and Causes of the Wealth of Nations, An (Smith) 13
intentio unionis, love as 81
intercourse 47
internal righteousness 180–81
intimacy 69
intuition 70–72
Irigaray, Luce (1930) 11, 92, 149; conception of love 149–53; ethics of love 150–51; *Ethics of Sexual Difference, An* 150–51; on love as horizontal transcendence 149–53; philosophy of love, contribution to 153; on sexuate difference 149–50; women and men, ethical relationality between 150

joy 40, 119
justice 36, 57–58, 130–31, 162–64, 172–77, 180, 182, 218; caring with 162; Christian thoughts 172–77; in love 162; of polis 163–64; restorative 218; in right-ordered love 172–77; self-serving 175; St Augustine on 172–77; true 182

Kagan, Shelley 20
Kant, Immanuel (1724–1804) 31; on benevolence *vs.* beneficence 68, 188–91; contribution to love 66; *Groundwork of the Metaphysics of Morals* 66–67, 188; on instrumental and non-instrumental values 66–67; on intimacy/closeness 69; on love as duty to care 187–92; love as valuing inherent dignity of persons 65–70; moral theory 67; nature, conception of 66; on pathological love *vs.* philanthropic love 67–68; philosophy on love as caring 187–92; on practical love 188–91; rationality for 66, 68; on respect *vs.* love 69–70; virtue for 66; on wishing *vs.* acting 69
key learnings 9–10
Kierkegaard, Søren (1813–1855) 192; on Christian love 192–93; *vs.* Kant's view of love 195; on love as caring act 192–95; on preferential love 192–94; *Works of Love* 192–93
King, Martin Luther, Jr. (1929–1968) 224
King-Core, Nat 14–15
Kingdom of God 173–74, 183
kingdom of world 183
knowledge 72; in love 55; self 33, 44, 55
Kraut, Richard 162

Leviathan (Hobbes) 116–17
Levy, Donald 35
Lewis, C. S. 24, 159
liberty 116, 122
life (good), human 2–5, 17, 73–75, 157–58, 217, 233; being-with/living-with 18–19; as continuum 2–4; cosmological/cosmocentric principle 3; of dignity 19, 65–70; doing work and 20–21; evolution 2–5; flourishing 20, 22, 30, 37, 44; freedom 4; humanist/humancentric principle 3, 6; instrumental values 18–22; lived 170; with love 5–6, 22–29; love as valuing 73–75; meaningful 18–19; nature of 18; non-instrumental values 19–22, 26; political community in 160; post-modernist individual-centric principle 4; subjective *vs.* objective values 22; theological/theocentric principle 3; transcendent model 3–5; understanding 18–22; values

18–22; as via redamationis 108; of well-being 101–2
Locke, John (1632–1704) 116–17; on human's state of nature 117; *Two Treatises of Government* 117
logos 37
Los Angeles Ecovillage 226
love 13–16; as acting righteously 180–83; active 205–8; in acts 16, 205–8; Agathon views on 38; Aristotle views on 13, 42–44; articulations of 5–6; Augustinian vs. Thomasian conceptions of 103–4; as bestowing 24; commercialisation of 15; commodification of 15; community of 224–27; of concupiscence 54; in cosmic vision 5; cupiditas vs. caritas 104–5; ecology of 230–31; economy of 219–23; education of 227–30; ethics of 5–6, 150–51, 216–17, 221; evolution 30, 60; vs. fear 134–35; as fellowship with God 104–8; as fusion of souls 111–14; gendered performance of 14; general feelings of 16; as generative caring force 161–64; and God 5, 16, 48, 50–53, 61–65, 104–8, 172–77, 192–93; good life with 5–6, 22–29 (*see also* life (good), human); as horizontal transcendence 149–53; in humanist tradition 5; as ideal/perfect friendship 42–44; as idolatrous 121; individualised 14–15; as *intentio unionis* 81; in its own right 77–80; knowledge in 55; lust vs. 46–47; as mutual indwelling 108–11; as mutual participation in generative relations 132–37; narrative of 2, 7–9; necessities of 205–8; with new-age spirituality 15; as passion of soul 109; passive vs. active 206; as pathway to flourishing 118–21; phenomenology of 195–99; Plato's philosophy of 13, 37–42; politics of 201–5, 216–19; in post-modernist multiplicity 5–6, 76–87; radical 144–49; relational force 137–42; religions and 15; with romance 14; self-conscious awareness and 27–28; in theological account 5; transcendence, act of 27; understanding 16–18, 29–30; value-appreciation, act of 22–24, 44; value-recognition, act of 22–24; as verb 23–24; virtuous 186; vulgar 186; well-being and 25–26, 127–32; Wolf's conception 22; works on, selection of 30–32
Love, Power and Justice (Tillich) 211
Love and St. Augustine (Arendt) 201
love as caring 28–30, 157–212, 214; acting righteously as 180–83; Aquinas's philosophy of 178–80; Arendt on 201–5; Aristotle's philosophy of 164–67; as caring action 178–80; Christian perspective on 172–83; as civic and political engagement and action 164–67; in classical Greek philosophy 160–71; d'Aragona's on 185–87; duty as 187–92; Epictetus's philosophy of 168–71; Frankfurt on 205–8; generative force 161–64; hope 168–71; interpretation 157; justice as 172–77; Kant's philosophy on 187–92; Kierkegaard's philosophy on 192–95; Luther's theology on 180–83; modernist philosophy on 184–99; politics of love as 201–5; post-modernist ideas on 200–208; responsibility for persons 157–58; Scheler's philosophy on 195–99; St Augustine's philosophy of 172–77
love as relationing 25–27, 29–30, 91–155, 214; Aquinas's thought on 108–11; Aristophanes thoughts on 94–95; Aristotle's thought on 97–100; Augustine of Hippo on 104–8; Christian conceptions of love's relationality 103–14; classical Greek conceptions of 93–102; at core of our well-being 127–32; as daemon/in-between-ness 95–97; de Montaigne's thought on 111–14; Diotima of Mantinea on 95–97;

Epictetus's thought on 100–102; as fellowship with God 104–8; force 137–42; friendship-love in flourishing life 97–100; as fusion of souls 111–14; in generative relations 132–37; harmonising amour-de-soi and amour-propre 122–26; Hegel's thought on 132–37; as horizontal transcendence 149–53; imperative 154–55; Irigaray on 149–53; Marcel on 144–49; in modernist humanism 115–42; mutual indwelling 108–11; Nietzsche's conception of 137–42; as pathway to flourishing 118–21; as perpetual yearning for union with beloved 94–95; post-modernist individualism 143–53; as radical love 144–49; Rousseau's thought on 122–26; self-belonging and/other-belonging 100–102; Smith's thought on 127–32; Spinoza's conception of 118–21; Western conceptions of 91–92

love as valuing 22–25, 29–30, 33–89, 213–14; *amor fati* 73–75; as appreciating God's goodness 50–53; Aquinas, Thomas on 53–56; Aristotle's thought on 13, 42–44; Augustine of Hippo 50–53; Christian theology on 48–59; de Beauvoir, Simone on 82–87; as desiring good 53–56; as disinterested agapē 56–59, 93; Epictetus's philosophy of 45–47; friendship 37, 42–44; Goldman, Emma on 77–80; good 37–42; Greek thought on 35–47; human intuition 70–72; human qualities/ virtues 42–44; inherent dignity of persons 65–70; as integrating transcendence and immanence 82–87; Kant, Immanuel on 65–70; life 73–75; love in its own right 77–80; Luther's theology on 56–59; nature of things 45–47; Nietzsche, Friedrich on 73–75; Plato's thought on 37–42; post-modern/ contemporary conceptions of 76–87; response 80–82; Schopenhauer on 70–72; Spinoza, Baruch on 61–65; totality of existence 61–65; von Hildebrand, Dietrich on 80–82

love in practice 213–32; community of love 224–27; ecology of love 230–31; economy of love 219–23; education of love 227–30; politics of love 216–19

love of persons 240–42
lovers as emotional beings 14
'lovers of sights' 169
loving-kindness, feminine virtue of 72
Lubich, Chiara 222–23
lust *vs.* love 46–47
Luther, Martin (1483–1546) 31, 49; glory *vs.* cross, theology of 59; on hidden God *vs.* revealed God 59; on justice as love 183; on love as acting righteously 180–83; on love as caring 180–83; political theology 182–83; responsive *vs.* creative love 56–57; *Temporal Authority* 183; theology of love as disinterested agapē 56–59; *Two Kinds of Righteousness* 180–81

man 3–4
Marcel, Gabriel (1889–1973) 92, 144, 145n144; conception of love as relationing 144–49; ideas of presence and availing (disponibilité) 147–49; *Mystery of Being, The* 144; on other as mystery 146–47; on radical love 144–49
marriage 14, 77–79; institution 78–79; *vs.* insurance policy 78
"Martin Luther's Political Theology: Freedom is Obedience, Justice is Love" (Tsonchev) 182
matrimonial love 112
Melanchthon, Philipp 58
Men in Dark Times (Arendt) 202–3
mental perception, values of 196
Metaphysics of Sexual Love (Schopenhauer) 71
Million Pollinator Gardens Challenge 231

Index

modernist humanism, love as relationing in 115–42; Hegel's conception of 132–37; Nietzsche's conception of 137–42; Rousseau's conception of 122–26; Smith's conception of 127–32; Spinoza's conception of 118–21
modernist philosophy on love as caring 158–59, 184–99, 210–11; d'Aragona's on 185–87; Kant's philosophy 187–92; Kierkegaard's philosophy 192–95; Scheler's philosophy 195–99
modernist thought in love as valuing 33, 60–75; Kant's philosophy 65–70; Nietzsche's philosophy 73–75; Schopenhauer's philosophy 70–72; Spinoza's philosophy 61–65
Montaigne's Dictionary of Love (Comte-Sponville) 112
moral sentiments 127–32
morality 22, 66–67, 187
moral/political inequality 123
Morgan, Kathryn 32
morir 17
mortality 161
mother's love 178–79
moving-outwardly (ecstasy) 110
multiplicity 5–6, 143–44, 202
Mutual Aid 226–27
mutual indwelling, love as 49, 106, 108–11, 154, 172, 178, 214
mutual-constituted-ness 133–34
mutuality 101–2
mutual-regarding 26
mystery 146
Mystery of Being, The (Marcel) 144

Nancy, Jean-Luc 26
narrative of love 2, 7–9
National Pollinator Gardens Network 231
natural love 53
nature 60; God with 62–63, 120; human 4, 72–74, 82, 116–17, 123, 127, 143, 154, 210, 244; as individual 120–21; of life 18; of things 45–47

Nature of Love (von Hildebrand) 80
Nature of Sympathy, The (Scheler) 196–97
necessities of love 205–8
Necessity, Volition and Love (Frankfurt) 205
negative emotions 216
negative virtues 130–31
neighbours 193–94, 226–27
New England Valentine Company 15
Nicomachean Ethic (Aristotle) 99, 164–67
Nietzsche, Friedrich (1844–1900) 72; *amor fati* 73–75, 137; *Birth of Tragedy, The* 137–42; on Christian aspiration for transcendence 73; on good *vs.* evil 74, 74n144; on humans as part of nature 73–74; on love as relational force 137–42; on love as valuing life 73–75; *Thus Spoke Zarathustra* 73, 142; will to power 73–74; *Will to Power* 137
noble savage 117
nomos 49
non-violence 173–74
Nozick, Robert 116, 235
Nussbaum, Martha 159, 216, 242–43
Nygren, Anders (1890–1978) 57

obedience 180
oikeiosis 100
On Christian Doctrine (Augustine) 50, 173
On Friendship (de Montaigne) 111–12
ordo amoris 81
organisation 215
Origin and Nature of the Emotions (Spinoza) 118
Origin of Totalitarianism, The (Arendt) 204
other beings 26
other-belonging 100–102
other-love 215
Otherness 7, 151
other-regarding 26, 100–102
Oxford Handbook of Montaigne (Guild) 113

paradigm of love 8–10, 12, 218, 223, 233–46; ascension 238–40; Christian love 235; cosmology of divine 237; emotions 242–44; good

life 233–36; human well-being 233–36; love as transcendent vision in humans 234–35; love of persons 240–42
passions 109–10, 118–19, 123, 201
passive desire 63
passive emotions 63–64
passive vs. active love 206
passivity 118–19
pathological love vs. philanthropic love 67–68
peace 128, 173
Peace of Babylon 174
Penia 96
perception 70–72
perfections 71
perpetuity 41
personal righteousness: *see* internal righteousness
personalised/individualised love 14–15
Phenomenology of the Spirit, The (Hegel) 135–36
philia 37, 42–44, 93, 99–100, 110
phrónēsis 44, 167
physical inequality 123
physical intimacy 14, 47
Plato (428–348 BC) 13, 35–36, 93; erôs 37; on love as generative caring force 161–64; philosophy of love 13, 37–42; *Republic, The* 40n23, 162–64; *Symposium* 13, 37–42, 93
Plato on Love (Kraut) 162
pleasure friendship 97–98
pleasure/agreeableness, values of 196
pleasures 91, 104–5, 192–93
polis 162–65
political community 160, 165–67; common good 179–80; flourishing life within 160–61; justice 179–80; love 179–80
Political Emotions: Why Love Matters for Justice (Nussbaum) 216
political forgiveness 203–4, 218–19
political friendship 202–3
political harmony 163
political life 162–63
politics of love 201–5, 211, 216–19; compassionate politics 217–18; ethic of love 216–17; political forgiveness 218–19; restorative justice 218
politics of resistance 200–201
Pope Francis 216–17
Poros 96
positive virtues 130–31
possessiveness 206–7
post-modern/contemporary conceptions of love 33, 76–87, 76n152; de Beauvoir on 82–87; Goldman on 77–80; von Hildebrand on 80–82
post-modernist ideas on love as caring 159, 200–208, 211–12; Arendt on 201–5; Frankfurt on 205–8
post-modernist individualism: Irigaray on 149–53; love as relationing 143–53; Marcel on 144–49
power 63, 63n101, 73; appetitive 110; apprehensive 110; love 110–11
practical love 188–89
praise 16
preferential love 192–94
primitive human 122
procreation 41
punishment 182

radical alterity 150
radical love 144–49
rational beings 117
rationalism 116
rationality 37, 66, 68, 141
Reasons of Love, The (Frankfurt) 205
refugee crisis 1
relationing/relationships 25–27; beings 91; connection 115; love as 25–27, 29–30 (*see also* love as relationing); ontology 152–53
religions 15, 141
Republic, The (Plato) 40n23, 162–64
respect vs. love 69–70
response 80–82
responsive vs. creative love 56–57
restorative justice 218
righteousness 180–83; Christ's 181; external 180–81; God's 181; internal 180–81; Luther's views on 180–83;

from soul/spirit 182–83; well-being and 181
romantic love 14, 61
romantic sexual attraction 16
romanticism 14, 61
Rorty, Amélie 31–32, 119, 121
Rousseau, Jean-Jacques (1712–1778) 116, 122; *Discourse on Inequality* 122; *Emile* 124; on harmonising amour-de-soi and amour-propre 122–26; human's natural goodness for 124; on primitive human 122; *Social Contract, The* 123; vision of natural state of being 117
Russel, Rinaldina 187
Russia's invasion of Ukraine 1

satisfaction 188–89
Scheler, Max (1874–1928) 195; on communal feelings 197; conception of love 195–99; fellow-feelings, categories of 196–97; *Formalism in Ethics* 196; holiness, values of 196; on infectious feelings 197; investigations of emotions 195–96; mental perception, values of 196; *Nature of Sympathy, The* 196–97; phenomenology of love 195–99; pleasure/agreeableness, values of 196; spiritual love for 199; value, categories of 196; on vicarious feelings 197; vitality, values of 196
Schoonheim, Liesbeth 203
Schopenhauer (1788–1860) 31; on feminine virtue of loving-kindness 72; on knowledge 72; on love as valuing human intuition 70–72; *Metaphysics of Sexual Love* 71; *World as Will and Representation, The* 70–71
Second Sex, The (de Beauvoir) 13, 83
self-actualisation 61
self-adjustment 158
self-alienation 104
self-aware consciousness 230–31
self-awareness 44, 99, 109, 130
self-belonging 100–102
self-completion 135–36

self-conscious awareness 19, 22, 27–28, 122
self-consciousness 4, 25, 115, 132–33
self-defining subject 115
self-dignity 19, 65–70
self-expression 73
self-forgetfulness 105
self-identifies 145–47
self-improvement 123
self-interests 34, 98, 104, 117, 124–26, 175
selfish people 116–17
self-knowledge 33, 44, 55, 99, 107, 109
self-love 5, 19, 25, 33, 43–44, 49, 55, 100–102, 123–26, 130–32, 215, 240–42
self-made man 4
self-negating 135–36
self-observation 158
self-other connection 99
self-overcoming 73
self-perfection 44, 123
self-preservation 123–26
self-realisation 135–36
self-reflection 158
self-regarding 26
self-relationship 99
self-respect 5, 19
self-serving justice 175
self-serving people 116–17
self-surrender 135–36
self-sustaining moral duties 190
self-transcendence 17, 29, 147, 152
sexual desire 93
sexual difference 150–53
sexual freedom 14
sexual pleasure 187
sexuate difference 149–50
shame 134
Short Treatise (Spinoza) 62
Singer, Ervin 5, 244–45
Singer, Irving 23–24, 40, 48
Smith, Adam (1723–1790) 13, 116–17, 127; on human nature 127–32; on justice 130–31; on love as relationing 127–32; reflection on love 127–32; *Theory of Moral Sentiments, The* 127–28; *Wealth of*

Nations, The 131–32; on well-being 127–32
Social Contract, The (Rousseau) 123
social justice 165
sociology of heart 195
Socrates 35, 38–39
soul 163, 174–75
Spinoza, Baruch (1632–1677) 31–32; *Ethics* 61–64, 118; on high-mindedness 118–19; ideal of love as relationing 118–21; on love as pathway to flourishing 118–21; on love as valuing totality of existence 61–65; on love of God as eternal 64; on nature of cause 62; on one's happiness 119–20; on one's place in nature 120; *Origin and Nature of the Emotions* 118; on power 63, 63n101; on recognition of nature 120–21; *Short Treatise* 62
spirit 26, 163, 182
Spirit of Christianity, The (Hegel) 132–33
spirit of goodwill 224
spiritual beauty 55
spiritual goodness 55
spiritual love 15, 55
spirituality 15
St. Augustine: A Harmonious Union (Torchia) 108
Stoicism 35–37, 46, 100, 168
Stories of a Generation 16
Summa Theologiae (Aquinas) 53, 108–9, 178–79
sympathy 127–28, 190–91
Symposium (Plato) 13, 37–42, 94

Taylor, Charles 132
Temporal Authority (Luther) 183
Theory of Moral Sentiments, The (Smith) 13, 127–28
Thus Spoke Zarathustra (Nietzsche) 73, 142
Tillich, Paul 211
totality of existence 61–65
Tragedy of Women's Emancipation, The (Goldman) 79–80
transcendence/transcendent model 4–5, 27, 36, 82–87; Aristotelean philosophies 168; Christian aspiration for 73; horizontal 149–53; and immanence 82–87, 210; of love 81; self 17; for Stoics 168
Tristan and Isolde 140
true justice 182
Truth and Reconciliation Commission 218–19
Tsonchev, T. S. 182
Two Kinds of Righteousness (Luther) 180–81
Two Treatises of Government (Locke) 117

UN Charter of Human Rights 214–15
unconditional love 62
union with beloved 94–95

value-directedness 28
value-response 80–82
valuing: *see* love as valuing
Varchi, Benedetto 185–86
vicarious feelings 197
violence 7, 9, 117, 122–23, 128, 130, 146, 173–74, 182, 202–4, 212, 218–19, 224, 226
virtues 42–44, 66, 130–31, 161–62, 174; cardinal 176; of good character of humans 165–66; of love as caring 176
virtuous friends 99
virtuous love 186
vitality, values of 196
volitional necessities 205
von Hildebrand, Dietrich (1889–1977) 80–82; *Arts of Living, The* 80; conception of love 80–82; on love as value-response 80–82; *Nature of Love* 80; *ordo amoris* 81; on self-interest of love 81; on transcendence love 81
vulgar love 186

war 173–74
Wealth of Nations, The (Smith) 131–32
Weber, Max 115
well-being 19–20, 22–23, 81, 111, 131–32, 164, 188–89, 217–18, 220–21, 230–31; definition 23; economy

220–21; life of 102; love and 25–26, 127–32; righteousness and 181
West, Cornel 32
whole Christ 104
wholeness 94–95
will to power 73–74
Will to Power (Nietzsche) 137
will-to-life 71–72
wisdom 161–62; lovers of 163
wishing *vs.* acting 69
with-ness 143
Wolf, Susan 21–22
women 40, 71–72, 77–80, 149–53; emancipation for 79; liberation movement 14, 86–87; in love 31, 83–85; marriage 14, 77–79; and men, ethical relationality between 150; oppression 83–84; philosophers 31–32; rights 77–80; Schopenhauer on 71–72; value of 83; virtue of 'loving-kindness' 72; wealth-seeking 14
Works of Love (Kierkegaard) 192–93
World as Will and Representation, The (Schopenhauer) 70–71

Zarathustra 73